GLORIOUS
IN SOLITUDE

GLORIOUS IN SOLITUDE

THE COURAGE OF ISOLATED REAR GUNNERS IN THE RAF DURING THE SECOND WORLD WAR

COLIN PATEMAN

FONTHILL

Fonthill Media Limited
Fonthill Media LLC
www.fonthillmedia.com

First published 2013

Typeset in 10pt on 13pt Sabon LT
Typesetting by Fonthill Media
Printed in the UK

ISBN 978-1-78155-221-6

CONTENTS

Acknowledgements 9

Foreword 10

Introduction – Historical Background 13

1. The RAuxAF and the RAFVR 23

2. Air Gunner Training 25

3. RAF Air Gunner's Cloth Brevet 31

4. Operational Training Units 33

5. Turret Gunsights 37

6. The Frazer Nash FN20 Turret 43

7. The Boulton Paul Type E Turret 48

8. Perspex Panels 50

9. Pigeons 54

10. Rear Gunner's Training Crash 56

11. Flight Rations 59

12. Armoury Duties 61

13. Combat Reports 65

14. Corkscrewing 72

15. Prisoners of War 74

16. Sergeant Neil Stockdale 78

17. Sergeant Eric Marvin DFM 85

18. The Call of Nature 103

19. Army Rear Gunners   106

20. Air Transport Auxiliary Rescue   111

21. Emergency Landings   115

22. Sergeant Ernest Wharton DFC, DFM   120

23. Sergeant Charles Boyce   138

24. Pilot Officer William Davies   144

25. Sergeant Alexander Barrie BEM   149

26. Sergeant Vaclav Spitz   153

27. Sergeant Frank Bell DFM   171

28. Flight Lieutenant John Darby DFC   184

29. Sergeant Brian Rogers   204

30. Flight Lieutenant John Hall DFC   211

31. Sergeants John McKenzie and Jack Cantor   225

32. Pilot Officer Virgil Fernquist and Sergeant William Crabe CGM   229

33. Sergeant James Hughes DFM   232

34. Night Hunters of the Reich   245

35. Luftwaffe Flak   250

36. Decorated by the King   259

    Epilogue   269

    Bibliography   271

Dedication

Glorious in Solitude is a tribute to the many thousands of air gunners who served in isolated vulnerability within rear gunner turrets during the Second World War. Amongst others, the hardships and bravery of fifteen individual air gunners is examined in this book. The author's calculations from their flying logbooks indicate that those fifteen men endured an estimated 2,750 hours in their gunner turrets, whilst engaged in some 416 operational intrusions over enemy occupied territory. The following words from Air Chief Marshal Sir Arthur Harris, Commander in Chief Bomber Command, written in 1947, epitomise the role of the rear gunner:

> There are no words with which I can do justice to the aircrew who fought under my command. There is no parallel in warfare to such courage and determination in the face of danger over so prolonged a period of danger, which at times was so great that scarcely one man in three could expect to survive his tour of thirty operations ... It was, furthermore, the courage of the small hours, of men virtually alone, for at his battle station the airman is virtually alone.

Bomber operations over enemy held territory were intensely stressful experiences with the survival odds stacked against rear gunners. This book is the author's attempt to create a testimony to the many thousands of rear gunners who took on the responsibility of protecting their crew despite the terrifying odds of never surviving a complete tour of duty.

An air gunner sculpted in clay by Philip Jackson. The large and imposing 9-foot sculpture was created to illustrate the emotion of an air gunner returning from an operation as part of a heavy bomber crew. This sculpture is one of seven incredibly detailed aircrew sculptures that were later cast in bronze to form the heart of the Bomber Command Memorial in London.

The air gunner is wearing a typical flying suit of the period supporting the observer parachute harness with the large clips which attached the parachute pack onto the chest. The observer type parachute pack is held in the left hand. The gauntlets are slipped behind one of the harness straps and slipped in the right boot can be seen the air gunner's cocking tool, imperative to any rear gunner who was confined within such restricted space and needing it to be immediately available.

Acknowledgements

Flying logbooks and ephemera from the Second World War have been used as the primary source of material to compile this book. The author would like to acknowledge the original recipients of such documentary evidence accordingly. In addition Jock Whitehouse, Martyn Ford-Jones, Alan Edmonton, Simon Muggleton, Roy Claridge, Norman Hood, Ian Simpson, Pavel Vancata, Tom Quinn, John Linnett, Gordon Leath of the RAF Museum, The Air Historical Branch and the exceptional work by Squadron Associations in compiling historical material is deserving of mention. I would like to identify 550 Squadron Association and the late Ron Bramley of the Air Gunner Association in particular for their assistance with photographic material.

In addition, I am earnestly indebted to Philip Jackson CVO. Philip created the impressive and inspiring sculptures of a bomber crew that now stand within the memorial to Bomber Command in London. The sculptures of the gunners in their clay form, prior to casting in the foundry, have been a most valued addition to this book.

In several instances, additional photographs have been included from the author's collection. The terms of the Open Government License facilitates the use of historic material from the National Archives whilst other material, particularly photographic work, sits within the public domain created by the Government prior to 1957. Wherever possible I have sought to credit material with due diligence and integrity.

Finally I would like to acknowledge the assistance of my wife Sarah-Jane who endeavours to support my passion for collecting, researching and writing and my nephew Tim Pateman who came to my rescue with his I.T. skills.

Foreword

The Royal Air Force and her Commonwealth forces are respectably credited with iconic images of gallant fighter pilots who participated in the Battle of Britain. In all cases those fighter pilots were young men who bravely engaged in collective and personal duels in the skies over southern England during 1940. These pilots controlled their own destiny – their hands firmly grasping the control columns of Hurricane and Spitfire aircraft. The ability to anticipate and react to instantaneous events, and the capability to shoot down the enemy with extremely narrow margins of advantage, was the slender difference between life and death. Clearly those young men deserve their place in the history of The Royal Air Force, and indeed for the survival of this country in its greatest hour of need.

It could be said that the flying service personnel furthest removed from the Fighter Command pilots were the Royal Air Force's air gunners. Historically pre-war, they came into existence as non-essential personnel – exceptional young men who volunteered from the most mundane duties at the lowest ranks possible to temporarily fill the gunner role and, when no longer required to serve this purpose in the aircraft, they would resume their station duties. Promotion and rank were never directly associated to these men and by default – academics frequently filled the remaining roles required in the early days of flying.

It was not until the 19 January 1939, that the RAF recognised air gunners as a specific trade, confirmed by an Air Ministry Order A17/1939 that enabled air gunners to be engaged on a full-time basis, with additional duties to be undertaken in wireless operation. Restrictions were still in place, however, in respect of rank and promotion, so as an aircraftsman, the only evidence of any qualification held was the small metal winged brass bullet badge worn below his shoulder eagle, indicating that he was an air gunner.

Things would soon change for these young air gunners. In September 1939, the RAF published an additional Air Ministry Order, which confirmed that after the completion of their training, air gunners would be issued with the rank of Sergeant, and the winged bullet badge was declared obsolescent and replaced by the air gunner's half wing brevet. This significant development saw the escalation in status and rank of air gunners within the Royal Air Force.

Pilots wore the full wing on their tunics and the air gunners displayed the half wing – both were instantly recognisable as aircrew personnel. The endurance and hardship experienced by the young volunteers had to some extent now been redressed and many thousands of young men were to follow them into the service of air gunnery.

A significantly high number of air gunners lost their lives sitting in the Perspex gunner turrets and in particular, the rear gunners who endured extraordinary conditions, unique to that most exposed location within an aircraft. This book explores some of the gallant actions taken by these individuals who volunteered to sit in solitude on the extremities of vulnerability. In many cases, their actual flying logbooks, composed at that time, have provided the detail of what they did night after night between 1939 and 1945.

From take-off to landing, at times for as long as ten or eleven hours, the air gunner constantly rotated their turrets, scanning the surrounding blackness, quarter by quarter, searching for the grey shadow that could transform instantly, into an attacking enemy night fighter. It was not unknown for some rear gunners to lose their lives within their first handful of operations, whilst others survived constant contact with the enemy. Likewise other men saw little if any combat with the Luftwaffe's night fighters – regardless, they all deserve a special place in aviation history. Always looking at where they had been, never seeing where they were going, and always devoid of human company. There can be no doubt whatsoever that all rear gunners possessed special qualities and a mental toughness, which they must have had in abundance, in order to cope and survive in these unique conditions.

Approximately 125,000 men served as aircrew within Bomber Command during the Second World War and from that number 55,573 lost their lives. The Commonwealth War Graves Commission maintains a significantly large proportion of those casualties' graves and will continue to do so in perpetuity. The Reichswald Cemetery near Kleves contains 3,971 RAF casualties alone, more than any other of the thirteen cemeteries within Germany. The Berlin 1939 – 1945 Commonwealth War Graves Commission cemetery was established in 1945 as a central burial ground for aircrew. About 80 per cent of those buried in the cemetery were killed during attacks on Berlin in the Battle of Berlin campaign, undertaken by Bomber Command between August 1943 and March 1944. The Commonwealth War Graves Commission has registered 347,151 recovered casualties from all services in the Second World War, with all of those personnel commemorated with graves and cared for in perpetuity. There are 232,931 personnel who are registered as missing and with no remains found, denied a grave. These casualties are commemorated by individually inscribed names upon many memorials across the world. The principal Air Force Memorials recording these losses are at Alamein, Singapore, Malta, and the large Runnymede Memorial in Surrey, South East England. The essential criteria in deciding where an airman is to be commemorated depends on where he was based, and not necessarily the area in which he was presumed lost. The Runnymede Memorial itself commemorates over 20,000 airmen and women of the Commonwealth Air Forces who died over northwest and central Europe, the British Isles, and the eastern Atlantic and who have no known grave. It is estimated that the average age of aircrew within Bomber Command was just twenty-two years and many of the casualties were air gunners who paid the ultimate and often solitary sacrifice fighting for freedom.

Colin Pateman

The two carrier pigeons are being loaded whilst the five remaining crewmembers wait to climb aboard. This 50 Squadron Lancaster was about to depart RAF Skellingthorpe for a raid upon Stuttgart on the night of 15 April 1943. Lancaster ED810 subsequently failed to return after its eighth operational raid to Oberhausen on 14 June 1943. The crew of seven perished including the 20-year-old Rear Gunner Sergeant Kenneth Bowerman. They are all buried in the Antwerpen Cemetery in Schoonselhof, Belgium.

The Historical Background

Little more than eight years after the Wright brothers took their primitive but capable flight machine into the air in 1903, the development of the aerial gunner commenced. In 1912 the experiment of firing a Lewis machine gun from an aeroplane proved possible and it was to become the adopted aerial weapon for many of the world's newly established air services. Before the First World War, aeroplanes were fragile, constructed of wood and linen, braced with wire and propulsion achieved using an underpowered engine with little reliability.

In August 1914, the Great War thrust itself upon the military services of Great Britain and its Empire and at that time only one aircraft had the capability to carry an air gunner – The Vickers No. 18. It was equipped with an engine that pushed the aircraft through the air and provided a position at the front of the aircraft from which it was possible to fire a machine gun. Despite this, the role of the air gunner was itself a long way from being recognised. In 1915 a machine gun school was created, and skills were established in aerial gunnery for the first time. It should be remembered that the men being carried in the primitive machines that flew in the Great War were venturing into unknown territory. The aeroplane was still an innovative invention and many long standing military personnel were entrenched in pre-war tactics where they felt there was no place for the Royal Flying Corp (RFC), which was ultimately commanded by the army. Safety was not seen as a priority in the early days. The brave men of the RFC were not issued with parachutes and the observer gunner was required to be agile in movement, frequently using his instincts alone to remain contained within the aeroplane and to avoid simply falling out.

In 1916, the FE2b aeroplane became available to the RFC and the observer gunner was an integral member of the crew, accommodated in a forward position, immediately in front of the pilot who in turn sat before the pusher engine and propeller. This particular aeroplane also heralded the birth of the rear gunner. It was equipped with two Lewis machine guns, one firing to the front and another available to fire to the rear. Defensive armaments to deal with offensive aerial attacks from enemy aeroplanes approaching from the rear, had been recognised as being immensely important, and was a role fulfilled by the gunner.

The requirement to carry gunners as opposed to observers saw the lowly ranked air mechanics frequently volunteering for such duties in the sky. These men would revert back to mundane duties, with status and pay consistently remaining on the bottom level regardless of any activity in the air. This historical situation regarding air gunners appears to have remained well into the inter-war period. Although there were consistent design improvements in both aircraft and engines, the Lewis light machine gun and the Vickers Maxim heavy machine guns remained the standard equipment for the air gunner.

The acute inter services rivalry resulted in the birth of the Royal Air Force in 1918. It commenced as a stand-alone service with its own rank structure and where the air gunner continued to function as a volunteer ground crewmember who flew part time when required. As the rapid development of aircraft took place, so did the air gunners' weapons, finally receiving the overdue attention they deserved in 1936 when they were updated. The American Colt Browning replaced the early Vickers, and the Vickers Armstrong K gun replaced the light Lewis machine gun. The change had been a long time coming but both weapons proved to be remarkably suited to the task, and the larger 20-mm Hispano Suiza gun followed in their footsteps. The Air Ministry Gun Section was headed by Major Thompson, a man who utilised his engineering and military background to great effect between the years 1918 – 1940. He worked with Captain Adams from the Royal Engineers who, remarkably, developed the British version of the Browning machine gun and was regarded in his area of expertise as a genius.

Another significant development that affected the air gunner was the enclosed turret designed by engineers at the Company Boulton Paul. Hydraulic or electrical engineering provided the means of power to enable rotation and directional control, the first of which was installed onto an aircraft just prior to the Second World War. Captain Frazer Nash was credited with designing the first power operated gunner turret, a name that has strong association to the history of Second World War air gunner turrets. He is also credited with naming 'Parnell Aircraft Limited' where Frazer's designs were constructed at their manufacturing units in Tolworth, Surrey. The natural progression of RAF guns saw the creation of the Armament Department at the Royal Aircraft Establishment at Farnborough who worked in collaboration with several companies. This establishment was also charged with bomb and other armament development. Consequently, due to the unique requirements of guns in the RAF the Gun Development Unit (GDU) was created at Boscombe Down, part of the Aircraft Armament Experimental Establishment.

Captain Adams had proposed that a gun be designed specifically for the use of rear gunners and it was this proposal that eventually led to the most important adaptation and modification of the Browning gun. The Browning gun was to become the most significant defensive weapon deployed by the Royal Air Force in its bomber aircraft. Vickers Armstrong and BSA Guns were engaged in the production of Captain Adams modified gun and produced nearly 20,000 units for delivery to the RAF by July 1939. It was regarded as being completely reliable and production figures of an estimated 2,000 guns a week continued to be delivered two years after the declaration of war with Germany.

The perceived status of the air gunner had remained in the shadows of pilots and other aircrew trades, despite the extraordinarily large numbers of young men required to service the needs of manning the turrets. There was never any shortage of young men who readily volunteered to join the trade of air gunner and these men were highly respected by their crews who tasked them with protecting their aircraft from the deadly night fighters that so actively sought to destroy them.

The Air Ministry intelligence summaries, AIR22 'Strength Reports', provide some statistics to illustrate the growth of Bomber Command and the number of fully trained aircrew and operationally available aircraft:

1 January 1941
Crews available – 350 with serviceable aircraft recorded at 357.
1 January 1942
Crews available – 569 with serviceable aircraft recorded at 581.
1 January 1943
Crews available – 557 with serviceable aircraft recorded at 547.

A Vickers Armstrong 'Wellington' rear gunner with his turret which is fully turned to expose the twin doors which provide access into the turret from the fuselage. He hopes to never bale out from those doors over Germany. Alongside, a piece of aircraft artwork painted on the dope canvas, expressing his opinion of the anti-aircraft defences over German territory.

Another photograph of the rear gunner in his turret. Notice the warning to bolt the doors securely. The confinement of space is apparent, especially as this gunner is wearing his thick Irvin flying jacket. The pull-tab to allow him to close both doors behind can be seen – once secure, the air gunner would be free to operate the controls and traverse the turret accordingly. The rear gunner's turret created a unique environment which required significant personal courage. (*Ron Bramley*)

The noticeable drop in establishment figures for 1943 was the result of Bomber Command's introduction of the large four engined aircraft and the withdrawal of outdated bombers from service. In addition the Luftwaffe had increased their night fighter and flak defences, both of which induced significant losses.

1 January 1944
Crews available – 1,126 with serviceable aircraft recorded at 927.
1 January 1945
Crews available – 1,904 with serviceable aircraft recorded at 1,486.

The infrastructure for training the steady and consistent growth of aircrew personnel was immense and it was recognised as being highly significant for the allies in ultimately securing victory. In relation to the personnel trained, the highest volumes of individuals were RAFVR air gunners and not all of these were young men. Arnold Talbot Wilson was without doubt one of the Royal Air Force's most renowned rear gunners and he was also the oldest gunner to squeeze into a rear turret having been born in 1884. In addition, he was without doubt the only rear gunner to have held court with Adolf Hitler.

Educated at Clifton College and then at the Royal Military College, Sandhurst, Arnold's abilities were recognised in the award of the King's Medal and the Sword of Honour in 1902. He was destined to become a highly decorated and honoured individual who gained a military commission from Sandhurst. He served with the Wiltshire Regiment before transferring to the Sikh Pioneers in 1904. Arnold was later employed in the Indian Political Department, southwest Persia until 1913 before returning to the UK. In the Great War he was appointed Deputy Chief Political Officer to General Gorringe, Indian Expeditionary Force, and was awarded the DSO. Arnold was appointed Deputy Civil Commissioner at Basra, and later at Baghdad, where he served until March 1918.

In 1932 Arnold decided to enter the political arena and was duly elected as the conservative Member of Parliament for Hitchin in June 1933 where he immediately pressed for rearmament and compulsory military service. He travelled extensively in Italy, Germany and Spain meeting amongst others, Hitler, Hess and Mussolini, names that went on to shape history and create devastation across Europe. Arnold recorded his meeting with Hitler in Berlin during May 1934 in his book, *Walks & Talks Abroad*:

> I was received by Herr Hitler at his office, a fine but unpretentious modern building close to the official residence of the President. There was no military display within or outside the portals, a couple of SS sentries at the door and two more on the first floor, were the only external indication that the building housed the ruler of new Germany ... Herr Hitler left on my mind an indelible impression of single-mindedness.

In the period 1936-38 Arnold remained a steady advocate for appeasement with his last speech to the House of Commons taking place on 31 July 1939, one which left no doubt as to his preferred plan of action:

> If Germany has not the courage to approach us, we, as the older, the senior, and the wiser power, must again take the initiative. Because we failed once, it does not follow that we may not succeed a second time. It is difficult – and no one realises it more than I – to speak of appeasement or to make suggestions for further negotiations. If these proposals were to be rejected I would fight myself, and I would urge others to fight to the utmost limit. I am no pacifist ... but the situation is such that we ought to be prepared to take the risk of approaching Germany once more, and to make specific

suggestions on the clear understanding that the alternative to agreement to confer is, in the long run, war.

The next time members of the House of Commons saw Sir Arnold, he was wearing the uniform of an RAFVR pilot officer having volunteered alongside young men, nearly forty years his junior, to serve in the Royal Air Force. His tunic supported an extensive row of medal ribbons, acknowledging his previous military and political achievements and, as an ex-Lieutenant-Colonel, he could scarcely hope to be treated on equal terms to the very youthful company he frequented. It was not long, however, before he came to be known to all as 'Sir Gunner', a title that sat happily with him and those that served alongside him. Arnold had made good his promise given previously to his Hitchin constituents – he had vowed, 'Not to shelter himself behind the bodies of young men.'

Aged 56, Arnold faced the unusual circumstances of matching his fitness alongside teenage and youthful men in their twenties. His advantage, if he had one, was his previous flying experience gained whilst serving in Persia. Without doubt Arnold was exceptional in many ways. His desire to serve as an air gunner commenced with training at RAF Manby in Lincolnshire and later at the Central Gunnery School at Warmwell in Dorset where the instructional staff were confronted with a student of such bearing and military service as well as a knighthood – a most interesting experience. Arnold was later introduced to the Wellington bomber during his conversion course at RAF Harwell where he gained the true experience of flying in the confines of a rear gunner's turret. The RAF recognised the leadership qualities within Arnold and he swiftly received a commission into the ranks as a pilot officer, which would have been a rare sight at that time, particularly with that rank supporting an air gunner's half brevet. As the development of air gunners progressed, Arnold was identified as a man suited to lead a squadron as a Gunnery Leader, a task that he held no particular interest in doing. He was focused on a personal level and serving in the rear gunner's turret was exactly where he desired to be.

In March 1940, Arnold was posted to 37 Squadron at RAF Feltwell. Equipped with Wellington bombers the Squadron were actively engaged in North Sea sweeps by day, searching for the German shipping and pamphlet or 'Nickle' raids over occupied France and Germany by night. Incredibly, wherever his service duties permitted, he continued to visit the House of Commons. Unbeknown to him, his last speech to the House took place on 7 May 1940, when he quoted the motto of the House, *Numini et Patriae Adsto* – 'I stand by God and my country' – his speech made a profound impact on the members who heard it:

> I count myself fortunate in having an opportunity to speak, for within an hour I must re-join my unit. The war is so close to our shores today that an airman can dine with his wife, proceed overseas over the North Sea to set fire to a hornets' nest, extinguish it with a pitch of high explosive, and be

back having breakfast, if he is fortunate, with his wife at the usual hour on the following morning.

Three nights later Arnold climbed into his aircraft and negotiated his way to the rear turret along the narrow walkway. He slid into his confined space and locked the twin doors behind him. It was a far cry from the political turmoil of Parliament, and in solitude, he flew on a bombing raid to Rotterdam where he had the opportunity to fire his guns with a sense of purpose, an experience which he later recorded:

> We came over the target at the precise moment laid down in our orders, just as the young moon was setting. Gray [the Sergeant-Pilot] was in no hurry. The hangar and buildings in the N.W. corner were blazing so brightly that it was hard at first to find out precisely where we were. Light clouds below us almost obscured the view. So he descended to 1,500 feet and nosed round for 20 minutes as far west as Dortrecht until he had satisfied himself beyond doubt we were over the aerodrome. As we arrived, a flare was dropped by another machine bent on a like errand. It fell off the aerodrome but showed clearly how the land lay. Gray sheered off and gained height before descending at 280 mph upon his chosen line. His first bomb, as observed by me, was just off, his second well within the aerodrome. Again he steered away and made a second run in a different direction. This time he dropped seven in quick succession. I saw flame which lit up a great troop-carrying aeroplane; it heeled over and a second later burst into flames which showed five smaller machines close by that must have been seriously damaged. I fired a few bursts from my machine-gun, hoping that they would pierce the hides of German sentries, but was chary of 'hose piping' lest any victims should be Dutch troops whom we knew to be close by. Gray made one more turn, climbing to 4,000 feet and descending rapidly to 2,000 feet before releasing his last 250-lb bombs. The heavy thud of each bomb shook the aeroplane slightly as if someone was hammering us with a gigantic wooden mallet. Then I heard the words, 'Door closed, power off'. We had done our job; we had dropped our stuff.

Arnold described a further raid from his gunner's turret, on the night of 14 May, this time to The Ruhr Valley where visibility tried to thwart his crews efforts on bombing their target:

> Again and again during the next half hour the searchlights got us … a burst of 'ack-ack' in front of us showed we were observed. We emerged from the clouds at 8,000 feet and were dazzled by a score or more of searchlights. At last Gray saw a bridge across the Meuse. We were at 4,000 feet. He dived to 1,000 feet, hoping to release a stickful over it. The bomb aimers were ready,

the sights adjusted, but again the searchlights foiled us. They got us and held us for two minutes … Nothing was left but to find a good Autostrade. This we succeeded in, hitting half a dozen times or more in succession at less than 1,000 feet. The machine rocked as the bombs found their mark. Then up and home, but not before we got a red stream of tracer within 20 or 30 feet – as it seemed – of my rear turret, showing that a machine-gun battery was trained upon us. I gave them 500 rounds from each of my guns, and they stopped, whether because we were out of range or because of my firing I know not.

Arnold completed further sorties against Givet, Namur, Aachen and Charleroi on the night of 20 May. Once again his penned words explain events witnessed from his perched position suspended in darkness:

Wellingtons are slow machines and good targets when they climb. Searchlights played on us; streams of tracer came up at us, so heavy and so near that they made the thin steel plate of my turret vibrate. It seemed very close to us, but in fact was probably further away than appeared, for there was not a hole or dent in us when we returned home three hours later. One very persistent searchlight was in range of my gun, as also a nest of machine-guns whose flashes were clearly visible. I 'hosepiped' them for some seconds and was cheered by a voice on the intercom: 'Oh good, Sir Gunner, a very pretty pattern right round them.' Gray turned quickly over the white streak, which marked the dam across the river where a canal takes off, and dived straight at the bridge. Six 250-lb bombs dropped on the river bank just clear, I fear, of the bridge … Then we banked steeply and, shaken by heavy air currents, climbed up and out, chased fore and aft by rather heavy fire. Again he turned and tried to drop his parachute flare. It failed to fall or, if it fell, to light. But he gave the bridge pontoon another half-dozen. I peppered our enemy whose position was revealed by their fire. One little burst and one alone came really near to us.

On the night of 31 May, Arnold went to France on what was to be no more than just another operational sortie. Tragically the mission proved to be his last and he was posted 'missing believed killed'. It transpired that Sir Arnold Wilson died in his rear turret along with his fellow crewmember Sergeant Brown, both having been killed outright during an attack on their aircraft over Eringhem, near Dunkirk. The rest of the crew had escaped with their lives and became prisoners of war, however, Sergeant Gray, the crew's likable pilot, later died of his wounds.

Sir Arnold Wilson was laid to rest in the Eringhem churchyard in France with his fellow crewmember alongside him. No commonwealth headstone anywhere celebrates the life of an air gunner with such bestowments. Following his name the precisely chiselled letters declare his status 'KCIE, CSI, CMG, DSO, MP'. He was in all probability the oldest rear gunner to lay down his life for his country, a country that had honoured him with the following orders and medals: The Most Exalted Order of the Star of India; The Most Distinguished Order of St Michael and St George; Distinguished Service Order; The Most Venerable Order of St John; Knight of Grace; 1914-15 Star; British War and Victory Medals; MID Oak Leaf; General Service 1918-62 with two clasps for Kurdistan and Iraq; 1939-45 Star; Aircrew Europe Star; Defence and War Medals; Delhi Durbar 1911; Jubilee 1935; and finally the Coronation Medal of 1937.

This inspiring man left a legacy to the United Kingdom, one that remains to this day. His extensive chronicle of bravery in non-combatant situations was published in 1939. Sir Arnold Wilson highlighted the restrictiveness of official recognition of bravery by civilians and military personnel in non-combat environments. It is without doubt, that his work subsequently influenced the King's initiative to institute two new awards. The George Cross, which was instituted in September 1940, and The George Medal which immediately followed. These medals continue to represent two of Britain's premier awards for gallantry. However, sadly they were instituted just three months after Sir Arnold Wilson lost his life.

Wellington bomber rear gunner with a fellow crewmember checking an ammunition belt for the guns. This was a similar scene set by Sir Arnold Wilson who served in this same type of turret.

Vickers Wellington Bomber and her crew making ready for flying. The crew entry ladder enables the air crew to climb directly into the forward section of the aircraft. The majority of crew are wearing the Irvin jacket, designed by the parachute pioneer Leslie Irvin, which was tested, assessed, and approved by the Air Ministry. Simply referred to as an 'Irvin', it was ordered in significant numbers, with production contracted out to many manufacturers. The Irvin jacket was issued in slightly differing forms to the Royal Air Force and Commonwealth aircrews during the Second World War.

The first examples went into production in 1931, and were manufactured with undivided one-piece body panels that required only the minimum of necessary seams. Although this facilitated easier assembly, it consumed much greater quantities of material. Irvin jackets constructed in that fashion are now referred to as 'Battle of Britain issue'. The early fighter pilots were all issued with this iconic design of jacket.

With the demand for jackets increasing, a more economic method of manufacture was devised. It was decided that the earlier pattern should be divided into smaller panels of sheepskin, resulting in better use of the materials, but this increased the numbers of stitched seams. Coastal Command and Fleet Air Arm crews were issued with an Irvin that had a modified full hood, designed to provide additional protection when ditching into the sea. The hood was yellow to help the wearer be spotted by rescue crews. Also manufactured by Irvin was the parachute harness as worn by the crew. The personal harness was worn at all times whilst in the air as seen, with no parachute attached. Crewmembers were able to move about with significantly less restriction. The parachute would be stowed and accessible at all times. Fitted with metal loops, it was simple to clip the parachute pack onto the harness hooks. This Irvin assembly was well liked by the vast majority of aircrews who wore it throughout the Second World War.

The RAuxAF and the RAFVR

The Royal Auxiliary Air Force, (RauxAF) was formed in 1925 as an extension to the well patronised military territorial associations that were in place across the country. The RAuxAF was the vision of Lord Trenchard, a man who was instrumental in and credited with establishing the Royal Air Force. Volunteers into the auxiliary were locally recruited in a similar fashion to the Territorial Army regiments. It proved to be a natural progression for the service, and many of the RAuxAF serving officers played an important part in the development of the Air Force during the interwar years.

The Royal Air Force Volunteer Reserve, (RAFVR) was formed in 1936. Initially the RAFVR composed of civilians recruited from the Reserve Flying Schools, which were operated by appointed civilian contractors, who engaged instructors from the Reserve of Air Force Officers (RAFO). These were men who had previously completed a four-year short service commission as pilots in the RAF. Volunteers into the RAFVR were men of between 18 and 25 years of age who undertook part time training as pilots, observers and wireless operators. The strategic vision was to create a reserve or pool of trained aircrew for use in the event of war. The Air Ministry employed the RAFVR as their principal means for aircrew to volunteer and enter the service. Following the declaration of war, eager volunteers signed up immediately hoping to be accepted for aircrew training. These men took an oath of allegiance to the King, and were formally inducted in to the RAFVR but generally they returned to their civilian jobs for several months until being called up for aircrew training. These men were able to wear the silver RAFVR lapel badge which proclaimed them as having enrolled into the RAFVR, a badge that was issued together with a document which explained the status of the 'civilian'. The document bore the number of the badge, which was stamped accordingly. On formal call up the volunteers were given a list of items they were to bring with them, which included the RAFVR badge and document so as to ensure that such badges and accompanying documentation did not pass into the hands of those not entitled to possess such important means of identification.

After the declaration of war most pre-war pilot and observer aircrew received a commission into the officer ranks, with the surviving regular officers and members

Above left: The RAFVR lapel badge.

Above right: The RAFAAF lapel badge.

of the experienced RAFO filling the roles of flight and squadron commanders. The many thousands of volunteer aircrew personnel that walked into the RAF recruitment offices and undertook the assessment and selection process were therefore all employed as RAFVR and eventually formed the vast majority of aircrew personnel who served in the Royal Air Force. Aptitude assessments, combined with the individuals preferred aircrew role or category, dictated the subsequent route of training that would follow their official acceptance into the RAFVR. Clearly many men were faced with accepting their second or third choices as the needs of the service were paramount. Air gunners progressed through the training route in the least time when compared to other aircrew categories and for men who desired to serve in that duty it was achieved in six stages:

Aircrew Reception Centre → Initial Training Wing → Air Gunnery School → Operational Training Unit → Heavy Conversion Unit → Squadron.

Brass 'VR' letters were worn on the uniforms of the RAFVR volunteers and as recruitment progressed, the numbers of air gunners required in Bomber Command increased dramatically and the vast majority of air gunners therefore wore the VR lapel and shoulder insignia. However, in 1943 the Air Ministry raised an order for members of the RAFVR to remove their brass and cloth 'VR's. This was an order that affected all RAFVR ranks, officers and NCOs. Surprisingly however, no similar order was raised for members of the Auxiliary Air Force resulting in ranked officers retaining their 'A' lapel badges and insignia throughout the war.

Air Gunner Training

The training of air gunners commenced in the lecture rooms with basic mathematic calculations applicable to triangles and velocities, both regarded as an essential requirement to learn. The lecture rooms held squads or classes of six students each and the instructors ensured from the moment the six-week course commenced, the purpose was training men for the harsh reality of war. Flying kit was issued along with a white flash to insert in the airman's cap; this was standard recognition for any airman undertaking aircrew training. In addition, the student was issued with a badge representing a propeller to be worn on their uniform sleeve, thus showing they had been promoted to a leading aircraftsman. Blackboard demonstrations were given on how to quarter the sky in search of enemy aircraft and for rear gunners in particular this was an essential skill. Demonstrations were given on the 'curve of pursuit' or 'bullet drop' that was required to be calculated by the gunner when aiming at an enemy aircraft. Exercises using hand-held reflector sights enabled the student to judge the speed of a target aircraft and all of these technically challenging matters were assessed by the instructors on a regular basis.

In addition to gunnery training, the students were also expected to carry out other duties which included guard duty, physical training and military drill. Self-study and associated reading material was issued to each student with aircraft recognition being a subject that required significant self-motivation to master. The ability to instantly recognise friendly from enemy aircraft was essential and the gunners needed to be accurate at both maximum and minimum distances, a skill that could only be achieved by hours of relentless study. The aircraft contours and how each individual design sat in the air were of utmost importance as the recognition of aircraft would eventually need to be made in split seconds and it would quite possibly be the difference between life and death for the gunner and his crew.

Recognition posters and model aircraft were hung in the classrooms as reminders and the plastics manufacturers, Curver, produced black moulded models that illustrated particular aircraft silhouettes in excellent detail. These were regarded as being a crucial training aid and instructors would examine

Students in individual gunnery turrets. Some are fully enclosed in Perspex whilst others are partially or completely open. Each unit has a compressor power unit to enable full hydraulic operation of the turret's movements. (*Air Ministry*)

students' knowledge in order to demonstrate their ability to instantly recognise enemy aircraft from all quarters.

The students also learned how to prevent a German aircraft from approaching them too closely, through early recognition. The gunners needed to judge the approaching aircraft's wingspan and length in order to insert those estimates into the reflector gun sight, alongside judging its speed, direction and angle of approach.

The RAF utilised synthetic devices, such as replica turrets which were designed to provide operating procedure exercises on the ground. The gun turrets were mounted on trolleys and fixed turrets were provided with full pneumatics so gunners would be able to learn the controls. These crude, but exceptionally useful, devices allowed the students to practice whilst wearing full flying gear – a step towards the reality of operational deployment. Back in the classroom, continual dismantling and assembly of the Browning .303 gun took place. They had to identify the weapon's mechanism even when blindfolded. At first, these large awesome weapons would have felt unnatural and terribly unwieldy to handle, however each individual gun (which weighed in at 24 lbs) soon became the air gunner's loyal and trusted friend. This level of ability was required because in combat the Browning could suffer from an ammunition feed problem, something they would have to rectify unconsciously. Progression towards using the training turrets and being able to track an aircraft in the sky was made using the fully powered synthetic units. Once more, this was undertaken in full flying clothing. It was essential that operating the turret, gun sight and the guns become second nature for the trainee air gunners.

Not all prospective air gunners arrived on courses with previous flying experience. For those novice students, the smells uniquely associated to aircraft – hot oil and exhausts – along with the engine noise and vibration were nearly always unexpected. This combined with the bumpy and somewhat alarming movements whilst accelerating down the runways, all built to a sinking feeling that preceded air sickness for a great many of the students. It was a common situation that inevitably passed fairly quickly, however some student air gunners failed to achieve the many and varied standards required, and were removed from the course in a sympathetic but quick process. The remaining students progressed to complete their initial training and took up duties at one of the many air gunnery schools distributed across the country alongside the Commonwealth student gunners who had arrived in Great Britain by troop ships.

The initial gunnery training commenced with students shooting at towed aerial targets. Canvas drogues were let out on a long cable, by a winch operator from within a towing aircraft. The crew were acutely aware of the dangers of excited air gunners, especially those who had not totally mastered the required skills. Fortunately, the aircrew flew boldly striped Lysander and Battle aircraft, painted in bright yellow and black livery, a paint scheme designed to ensure that student air gunners were given every opportunity to recognise the towing unit. The pilots posted to air gunnery schools were frequently frustrated at having to carry out towing duties. One such pilot was Rudolf Marczak, a pre-war Polish Pilot who had escaped the invasion of his country and reached England thanks to his fantastic stealth and tenacity. He joined the RAF and undertook training to establish his flying ability, something that was subsequently proven beyond doubt. He was awarded his RAF wings, but to his disappointment he was posted as a target tow pilot to the Gunnery School at Morpeth and not to an operational base. As such, he was unable to fulfil the desire to fly over his occupied homelands, frustrations experienced by others in similar positions. For Rudolf, the duties were mundane and predictable, however small consolation could be found in the fact that RAF Morpeth was used as a pool for Polish air gunners, therefore he was surrounded by fellow Poles.

Sitting behind Rudolf in the towing aircraft, would have been his regular winch operator, Leading Aircraftsman Leonard Ashton. Leonard had enlisted in the RAF with the intention of volunteering for aircrew duties but frustratingly for him, he had failed to progress through the selection procedure. However, as a general duties aircraftsman, he volunteered for the duty of winch operator at the gunnery school. His aircraft was fitted with a heavy metal cable with one of four types of drogue target attached; a 4-foot open sleeve, a closed low drag sleeve, a cone

Above and below: The Royal Air Force deployed several types of aircraft to perform 'Towing Duties'. The common feature amongst them was the bright yellow and black stripe identification markings seen on the 'Lysander' and 'Battle' aircraft illustrated.

sleeve or the smaller 3-foot cone and once in the air, targets could be let out by the winch or driven by wind. When the target was fully extended, Leonard would advise by radio that the target shooting exercise could commence. The usual flight path at Morphett took the aircraft over the coast at Blyth, out to sea for gunnery practice and back inland over the estuary. In order to maximise the time in the air, student gunners would interchange in the turrets and the instructors would record the rounds fired by each individual. The ammunition was painted with coloured tips so that the targets that were hit, had sufficient colour retained on them to enable the hits to be correctly allocated to the appropriate student, and scored. Communication between the target operator and the student's aircraft was of paramount importance and on completion of the exercise the drogue was dropped over the airfield and collected by a motorcyclist. Once recovered the instructors counted the scores, marking each hole with a cross to ensure that the hits were not marked twice.

Leading Aircraftsman Ashton served in the capacity of 'target tow operator' for four years and accumulated nearly 800 hours in the air. His dedication was rewarded with the award of the Air Force Medal in 1944. His pilot, Rudolf Marczak completed his service at the gunnery school and became operational, serving with a Polish unit – 304 Squadron, Coastal Command.

For the student air gunners, although they were trained and wearing the AG half-wing brevet on their uniforms, they were not yet regarded as being

Polish air gunner students posing for a photograph. They are examining the target drogue for their individual scores which were indicated by paint marks on the entry holes of the target. (*Marczak*)

fully competent for operational flying and were required to pass additional examinations before progressing onto an operational training unit. The white cap flash worn by the students was handed in, and the single propeller leading aircraftsman rank was replaced by sergeant stripes. Operational Training Units were crucial in ensuring that all gunners achieved the required skills ready for becoming fully operational. It was also where they would mix with navigators, bomb aimers, engineers and pilots and by mutual consent amongst themselves, form into fully operational crews.

Podpis właściciela legitymacji

Rudolf Marczak wearing the metal Polish pilots' wings attached under his left lapel. The RAF cloth wing is uniquely worn by Polish pilots on the right side.

RAF Air Gunner's Cloth Brevet

In December 1939, Air Chief Marshal Sir Edgar Ludlow-Hewitt, the officer commanding Bomber Command, instigated the concept of a new aircrew flying badge. Wing Commander E. H. Hooper, serving in the Directorate of Personal Services, designed the draft new-style half-wing air gunner's badge. It was seen as innovative at the time and proved to be a design that was accepted with little reservation by the Air Council. The featured half-wing was positioned on a slight upward and diagonal aspect. At the root of the wing there was a brown-coloured stitched laurel leaf wreath, which was open at the upper part and sitting within the wreath were the letters 'AG' in white silk. Someone observed that there were a total of thirteen white feathers that formed the half-wing. On realising, Wing Commander Hooper reduced the number to twelve.

The half-wing design received royal approval and quickly became the standard worn by all the Commonwealth air forces. It was a complete turnaround for the Royal Air Force air gunners. Not only were they now leading the service, the new badges meant that the aircrew could now be easily identified and their specific trade illustrated. The RCAF air gunners wore the King's crown and had the additional lettering in the same way as the RAAF, thus differentiating them from their RAF colleagues. In all cases the early WAG (Wireless Operator Air Gunner) configuration can be seen within the brevet's wreath.

The original 'O' Observer's wing worn by the Observer Navigator remained in service until 1942 when it was replaced by the 'N' Navigator's wing. The additional crew position of the Flight Engineer, required on the larger bomber aircraft, saw the 'E' wing come into being in 1941. Wing Commander Hooper remained in service with the Royal Air Force and later received the CBE for his services. In 1946, he acted as joint secretary for the military justice Court Martial Committee.

Cloth air gunner brevets, as
worn by the RAF and the RCAF.

A young sergeant air gunner
wearing his newly presented half
brevet on his tunic.

Operational Training Units

Bomber Command operational training units were set up as fully operational airfields, many of which were built on requisitioned land. Approximately 600 acres was required to enable the construction of a 'type A' three hard runway design, including the 50-foot wide perimeter track which circumnavigated the runways. Several of these aerodromes were constructed on sites with good rail and road connections. An estimated 130,000 tons of hard core, cement and other surfacing materials were needed to lay the 40,000 square yards of runways, taxiways, aircraft standings, roads and foundations for the Bomber Command's airfields. In common with every airfield, a primary runway would be constructed in the direction of the prevailing winds to run for approximately 2,000 yards in length with two ancillary runways crossing the primary runway at an angle of approximately 60 degrees. These runways were shorter in length, normally around 1,400 yards. The government tendered for airfield construction. One of the major companies to get involved was George Wimpey, one of the country's long established building companies, as well as John Laing and Sons Limited.

An estimated £850,000 was required to build a basic establishment in the 1940s, which was considered a monumental sum of money. Pre-war RAF aerodromes had generally been constructed to a high standard with brick-built buildings and accommodation, whilst wartime operational training unit sites tended to deploy the use of prefabricated building methods and materials. Amongst the array of new buildings were the large water towers and huge steel hangers, which were a feature of every RAF aerodrome and built to standard designs and construction methods. The company Redpath-Brown, who were normally employed on a sub-contracted basis, often built the enormous aircraft hangers known as type J or T2.

Student aircrews would spend a great deal of time in the instructional buildings where there would be a configuration of crew rooms, lecture rooms, gunnery and turret instructional blocks as well as a flight armoury and locker rooms where their flying equipment was stored. Students were normally on site for about six weeks with the first two weeks consisting mainly of ground instructional duties, followed by four weeks of flying to hone the gunner's skills. The new intake courses would overlap with those already going through training resulting in the OTU (Operational Training Unit) bases being intensely busy with students arriving, and full crew's departing regularly.

An OTU equipped with Wellingtons, had four individually commanded flights generally identified from A to D with each facilitating between six and eight aircraft. All student air gunners were the responsibility of the Station Gunnery Leader who worked closely with the Chief Armaments instructor. The vast majority of instructors were known as 'screened' having completed a tour of operational duty, and thus regarded as permanent members of staff. This was despite the fact that the status of being screened would only last for six months before a further operational posting would fall upon them. It was known for some instructors to remain on station for up to a year, but this was a far from common practice.

The instructors were identified by wearing a small white triangle on the sleeve of their tunic or battledress. The other, and probably more identifiable, means of identification were the ribbons of the Distinguished Flying Medal and Distinguished Flying Cross, which were sewn on their battledress jackets. The casualty rates in Bomber Command were so horrific that completing a full tour of duty was regarded as exceptional – hence, men were frequently bestowed with such awards. The screened air gunners conducted a lot of their instructional duties in what was known as the 'Free Gunnery Trainer', a rear gunner's turret with a domed or curved screened wall that surrounded it. A film would be projected onto the walls with images simulating flying and fighter aircraft attacks. This concept of air gunner training continued to be developed and refined during the entire period of the war. Some airfields had purpose-built, small-domed buildings constructed which were regarded as state-of-the-art training aids – the forerunner to modern screen shoots which are used in police and military gunnery training today.

The operational training units saw the formation and consolidation of actual crews. Every aircrew trade and ability was posted into the OTU. Once the system was established, a typical course intake might have consisted of twenty crews of six-man units. One hundred and twenty young men were pooled together, and left to create a full crew compliment themselves. The pilots would mill around, and on seeing a brevet for the trade he needed to complete his crew, he might introduce himself and invite the individual to join him. It was then, not uncommon for the individual, a gunner for example, to advise the pilot that he knew another excellent mid-upper gunner who had been on a course with him. This would result in him being approached to join the crew. Some evidence exists to indicate that some crews were formed by selection alphabetically but from research undertaken by the author this appears to have been in the minority.

These novice crews initially flew intrusion raids in order to gain experience of flying over enemy-occupied territory, with instructions to drop propaganda leaflets. The value of dropping propaganda leaflets had been well established and developed by the Political Warfare Executive. Raids, where these leaflets

Le Courrier de l'Air

Apporté par vos amis de la R.A.F.

1941   No. 38

Distribué par les patriotes français

Crise en Allemagne

HITLER DECLARE: "Désormais c'est mon intuition qui vous mène"

UNE crise politique et militaire est ouverte en Allemagne. Il est impossible, pour l'instant, d'en apprécier exactement l'étendue et les conséquences. Mais il est impossible, également, d'en surestimer l'importance.

Hitler, écartant le maréchal von Brauchitsch et d'autres chefs militaires, a pris le commandement " personnel et direct " des forces allemandes. Il prétend exercer *pour la première fois* (ce qui est faux) le contrôle absolu des opérations, sur lesquelles il n'avait jusqu'à présent qu'un contrôle " théorique."

Selon sa propre expression, il compte désormais sur son " intuition " et sur sa " vocation intérieure," plutôt que sur l'expérience et la technique des militaires, pour conduire l'Allemagne à la victoire.

Autrement dit, si l'armée allemande n'a pas réussi à gagner, *en 1941*, la victoire finale, c'est parce que Hitler, n'était pas le maître absolu dans le domaine militaire, et parce que son avis ne fut pas toujours accepté par l'état-major. Maintenant qu'il prend les choses en main, l'armée allemande (selon lui) n'aura qu'à fournir un effort de plus pour vaincre.

L'annonce de la décision de Hitler fut accompagnée d'une proclamation à l'armée et aux formations des S.S. qui est certainement unique en son genre. Qu'un Chef d'Etat décide de limoger le Commandant-en-Chef des armées au milieu d'une bataille critique, c'est déjà bien grave, quoique compréhensible à la rigueur. Mais que le Chef de l'Etat assume lui-même la direction des opérations, *et fasse en même temps une espèce d'appel in extremis à ses troupes pour qu'elles tiennent* un peu plus longtemps, en attendant " de meilleurs équipements " et " de nouvelles mesures défensives," voilà un fait sans précédent, et qui montre bien à quel point la situation de cette armée " victorieuse " a dû se transformer depuis quelques semaines.

* * *

Hitler se répand en assurances personnelles et sentimentales envers ses chers soldats — ces chers soldats qu'il a lancés *sans nécessité* dans l'aventure russe, et qui périssent aujourd'hui, grâce à lui, par centaines de milliers dans des souffrances inimaginables. Au milieu de la neige, de la peste, sans abri et sans vêtements chauds, traqués par les guérillas, mitraillés par les nouveaux avions russes, poussés hors des villes et des villages vers les marais glacés du Pripet, ces malheureux doivent se réconforter de phrases comme celles-ci :

" Rien qui vous tourmente, qui vous opprime, ne m'est inconnu . . . Par ma volonté fanatique, moi, un simple soldat allemand, j'ai libéré l'Allemagne de Versailles . . . Mes soldats, mon cœur est à vous seuls . . . Tout ce que je puis faire pour vous sera fait . . . Je sais ce que vous pouvez faire et ce que vous ferez pour moi."

Sans doute, les Allemands ne ressemblent pas aux autres peuples, et leur instinct d'obéissance est presque sans limites. Mais peut-on vraiment croire que même en Allemagne, une telle proclamation ne sera pas plus apte à semer la panique dans une armée battue qu'à la redresser pour une nouvelle offensive ?

* * *

Hitler, on le voit bien, mise sur sa réputation d'infaillibilité, sur la mystique qu'ils s'est créée par ses succès politiques. D'où la recherche d'un bouc émissaire (Von Brauchitsch) pour la faillite de " l'offensive suprême " en Russie *sur*

Guidé par son intuition, Adolf guide ses généraux.

Guerre unique : plan unique

L'ARRIVÉE de M. Churchill à Washington, annoncée le 22 décembre, marque l'importance des consultations qui ont lieu pour coordonner l'action des Alliés dans tous les théâtres de guerre, anciens et nouveaux.

M. Churchill est arrivé à Washington en avion, accompagné de Lord Beaverbrook, Ministre de l'Armement, de l'amiral Sir Dudley Pound, Premier Lord de l'Amirauté, de maréchal Sir John Dill, chef de l'Etat-Major Impérial, du maréchal de l'Air Sir Charles Portal, chef de l'Etat-Major de l'Air, de M. Winant, ambassadeur des Etats-Unis à Londres, et de M. Harriman, représentant personnel de M. Roosevelt.

Des consultations parallèles et non moins importantes ont lieu en même temps à Moscou et à Tchungking, où les gouvernements britannique, américain, russe, chinois et hollandais étudient un programme en commun pour la conduite future de la guerre.

Après avoir reçu M. Churchill, M. Roosevelt a fait la déclaration suivante :—

" Les conversations qui auront lieu pendant quelques jours entre le Président et le Premier britannique, et entre les états-majors, n'ont naturellement qu'un but principal. Ce but, c'est la défaite de l'hitlérisme à travers le monde.

" Rappelons-nous que beaucoup d'autres nations ont maintenant entrepris cette tâche commune. Les conférences actuelles de Washington doivent donc être considérées comme une préparation à d'autres, conférences qui comprendront officiellement la Russie, la Chine, les Pays-Bas et les Dominions britanniques.

" Nous pouvons nous attendre à ce qu'une unité générale dans la conduite de la guerre en résulte. D'autres nations seront invitées à participer à la recherche du but mentionné ci-dessus, dans la mesure qui leur sera possible."

Suite à la page 4

A French text propaganda leaflet typical of those dropped by the RAF across France and other occupied territories.

were deployed, were known by the RAF as Nickel Operations. These 'nickels' or 'leaflets' were, on occasions, specifically created to lower the morale of enemy troops and a large quantity of them were produced for dropping from the air by the RAF. A number of motivational leaflets were produced also. The publication *Le Courrier de l'Air,* a French language newspaper, was intended to boost morale and give information to inhabitants across France. Miniature magazines often had a camouflaged cover to hide the true contents, as the German authorities were strict in enforcing that such material was illegal to possess and read.

The RAF was well aware of the value and responsibility of delivering the propaganda material. Bundles of leaflets, several inches deep, were banded together and thrown out of the aircraft at dedicated and precise locations. Rear gunners were also engaged in this practice and were known to carry the odd bundle, which they independently tossed into the aircrafts slipstream from their turret. At some 12,000 feet, these bundles of printed pages or booklets took up to an hour to gently flutter to the ground. Thousands of leaflets would cover a huge built-up area and prove almost impossible for the German authorities to collect and destroy. Nickels were also dropped on regular bombing raids by operational crews throughout the entire war as well as a number of other moral-boosting items, which included small packets of cigarettes, dropped over Holland on Queen Wilhelmina's birthday on the 31 August, 1941, and again in 1942. Pseudo currency and ration books were also printed and dropped to create financial instability over occupied countries.

5

Turret Gunsights

The early air gunners were accustomed to the old and established ring and bead sight that was used on the Vickers gas-operated guns. The reflector gunsight became the standard RAF turret gunner's equipment until the development of the gyro gunsight. The gyro device solved the single most difficult problem faced by air gunners: that of finding the correct angle of deflection. Once the gyro sight was perfected, it removed any error or enforced operator guesswork. The sight created an aiming system which calculated both range and deflection. The range calculation also accounted for the gravity drop of the rounds fired into the air.

The historic development of the gyro gunsight took place over many years. The problem had been recognised during the First World War but it had never been successfully rectified and developed. Dr Cunningham, an academic and education officer in the Royal Air Force, had studied the trajectory of falling bombs and created a PhD thesis on the subject. He was in charge of the Air Warfare Analysis Section, which operated under the Ministry of Aircraft Production. Cunningham was greatly interested in the RAF bomb and gun sighting equipment and he became the first patentee of the gyro gunsight. Dr. Cunningham was responsible for putting forward the idea of inserting a gyroscope into the reflector gunsight. His theory was based upon on the fact that a gyroscope would resist any rotation of its axis and if was clamped onto a fixed structure within the air gunner's turret. Gun sight stability would be created, providing the air gunner with a sight line for the target held back by the gyro. In other words, if the air gunner kept to the sight line indicated by the gyro, his guns would automatically point correctly and in direct relation to the rate of turn and direction of the attacking target.

By the summer of 1940, a potential operational sight had been created and identified as the Mk.I GGS (gyro gunsight). It was regarded as being an item of utmost secrecy and was given the code name, 'Type 6 mechanism'. Doctor Cunningham has created a working device that had an electric motor driving a rotor and the motor ran at a constant speed of 4,000 rpm. Within the device were four electro magnets and the speed of the gyro provided the stability to resist any angular movement. A celluloid strip in the optics of the sight had a black ring engraved at the end of the strip. When the air gunner looked through the device he would see two rings – one larger, fixed and bolder outlined ring and the other on another celluloid strip which moved across the sight line. The smaller ring in effect, was the sighting ring which held the actual target within its inner circle. Once it entered the larger ring or was calculated to just about enter the large ring, the guns could be fired.

Ferranti and Elliot Brothers began production of Doctor Cunningham's device in April 1941 and the device was initially deployed within Fighter Command to combat the German intrusion raids over Great Britain. Initially, the new concept of using the gyro gunsight was not met with great enthusiasm by fighter pilots because they regarded it as rather unstable. However Bomber Command had been testing the sights as well, as they had been fitted into the rear turrets of their Wellingtons. Reports from squadron gunnery officers were more enthusiastic and they reported that once the gunners had mastered the new techniques required, they had recorded significant improvements in accuracy. The small target ring on the sighting ring was at times difficult to follow, but primarily Bomber Command wanted the device to be illuminated to enable its use at night. Limited production by Ferranti continued and the few units that had been built were integrated into the command's training gunnery units. At that time the air gunnery students were required to follow these instructions when using the device.

> To prevent unnecessary wear, the sight should be switched on only when hostile aircraft are expected. You then set the aircraft's height and speed on a control box on the left side of your turret. Looking through the eyepiece you will see two black circles. The larger graticule is fixed and indicates the direction in which the guns are pointing. The smaller ring is the point of aim computed to allow for deflection and bullet trail. When the turret is stationary and the gun is pointing in any direction other than astern, the moving graticule will be seen as being displaced from the fixed ring by the four electro magnets. When you turn your turret to follow a target, the gyro will make the moving graticule lag behind in relation to the rate of turn or rotation. This lag, added to the bullet trail allowance, gives the point of aim required to hit the target.
>
> The target – in other words, you can't miss – provided you can manipulate your turret controls accurately. The range of your sight is fixed at 274 metres (300 yards), which has been found to be the optimum – you merely place the graticule round the target. The sight is protected from misting by a filter of silica gel, which dries the air as it enters an inlet at the bottom of the sight. Two adjusting screws harmonise the guns with the sight.

The Heavy Conversion Unit No. 1657, equipped their Stirling Bomber rear gunners with compact 16-mm camera guns, and student air gunners operated the camera in the same way as firing the Browning machine guns. The cameras recorded their ability in using the gyro gunsight. Fighter affiliation exercises

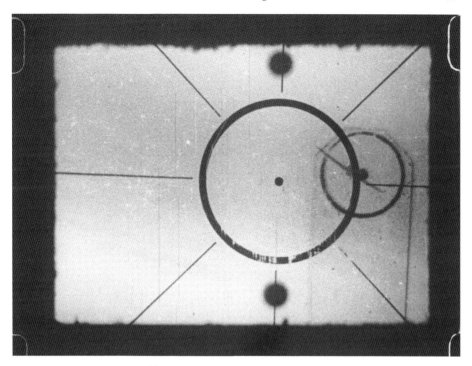

Rear gunner camera gun film exposure. This single frame illustrates the small aiming circle perfectly positioned. The turret needed a minor adjustment to bring the target into the gunner's field of gunfire for what would have been an excellent result.

were flown with RAF Spitfires acting as aggressive fighters, engaged in various attacks whilst being filmed. The gunnery training was much improved by this development, thanks to the fact that no ammunition needed to be fired and the camera film provided an excellent means to examine the use of the two graticules present within the sighting mechanism.

The gunnery schools were very impressed with the Mk.I sight, which had proved invaluable for instructional purposes. The development solution to the initial problems with the gunsight were subsequently solved by some of the most gifted academics in the country who devised a simple solution which proved to be most effective; a mirror was fixed to the end of the gyro device which reflected an illuminated graticule onto a reflector to be viewed by the gunner. The graticule consisted of a ring of six small diamonds, the diameter of which could be set to correspond with the target width or wingspan. The type of enemy aircraft was set on a dial, enabling the sight to calculate the range. The reflector screen was a large glass plate with the two illuminated graticules still present, similar to the early design. The one on the left was a fixed ring with the gyro-controlled ring of six diamonds, which had in effect replaced the previous smaller one. Both graticules could be dimmed for night use, or used singly by switching either on or off. The Armament Research Unit tested the first Mk.II gyro sights made at Farnborough

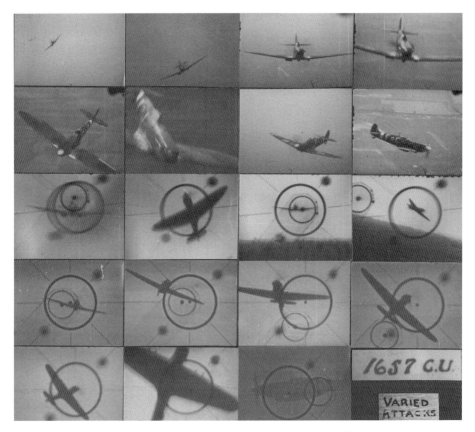

These prints were obtained from an original length of camera gun film exposures provided by a Stirling squadron historian. The Spitfire is clearly seen acting as an attacking fighter and the frames expose how the gunner has tracked and initiated the camera at the point of compatibility with the sight. What must be realised is that significant speeds were involved and the guns were fired for no more than a few seconds, illustrating the requirements of alertness and skill imposed upon the gunners.

in July 1943, and it was clear that the initial problems had been solved. The sight became known as the GGS Mk.IIC (turret) and deliveries from a purpose-built factory in Scotland commenced towards the end of 1943.

In most turrets, the sight was mounted at the gunner's eye level and connected in elevation to the gun cradle by rods and other connectors. Air gunners using a Nash & Thompson FN4 tail turret often used the sight as a convenient handhold when getting in and out of their confined turrets. This was likely to put the sight out of alignment so a prominent 'Hands Off' sign was attached and can be seen in the photograph at the gunner's eye line. The air gunner in this posed photograph is holding the firing mechanism. Above his hand is the roller device, which would have the .303 ammunition belt running over it, which would then feed into the Browning machine gun to the right.

The rear gunners were now required to operate the new sight in the following

The rear gunner of a Stirling sitting in the rear turret, the gunsight traversing bar holds the sign 'Hands Off', warning the gunners to not use it when extracting themselves from the turret.

sequence; set the height and speed via the dials fitted to the control box, which was conveniently mounted close to his right hand position, and then the enemy aircraft was estimated and its span set by the span handle control. The gunner's left foot was used to depress a pedal that opened the ring of diamonds to the range setting. This was retained upon the target aircraft until it filled the pre-set dimensions in the diamond ring. Once within the set area the gunner used the right pedal to control the diamond ring to keep the aircraft within its dimensions. This tracking remained constant with both foot pedal manipulations until the aircraft reached the estimated 200 yards prime distance (183 metres) the guns were fired and if still within the harmonised areas the enemy aircraft would have sustained serious if not fatal defensive fire resulting in its probable destruction. These skills and capabilities were only achieved with continuous training and dedication of the individual. Rear gunners were truly valued within each and every crew, and from such humble beginnings, they became an important member of both Coastal and Bomber Commands operational capabilities.

The King viewing the rear gunner's sight mounted on a frame with a battery power supply to illuminate the device. The air gunners with him are seen wearing the early full Sidcot flying suits. (*Press photograph dated 31 July 1940*)

6

The Frazer Nash FN20 Turret

This turret was an effective hydraulically powered turret produced for use prior to and during the Second World War. Some of its success may well be credited to the valuable information that had been fed back to the manufacturing company by RAF Gunnery Leaders and instructors from across Bomber Command. They informed the company of areas for potential improvement on the earlier design, which resulted in a number of modifications. Whilst the modifications centred on several aspects of the turret, the reliability of the capable browning guns remained a consistent factor. The designers provided metal plated protection for the air gunner in the turret and a clear-vision central panel became an official design characteristic. One of the main improvements had been in the ammunition supply to the guns. The ammunition boxes in the previous FN.4 had been fitted within the actual turret under the gun mountings. This limited the supply of ammunition and additionally affected the trim of the aircraft. A new supply system was devised which created large capacity ammunition boxes fixed to the sides of the aircraft's rear fuselage which enabled the ammunition belts to be taken from the boxes along steel tracks to the base of the turret. A method of feeding the ammunition into the guns was achieved by individual booster units that supplied enough energy to feed the heavy ammunition belts into the guns. The ammunition available to the gunner was 2,500 rounds per gun – 1,900 in the fuselage storage and 600 in the feed tracks.

The booster ammunition feed unit was driven by a hydraulic motor with two pipes connecting it to the pressure and exhaust lines of the turret feed system. The drive was transferred to the sprockets by four friction clutches so when the guns commenced firing, the belts between the sprockets and the guns tightened and the platen arms moved across, engaging the clutches. If a belt jammed, an overload device would disengage the clutch and, once the obstruction had been cleared, the clutch could be re-engaged by hand. This sounds more complicated than it actually was; in practice the air gunners had no problems in operating the machinery. The original design, created by Power Mountings, handed the patent rights to Frazer Nash for aeronautical purposes during the pre-war years. Frazer Nash turrets were subsequently built by the Parnall Company.

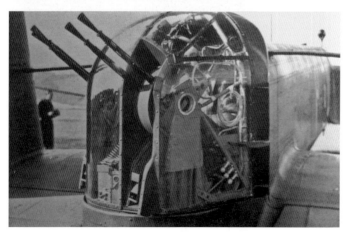

The Frazer Nash
turret seen from
the exterior and
interior perspective.
The gunner's
hand grips and
firing buttons are
clearly seen on
the central control
column, with
the ammunition
feed running into
the guns. The
gunner's simple seat
arrangement and
the wide lap belt
fastenings are seen
over the threshold
into the turret.
(*Ron Bramley*)

The protective metal sheeting mentioned in the improved design was detrimental to the gunners' field of view and in addition, it limited the amount of ammunition that could be carried on some of the long-distance sorties because of the additional weight. These were the two most significant issues for the rear gunners – any impairment of view was likely to herald tragic consequences. Some air gunners made it known that they valued better vision and more ammunition over and above the additional protection that had been provided. In common with most turrets, when operating at the very low temperatures on night operations, the gunner's view was often restricted by misting and frost glazing over the Perspex panels. The removal of the front panel soon became widespread and this led to an official modification to the turret whereby the front panel was mounted in side grooves, allowing it to be dropped down to give a clear view to the front. The technical field of view available to the rear gunner was traversed 94 degrees to each beam, an elevation of 60 degrees and depression of 45 degrees.

The gunner would enter the FN.20 turret from the fuselage of the aircraft. After clipping his parachute to the quick-release hooks just inside the turret, he would climb into his seat and close the sliding doors behind him. An Air Ministry pamphlet, No. 132 Gunnery Sense, advised rear gunners to check the security of the rear gunners doors to make sure that they secured the locking catch properly. On early models of the turret, the catch would sometimes give way and this allowed the doors to open with the result that, without a backrest, the gunner was always likely to fall back into the fuselage or when traversing the turret to its full capacity the two doors would be torn away into the slipstream.

Gunnery Sense booklet produced by The Air Ministry.

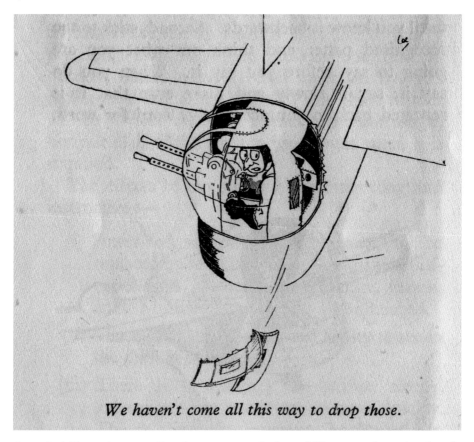

We haven't come all this way to drop those.

A comical illustration regarding the rear gunner's doors falling away from the aircraft. Despite this comical representation this was a serious problem in the early years.

Turret controls for the rear gunners were basically the same as in all Parnall turrets. The triggers on the twin-handled control column operated the four Palmer hydraulically gun-firing valves. The gunsight was the Mk.III, free mounted reflector sight with Mk.II C gyro gunsight.

The four Browning guns were harmonised to a point, 229 metres distant into a 3-metre square for night operations, and 366 metres on a 2-metre square for daylight sorties. The FN.20 turret was popular with gunners, and apart from the clear-view panel and door catch, few major modifications were undertaken. The .303 ammunition harmonised to the above guidelines created significant and impressive firepower from what may have been regarded as fairly light ammunition, so it became the responsibility of the individual air gunners to ensure the sights had been harmonized every day.

Problems had previously occurred with air gunners and other crewmembers reporting the old Type E oxygen masks being troublesome. Any oxygen deprivation was a serious matter when flying at height and a new mask, a Type G, was issued at the time of the introduction of the FN.20 turret. This mask also fitted the original Type B helmet which made it acceptable for a great many helmet combinations that existed and were already in use. As a result of the change, fewer problems were encountered with the oxygen equipment. By way of example as to the dangers associated with oxygen failure, the following account confirms that tragedies did occur. Flight Lieutenant Keith Thiele DFC, captained a Lancaster from No. 467 Australian Squadron on one of the Berlin raids in early 1943. During the approach to the target his rear gunner lost consciousness through lack of oxygen. It is assumed the pilot became aware of this as a result of a failure in communication. Thiele went on to attack the planned target whilst two of his crew endeavored to assist the rear gunner by removing him from his turret and rendering first aid. As soon as the bombs had been dropped the pilot took the Lancaster down through the flak and searchlights in order to reduce altitude in an attempt to save his gunners' life. This action was exceptionally dangerous and unfortunately it did not succeed in reviving the gunner. Artificial respiration was then continuously applied during the long return flight back to base during which the aircraft was maintained at low level. Unfortunately the crew's endurance and monumental effort in attempting to save the rear gunner's life were unsuccessful. He was pronounced dead on arrival by the medical officer. The squadron diary recorded that Sergeant Alvin John Broemeling RCAF had trouble with his face mask and its oxygen supply resulting in his untimely death.

When required to do so, rear gunners could abandon the aircraft by opening the turret doors, grabbing and clipping on their parachute then traversing the turret to the furthest position, pulling the pin from his seat harness and falling out backwards. In the event of the gunner being injured, another member of the crew could release the door catch from within the fuselage. There was also a manually operated hydraulic valve situated in the fuselage which enabled the turret to be turned from the outside. This facility was added after injured Gunners had been trapped within their turret with fatal consequences. If the hydraulic supply to the turret failed, the gunner could turn the turret by means of a turning handle from within the turret. All of these were designed in the hope that they would create a safe means of escape from the confined turrets. One of the ever present threats to a gunner was that of fire from within the fuselage. These fires would gain in intensity from the movement of air, fanning flames towards the tail section with the likelihood that it would destroy the rear gunner's parachute stored in the fuselage, resulting in tragedy.

7

The Boulton Paul Type E Turret

The Boulton Paul Type E turret proved to be one of the most successful turrets designed and produced during the Second World War. The Type E turret was easily fitted into the Halifax fuselage and its maintenance on station proved to be uncomplicated for the ground crews. Over 8,000 turrets were produced and fitted to all of the Royal Air Force's Halifax aircraft. The Boulton Paul Company used individual pumps operated by a 24-volt electrical supply feed to power the turrets. The turret was capable of traversing at two speeds as selected by the gunner, generally 3 mph but over short durations it could be switched to function at 5 mph. When compared to the Frazer Nash – Parnall turret which everybody was familiar with, the Type E turret looked rounder in its form and produced a more moulded profile. This particular turret was popular with the men who operated within it but that said, any design modernisation that created ease of use, comfort, or safety was well received regardless of the model or type.

When the air gunner was seated within this particular turret, to his front was the control table through which the operating stick or column protruded. There was a panel facing the gunner with the primary controls – the main motor switch, sight switch and oxygen supply socket – easily accessible. Directly in front was the Mk.III reflector sight fixed to an arm, which in turn was connected to the gun arm assemblies. Two armrests were provided, which were able to be lowered into position once the gunner was seated. These were required to provide some support to the air gunner's arms which were constantly controlling the operating column. The visibility that the Perspex panels provided, was fairly good apart from the downward perspective which was restricted by the equipment and the gunner's seating position. This problem was partly overcome by incorporating a feature deployed on other turrets – when the guns were depressed, two small hydraulic rams automatically raised the seat, keeping the gunner's line-of-sight parallel with the gun barrels and giving him a good view downwards. The gunner's body weight on the seat would inevitably cause the seat to gradually sink as a result of leakage through the hydraulic valve. To prevent this, a hydraulic lock was fitted which could be manually operated, should the gunner wish to lower the seat when power was not available. The four Browning Mk.II 0.303 guns

A Boulton Paul Type E rear gunner's turret photographed on what appears to be a newly delivered Halifax bomber. The immaculate Perspex glistens in the light. Note the applied external Perspex shelf fitted to the lower central panel and the smooth design around the entire turret. The early tail fin design dates this *c.* 1943.

The later design of tail fin illustrated in this evocative picture of two air gunners from 434 Squadron RCAF. Sergeants Nowlan and Dunlop celebrate their successful engagement shooting down a Ju88 during a mine laying operation in 1944. Sergeant Yvon Nowlan is sitting on top of his Type E turret. (*Canadian National Archives* PL29693)

were mounted on their sides in pairs and sat either side of the gunner. The guns cocking handles were within easy reach, essential for stoppage clearance and each gun was provided with 2,500 rounds of ammunition with the ammo boxes fixed on the port side of the fuselage, well forward and remote from the actual turret.

8

Perspex Panels

Bomber Command air gunners were encapsulated behind clear glass-like panels of Perspex which formed the exterior surface of their turret construction. Perspex provided the utmost visibility and fields of view possible, both essential requirements for the gunner to be able to scan the sky for enemy fighters. Hours were spent polishing the Perspex in order to remove smears or debris that would impair the gunners' visibility. The RAF bombers were primarily operating on night operations and inevitably at heights which induced low temperatures. The air gunner's view would often be restricted by frost on the Perspex panels. It became common, despite the added discomfort for gunners, to request the removal of the centre panel of Perspex to ensure the best possible visibility at all times. However, the removal of the Perspex created further exposure of freezing conditions for the occupants of the turrets. In particular there was a small area of exposed skin on the forehead between the leather flying helmet and the facemask and the rear gunners would treat this area with an anti-freeze ointment applied directly on the skin. This ointment, which was provided by the station medical officers, worked very effectively.

In all the hours spent gazing through the Perspex with strained eyes, very few, if any of the young men knew how or where it had originated from. The discovery and production of acrylic acid in 1843 was the key to its creation. Other developments followed, particularly the discovery of polymethyl methacrylate, now commonly called acrylic. In 1901, Otto Röhm wrote a thesis, 'On the Polymerization Products of Acrylic Acid.' Otto Rohm's research established a new set of polymers and this product was researched and eventually led to the creation of a flexible material that would become Plexiglas acrylic. In 1933 Rohm and his associate Haas, polymerized raw materials between two pieces of glass. They created a transparent and break-resistant material which was soon trademarked as Plexiglas acrylic. Patented in Germany in 1933, Plexiglas became a well-known brand name. Commercial production of acrylic occurred in 1936 and other brand names such as Lucite and Perspex became common place in the industry.

In 1937 Plexiglas was exhibited at the World Fair in Paris. It opened new possibilities of design and application to a great many manufacturers and was

A Frazer Nash turret with the central Perspex panel having been removed by the ground crews. One of the lower sections of Perspex has been left installed which has been fitted with an edge strip, most likely designed to prevent rain or moisture being driven up and into the actual turret opening by the slip stream of air from beneath the turret. (*Real Photographs Ltd*)

subsequently used on a large scale during the Second World War. For security reasons, little publicity was initially given to this innovative product and in 1939, the British Government set up a technical services department to act as a link between the military and industry. This led to the appointment of a Plastics Controller who reported to the raw material department in the Ministry of Supply. The RAF, Air Ministry and Ministry of Aircraft Production oversaw the deployment of Perspex in the production of bomber cockpits, gunners' turrets and nose compartments. In the United States, the Army and Navy Air Corps authorised the exclusive use of Plexiglas acrylic sheet in the construction of its aircraft, leading to an intense collaboration between Rohm and Haas, the armed forces and the aircraft manufacturers. Plexiglas and Perspex acrylic sheet found a strong market in all military aircraft due to its strength, being shatterproof, weather-resistant and providing excellent optical properties.

The Air Ministry subsequently issued contracts to several companies to supply materials to the most specific and exacting specifications imposed by the Ministry of Aircraft Production. In 1942, *Flight Magazine* published the list of approved plasticised material suppliers to DTD specifications. DTD 339A – known in England under the trade name of Perspex, was supplied in various thicknesses and the tensile strength was required was to be not less than 2.75 or more than 4.25 tons per square inch. The list included the following:

Gregory and Co. (G. H.) (Plastics) Ltd., 79, Lea Bridge Road, London, E.10. Gregory and Co. manufactured moulded Cellulose Acetate and other thermoplastic sheeting in connection with Air Ministry contracts. [Their range of components included gun heating pipes and other parts from Celastoid (Spec. DTD 315), windows, light covers, wing tips, etc., from Novellon (Spec. F. 56), Perspex (Spec. DTD 339A) and Rhodoid in green, red and blue (Spec. E. and I. 550). They developed a metallizing process which opened new possibilities for cellulose acetate mouldings in the aircraft industry for parts needing greater strength and fire resistance.]

Hadley Co. Ltd. Surbiton, Surrey. Hadley Co. Ltd. [who manufactured all types of mouldings from cellulose acetate and Perspex, to Air Ministry specifications, including windows, fairings, navigation and landing light covers, moulded ammunition chutes, goggles, and eye-shields.]

I.C.I. (Plastics) Ltd. The Hall, Welwyn, Herts. [I.C.I. Plastics were suppliers of Perspex brand transparent synthetic resin in sheet form to the Air Ministry's Specification DTD 339A.]

Plastilume Products Ltd., Station Works, High Wycombe, Bucks. [Plastilume Products moulded or shaped, machined and glazed aircraft parts such as windscreens, cabin windows, landing and navigation lamp covers in I.C.I. Perspex (synthetic resin), or in any of the acetate sheetings as well as other parts, such as spats and fairings, in opaque acetate.]

Splintex Safety Glass Ltd. Splintex-Noctex Works, Nightingale Road, London, W.7. [Splintex Safety Glass manufactured all types of Splintex safety glass for aircraft, specialising in both flat and curved multi-ply bullet-proof safety glass for pilots' screens, smoke tinted dimming panels and instrument glasses in all shapes, sizes and thicknesses. They specialised in moulding and trimming transparent Perspex (DTD 339) and Acetate (F.56) for curved front, side and roof windows, sighting domes, wing tip and landing light panels, and all panels, flat and moulded where clear vision is essential.][1]

As a new and innovative material which had rarely been seen, air gunners and ground crew eagerly recovered sections of the material whenever the opportunity presented itself. Aircraft engaged in action with the enemy, frequently returned with shattered turrets and cockpits. Scrap sections of the Perspex were crafted and polished into all manner of keepsakes and sweethearts. Brooches in the shape of hearts were most popular for mothers and girlfriends. Other more time consuming, exquisite models of aircraft were made by the more skilled individuals and the manufacturers themselves used offcuts to make bracelets which were sold to fund 'Weapons Weeks' or similar governmental savings schemes. Trimmings from large cockpit sections were heated and twisted into child size bracelets which proved to be immensely popular with the general public.

Carved pieces of Perspex crafted into various keepsake or sweethearts. The label attached to the bracelet clearly identifying that these off cuts were sold for war funds. The skill required to create some of these exceptional pieces is remarkable.

During the war years, the British surgeon Harold Ridley operated on several pilots and air gunners who had suffered with splinters of Perspex material in their eyes. Despite being an innovative material and absolutely ideal for use in cockpits and gunners' turrets, once Perspex had shattered as a result of enemy gunfire of flak, small shards of Perspex would easily penetrate any exposed area of flesh. Harold noticed that the eye had tolerated this material surprisingly well and the product itself appeared to avoid any infection being created. Based on this discovery, which proved to be well established following further experimentation, he later developed the first artificial eye lens which he implanted in 1949. As a result of this innovation, millions of modern day cataract patients now benefit from this unexpected development.

9

Pigeons

At the beginning of the Second World War the British National Pigeon Service supplied birds to the RAF. Both Coastal and Bomber Command carried these birds in long oblong boxes with drinkers and food containers. Some early containers were made of wicker and these remained in service for quite some time. If radio communication methods failed, (which often occurred in the early years of the war), and an urgent message needed to be sent, messages were written and secured within tiny containers attached to the birds' leg. This rather primitive system of emergency communication was responsible for saving many bomber crews that ditched into the sea whilst returning from operations. Within the operational crews, nominated members were responsible for the birds' welfare, often the turret gunner. In the event of unforeseen circumstances, it became their responsibility to ensure the birds were recovered from the aircraft and placed in the life raft. The crew of the Hudson shown in the illustration, includes a turret gunner who had the responsibility of the pigeons and he is seen carrying the wicker box.

Two Canadian air gunners, James D. Drennan and Gerald M. Drennan, twin brothers from Quebec served in a Hudson aircraft, and shared the responsibilities connected with carrying the crew pigeons. The twin brothers volunteered together and in 1941, the brothers unexpectedly served in the same crew in 407 Squadron, Coastal Command. On 5 December 1941, James was manning the rear gunner's turret of Hudson aircraft AM556, whilst his brother was acting as the wireless operator. The crew was undertaking a shipping strike sortie when their Hudson was shot down by flak. The Hudson aircraft crashed into the North Sea and the entire crew was lost beneath the waves. It was a rare example and a tragic loss – twin brothers who served together within one aircraft. It was also an example of circumstances that saw the demise of pigeons restrained in their baskets when aircraft crashed or became engulfed in flames.

The RAF established an extensive bird breeding programme which included the training of young birds to supply the service. Inevitably, the introduction of better quality and reliable means of electronic communication saw the pigeon service cease in 1944. They were however, still deployed and dropped to agents and

The Hudson aircraft was fitted with a Boulton Paul C Type gunner's turret which sat towards the rear of the fuselage. The two crewmembers standing left are wearing the early Irvin combined suits and carry their parachutes in the large holdall. The aircraftsman wearing his tunic is the air gunner. He has been given the responsibility of the two pigeons contained in the wicker bird basket. (*Air Ministry*)

into underground movements in occupied territory by the RAF throughout the entire war. They were normally sent in small containers and parachuted into pre-arranged dropping zones where they were retrieved by the resistance operatives. Needless to say, some pigeons fell into German hands and the German *Wehrmacht* in Denmark, issued a standing order in early 1942, signed by the Chief of Staff of the German Forces. The orders ensured that all Allied forces pigeons were to be given food and drink before being delivered to central collection points run by the *Abwehr* (German counter-intelligence). Next, the pigeons were transported to a further location where bogus information was inserted into the message containers and the pigeons were released to fly back to England.

10

Rear Gunners' Training Crash

In many instances fate would play a part in taking many young potential gunners' lives before they had even commenced operational duty. Flying during the Second World War, even when not engaging the enemy, was inherently dangerous and there were many fatalities among young student air gunners. These were not always fully recognised and they became inconsequential when compared to the enormous losses whilst flying operationally, for example being shot down, killed by flak shrapnel, or suffering the terrors of crash landings along with the ever present dangers of flying with hundreds of gallons of aviation fuel and bombs over enemy territory.

Elsham Wolds aerodrome was just one of many bomber bases that spread across Lincolnshire during the war. The airfield was situated approximately 7 miles north-east of Brigg, on the A15 road near Elsham village, North Lincolnshire. RAF Elsham Wolds opened as a heavy bomber station, part of 1 Group, Bomber Command in July 1941. 103 Squadron moved onto the station and, unusually, remained there throughout the war. 103 Squadron flew many and varied operations within Bomber Command and in 1942, the squadron formed its own Conversion Flight at the station. The resident conversion unit facilitated the training of new crews within the large four-engined Halifax aircraft, in effect providing experience on the Halifax before being absorbed into the operational strength of the parent 103 Squadron itself.

Sergeant Christopher Morgan was a fully trained and operational rear gunner who served within the conversion unit strength. He was 27 years old, and would have been regarded as an old-boy compared to his pilot Sergeant William Bagley, who was just 19, and his flight engineer Sergeant Joseph Henson, aged 20. 103 Squadron had been operating with the two-engined Wellington bombers, only converting onto the larger Halifax in July 1942. The conversion onto the Halifax bombers was therefore in its early stages.

On 1 August 1942, the pilot Sergeant Bagley with just nine hours experience flying the Halifax, took aircraft R9379 on a training sortie. His crew of six included a second pilot, a term used to identify a pilot under training, who had the rather impressive name of Squire Lightowler. The training sortie authorised the Halifax to leave Elsham Wold and gradually climb to a height of 17,000 feet where the Pilot was to remain for some 30 minutes. The sortie was scheduled to take an estimated two and a half hours in total. Sergeant Morgan was manning the rear gunner's position with his Browning machine guns armed, despite the remote possibility of his guns ever being used. The Halifax was carrying an additional six persons, three newly qualified air gunners and three observers – navigators, all who had been recently posted onto the conversion unit. Trainees would be taken up to experience the effects of a reduced oxygen supply, however events overtook the objectives of this particular sortie, when within an hour of taking off, the Halifax was sighted in the neighbourhood of the aerodrome. Smoke was seen to be trailing from the port mainplane area and approximately a quarter of a mile from the airfield, the port-wing dropped suddenly and the Halifax spun directly into the ground from a height of approximately 500 feet. A massive fireball was sighted which was followed by a cloud of thick black smoke rising high into the air.

Constable Herbert Sanderson, the local Elsham Wolds policeman, witnessed the Halifax approaching the airfield. It was clear to him that the aircraft was in trouble and as the aircraft crashed into the ground, he commenced running through a farmers' summer pea crop to reach the scene. Herbert arrived to see the fuselage had broken open which enabled him to climb inside as best possible. The aircraft was blazing, but in the smoke and carnage he managed to disengage the straps of the first man he came across. With great bravery Herbert extracted the two bodies he could reach and despite the danger of exploding fuel tanks and ammunition, he returned into the wreckage many times. Despite his courageous

Constable Herbert Sanderson, the King's Commendation silver emblem can be seen alongside his service medal ribbons. The sleeve insignia is the Chief Constable's Commendation also awarded for his gallant rescue attempt in 1942.

efforts, no further bodies could be recovered. It became obvious to Herbert that all twelve members of crew had tragically perished in the incident. Later that day the airmen's remains were recovered and taken to the station's sick-quarters mortuary. The grim task of caring for the casualties and advising the next of kin commenced. Accordingly and in compliance to the family instructions, on 4 August the bodies of Sergeant Hancock, Sergeant Langan, Sergeant Bagley, Sergeant Lightowler, Sergeant McDonald, Sgt Munro and Sergeant Dinsdale were respectfully removed from the mortuary at Elsham Wolds and taken to the railway station for transit to their respective home locations. The following day the bodies of Sergeant Henson, Sergeant Morgan, Sergeant Keane, Pilot Officer Simons and Sergeant Finney were buried with full military honours in the nearby cemetery at Brigg.

Group Captain 'Connie' Constantine, the Officer Commanding Elsham Wold, personally sought out Constable Sanderson in order to thank him for his rescue attempts and brought Herbert's act of bravery to the attention of the Chief Constable. Constable Sanderson was duly awarded the Kings Commendation, announced in the *London Gazette* on 4 January 1943.

The crash investigation findings reported that the Halifax had stalled at the low height while the pilot was attempting a forced landing onto the aerodrome, following failure of the port outer engine. The engine failure was due to a very rapid loss of coolant, a simple set of circumstances that claimed twelve lives, four of which were trained rear gunners. Christopher Morgan was still manning his rear turret when the aircraft dived into the ground.

11

Flight Rations

All operational crewmembers were provided with much needed flying rations, made by WAAFs who would wrap up individual packs. These tended to include sandwiches, two packets of chewing gum, two bars of chocolate, two ounces of barley sweets, a packet of raisins and on occasions a small tin of Florida orange juice or a piece of fruit whenever available. The barley sugars were particularly desirable as once the crew had been flying for several hours on oxygen, their mouths would taste of rubber from the oxygen mask strapped across their nose and mouth, so by sucking on the barley sugars, it provided some relief in taking away the unpleasant taste.

The British Medical Association produced scientifically based air ration suggestions for aircrew consisting of health biscuits and fruit blocks but these were universally disliked by the men. The men preferred sandwiches made by the WAAFs with Spam being a favourite filling alongside hot, sweet coffee from cylindrical Thermos metal flasks, which were fitted with a wire handle and screw top lid. The filler was a cork stopper which fitted into the lip of the glass liner and it was fairly effective but regardless, fluids did not remain hot for more than two to three hours.

It was a common occurrence to label crewmen as pessimists if they consumed much of their rations on the outward portion of the sortie prior to reaching the flak and fighters. Optimists however, were those who saved their rations for the return flight back to base. A small tin of Horlicks energy tablets was always available to supplement the flight rations and the manufacturers produced these in small tins with 'As supplied to the Air Ministry', printed on the lids despite the fact that they were available to the general public and described as a general food.

Each aircraft would carry a British emergency ration tin that contained a large block of chocolate. Each tin had a package date on the label with text on the lid which read, 'Emergency Ration – Purpose of Contents – To be consumed only when no other rations of any kind are procurable.' These tins also carried a formal notice: 'Not to be opened except on order of an officer', clearly making them an accountable item and not for general consumption.

In addition to flight rations, the Air Ministry issued bomber crews with tablets that were designed to assist in keeping the crew alert and effective in operations.

A Stirling crewmember Sergeant Len Tonkin, 214 Squadron, exiting the rear access door carrying his parachute and holding his personal issue Thermos flight ration flask. He is wearing the early 1940 sheepskin-lined flying boot renowned for falling off during any parachute descent. (*Ian Tonkin*)

These originated from research carried out by the Flying Personnel Research Committee. They had established that a German pilot captured early in the war, had been in possession of a small amount of tablets which following analysis, showed them to be sugar with a small quantity of an amphetamine like substance. It was clear that these were issued by the Luftwaffe for a reason, so it triggered the department to conduct research on the subject. The results of the research, which included operatives at the Medical Research Council based at Cambridge University, subsequently led to the Air Ministry issuing Benzedrine to aircrews during the war. The small tablets were used by some men to help with the serious fatigue that was likely to overcome them, particularly rear gunners who had the responsibility of keeping awake and alert in all extremes. The use of Benzedrine helped them to maintain a satisfactory level of concentration. Benzedrine was by no means mandatory and the responsibility to take or otherwise, rested with each and every individual. Benzedrine, which was the trade name for amphetamine, was also incorporated into the escape packs carried by individual airmen. Evidence exists in a number of post war evader reports, that Benzedrine tablets helped some men to escape from dire situations and they were recognised as being of great assistance in securing freedom. The RAF Type 2 rations and escape packs were made from two sections of clear acetate plastic. They contained food rations sufficient for 48 hours and included high-energy foods such as the Horlicks tablets, chocolate, barley sugar sweets, a tube of condensed milk and chewing gum. The survival aids included matches, magnetised razor blades a small compass, a heliograph signal mirror, Benzedrine tablets, water-purifying tablets, a rubber water bottle, needle and thread and fishing twine.

12

Armoury Duties

Rear gunners were responsible for the maintenance of their guns, a serious responsibility as they were required to be in prime condition at all times. The Station Armoury was a place where the air gunners and the armoury staff frequented on an almost daily basis. Aircrew personnel would generally pedal cycle around the aerodrome and a row of cycles left by gunners was always present, propped up adjacent to the armoury's gunnery section.

The gunner who ensured the guns were uncocked and safe generally removed the Browning guns from the turret after every operation. The fire and safe unit, mounted on the side of the gun body, was operated by a pneumatic actuator. Turret guns were fired by hydraulic units or electrical solenoids controlled by triggers or push buttons on the turret control handle. The guns were made safe by pressing a release pin at the back of the fire and safe unit and that procedure always took place prior to the removal of the guns from the turret.

At the armoury, the guns would be stripped down, cleaned, oiled and made ready for the next operation. Each gun was marked with its number and type designation making them individually identifiable. With sufficient maintenance, malfunctions in firing were reduced to a minimum although the most usual stoppage was likely to be caused by rogue ammunition or badly made-up ammunition belts. It was also possible that the links could, on occasions, jam in the ejection outlet of the gun. Turret gunners could identify and clear stoppages with a hooked tool kept handy in the turret, and it would also be frequently seen tucked down into one of their flying boots. Clearing a gun jam was something that all gunners were trained to perform instinctively, a skill they should be able to perform with their eyes closed. The gunners also kept a looped wire or cocking tool which was used to clear the gun – this was normally retained in a pouch to the side of their seat within the turret so that it was always available.

Browning ammunition belts were made up in the early war years by the station armourers, using hand-wound belt-making machines. On some occasions the bullets would be inserted into the links by hand. The make-up of the belts varied with the unit or upon direction by the gunnery leader. In the majority of Bomber Command groups, one in five rounds was a tracer round but this

Ground crew personnel loading a newly cleaned and prepared Browning gun into the rear turret in preparation for an operation that night. The rear doors of this Whitley turret illustrate the additional room created to allow the rear gunner better headroom when escaping from the turret in emergencies. (*Ron Bramley*)

was by no means a universal rule. Various types of tracer were designed by the munitions manufacturers; one type burned red for approximately 400 yards then changed to a brilliant red, indicating that the ammunition was nearly spent whilst another tracer round was designed to delay a trace until it had travelled 200 yards so as to avoid giving away the position of the aircraft. Station armourers had an instant way of identifying ammunition by colouring the tips of the bullet rounds and it became standard practice within the command to do so. Red tracer rounds had white or grey colouring, depending on day or night use, whilst the incendiary rounds designed to create inflammable damage were identified with blue paint. The manufacturers impressed each individual round on the rim to provide identification between the various rounds: 'BIV' for incendiary and 'GVI' for daylight tracer. The standard armour piercing rounds was marked 'WI'.

When the Browning machine guns were carried in the aircraft, differing moisture conditions and more specifically rain were always likely to be present. Any gun was capable of suffering from water penetration but fortunately the movement through the air by the aircraft, created a significant slipstream which tended to force any water away from the rear gunners' turrets. However on the ground, the opposite was true and rain easily penetrated the actual turret and

An RAF Corporal holding a belt of Browning ammunition and the RCAF air gunner discussing the configuration of the round to be loaded into his turrets supply. The crest worn on the air gunner's right sleeve indicates his rank of Warrant Officer. (*Ron Bramley*)

guns. Ground staff in many instances used wax covered tarpaulins that were able to cover the turrets or covers used specifically to simply cover the actual gun barrels alone.

Rear gunners were always likely to have a damp seat after inclement weather as rain easily penetrated the turret so they frequently took personal measures to avoid their small seats from getting wet. To add to their discomfort, the electrically heated clothing that the rear gunners wore was susceptible to malfunctions due to the independent plugs that were attached to the trousers, jacket and gloves. Water or moisture were the last thing that these men wanted to see when their lives, to a certain extent, depended upon the protection from the heated clothing they wore. The favoured gauntlets worn by the rear gunners had electrical inner white, fleece-wool lining and two electrical contacts on the inside forearm. These frequently had a black, silk outer-glove, which was worn inside the leather full gauntlet.

Rear gunners frequently favoured the 1941 pattern Sidcot Flying Suit. It was identical to the early suits used by aircrew personnel, a product of the First World War designed by Sidney Cotton, from whom the suit got its name. The 1941 pattern suit was fitted with electrical heating elements but the garment required looking after with some care as the elements could easily be damaged. The sculpture of an air gunner, which forms part of the impressive Bomber Command Memorial in London, illustrates the late Sidcot suit in great detail. It was also not an uncommon sight to see an air gunner wearing the Taylor flying suit, also known as the 'buoyancy suit'. This was very similar in design but was made with a yellow fabric and lined with kapok, which acted as a means of flotation should the wearer find himself in a sea ditching situation.

One of the seven impressive Bomber Crew sculptures created by Philip Jackson. Each figure was later cast in bronze from the original clay works and now stand nine feet tall within the Bomber Command Memorial which was unveiled in London in 2012. This is the individual clay sculpture of an air gunner, wearing a full Taylor buoyancy suit and 1940 pattern flying boot fitted with the ankle strap, which were added to help stop the boots falling off when bailing out of the aircraft. (*Philip Jackson*)

The Birmingham Small Arms Company Limited (BSA), supplied the majority of the 460,000 Browning guns during the war, however an extensive sub-contract scheme had been set up by 1941 in order to support the orders received from the War Office. Production of the Browning guns started in late 1938, when 3,809 were produced, and subsequent production figures steadily rose until 1942 when an impressive 16,300 units were completed. Production contracts with the War Office were completed at the end of 1944 and by this time, BSA had produced more than half the small arms supplied to Britain's forces during the war, which included nearly half a million of the Browning machine guns, one and a quarter million service rifles, 400,000 Sten guns, machine guns, anti-tank rifles, gun carriages, ten million shell fuses, over three and a half million magazines and 750,000 anti-aircraft munitions. Producing the small arms was not without risk. Several factories within the BSA group sustained damage from targeted raids by the Luftwaffe and more than fifty employees lost their lives whilst working in the BSA small arms factories.

Combat Reports

Royal Air Force combat reports were written by pilots and air gunners who engaged in aerial combat with the enemy during the Second World War in order to provide official records conveying the offensive action by the squadrons, wings and groups serving with all commands including the Fleet Air Arm. The records that have survived are now held at the National Archives in series AIR 50. During the war the air gunners in Bomber Command were unlikely to know that the information they wrote within these documents was providing significant intelligence, that was cascaded down to a plethora of official departments. The methods of attack, weapons and ammunition deployed were of key importance, but equally, the height and locations of where enemy engagements took place provided vital strategic intelligence. For air gunners, the submission of a combat report not only provided evidence of their engagement, but the probability of claiming a damaged or destroyed enemy aircraft. The gunnery leaders would additionally forward written reports to the station intelligence officer which concentrated on details relative to the air gunnery aspects and outlined the experience of the air gunner or gunners involved. To provide an example, in June 1943 the Lancaster 'Minnie the Moocher', captained by Sergeant A. H. Moores, was subjected to a night fighter attack that killed the rear gunner. The official combat report of that incident:

Public Record Office Air 50/190 Combat Report for 14/15 June 1943:

Lancaster M (ED413) of 57 Squadron on way to Oberhausen on night 14-15 June 1943, 22,000 feet (altitude ineligible obscured) 08.50 E, I.A.S.150. Three-quarters moon, many searchlights to port and starboard, no cloud or any unusual phenomena.

Air Bomber saw two twin-engined enemy aircraft, which he identified as Ju.88s flying 500 feet below. He reported these to the skipper, who continued in his barrel search. Rear gunner [Sergeant Reginald Frank Haynes, service No. 1205271] was then heard and seen to fire by Mid-Upper [Golding], but apparently the attack was too sudden for him to give the skipper any evasive

Lancaster ED413 'Minnie the Moocher' clearly illustrating the rear turret occupied by Sergeant Haynes and after being traversed to the starboard quarter, the enemy cannon fire penetrations through the side and rear sections are clear to see. A large section of Perspex has been destroyed and fallen away from the turret.

action. Mid-upper, who was unable to get his guns to bear on either enemy aircraft, then observed that one enemy aircraft climbed up to attack on starboard side and opened fire on rear turret. This fire must have killed rear gunner instantly as he ceased firing abruptly. It is assumed that the second enemy aircraft dived underneath Lancaster to port quarter and turned in to attack from port side. Lancaster was carrying out barrel search at time of attack and then turned to starboard losing about 800 feet.

Damage to Lancaster amounted to: twenty holes in port fin, one cannon shell in tail plane; rear turret riddled, unfortunately killing rear gunner outright, tyre of tail-wheel burst, main-plane peppered, also bomb doors, several holes in mid-upper turret but mid-upper gunner not injured – all hydraulics rendered unserviceable.

The loss of a life in these circumstances would have been devastating to the crew and also to Reginald's wife Annie, whom he had married in 1937. Reginald would have been seen as a father figure to the crew as he was aged 35 when he lost his life, an 'old' age for a crewmember. Annie together with his parents,

Frank and Sarah, took Reginald home to lay in rest in the Nuneaton cemetery, a Commonwealth war grave headstone fittingly marking his final resting place. Extensive repairs were required for the aircraft in which Reginald had lost his life, in order to return it to airworthy status. Approximately twelve weeks later it recommenced operations with 57 Squadron with a raid to Mannheim.

Combat report forms were always completed in a prescriptive format, with numbered sections. The account of George Meadows R191205, a recipient of the Conspicuous Gallantry Medal whilst engaged as a rear gunner with 166 Squadron provides an opportunity to see what information was included within a standard combat report submission. George William Meadows was born in Bowsman River, Manitoba, Canada, in June 1913. He enlisted into the Royal Canadian Air force during 1942, and completed his initial training as an air gunner in his home country. His final training was completed in the United Kingdom following a nine-day passage by Allied convoy that took place in June 1943.

The system of training at that time allowed George to pass through an Operational Training Unit, and then directly onto a Heavy Conversion Unit. He served at No. 1656 HCU, RAF Lindholm in preparation for operational duties in one of the Lancaster squadrons within Bomber Command. It must have been an exciting prospect, waiting for the final posting and wondering where he would be stationed. Eventually the posting arrived, and George and his newly formed bomber crew reported to 166 Squadron, at RAF Kirmington on 12 November 1943. He arrived at the commencement of the Battle of Berlin a concentrated period of attacks upon the German capital. George was to be introduced to operational flying just two operations before his first sortie to Berlin.

As the rear gunner to Flight Sergeant Fennell's crew, George was ready for the ultimate test – Berlin was always going to be a challenging target. In common with the main bombing force, slung underneath in the Lancaster's bomb bay was a large 'cookie' surrounded by the small bomb containers holding incendiaries.

The mid-upper gunner was Sergeant Cushing and both he and George had no idea what lay ahead of them. Lancaster DV365 appeared to be a reliable aircraft and this would have reassured both air gunners as they sat within their turrets. George would have, as was standard practice, checked the ammunition stowage and tracking system that fed his four Browning guns. The weight of the bulk ammunition was balanced in the aircraft by being forward from his turret and held in the main fuselage. This meant that the tracking that fed the long ammunition belts, ran along the fuselage into his actual turret, rising up before being fed into the actual guns.

The long November nights allowed for relatively early departures for the bombers. On this operation, Lancaster DV365 left the runway with all four engines straining to lift the aircraft with its full fuel load and the payload of bombs. DV365 rose into the air at 1723 hours and George was provided with an opportunity to see the airfield at Kirmington swiftly fade into the darkness. Their route, once the aircraft had formed up with the Bomber force, would cross the

English Channel and then into enemy held airspace. Any deep penetration raid into Germany provided the Luftwaffe night fighters, opportunities for attack, and for George it was no more than two hours into the operation before the enemy struck. The first attack set the precedent for further persistent efforts in an attempt to destroy their Lancaster. During the aerial combat that ensued, George sustained a bullet round that entered into his back and traversed through his body, exiting through his left groin. This was a traumatic injury which must have created intense pain, yet he remained in his rear turret and continued with the engagement against the night fighter on at least a further eight occasions during the operation.

The National Archives Air 50/292 holds the following combat reports relevant to this night's action. They are reproduced in the sequential numbering format as compiled on the official forms after the crews amazing survival and emergency landing at the airfield at Ford, Sussex:

First Combat:

 1. Night 26/27 November 1943; Lancaster I, ZZ/166, DV365, Berlin.
 2. 5017 North, 0437 East, 1930 hours, 19,500 feet.
 3. No cloud. Visibility. Hazy no moon.
 4. No searchlights or ground activity observed.
 5. No unusual phenomena.
 6. Enemy aircraft not seen.
 7. Not observed.
 8. Cannon and machine guns used.
 9. Enemy aircraft not observed.
 10. One attack. Enemy aircraft attacked from dead ahead. Breakaway not seen.
 11. No evasive action was taken.
 12. Our gunners did not open fire.
 13. No damage to enemy aircraft. D.R. compass and master unit hit, also mid-upper and rear turrets hit. Rear gunner wounded.
 14. No rounds fired.
 15. Mid-upper: 1615703 Sergeant Cushing. Rear gunner: R191205 Sergeant Meadows.
 16. Monica fitted. Warning received approximately five minutes before attack.
 17. The attack definitely took aircrew by surprise and the pilot stated that it was all over before he could take evasive action or do very much about it. Rear gunner and mid-upper did not see enemy aircraft during this attack. All crews have been warned of the possibilities of the enemy carrying out a head on attack.
 18. Tracer first observed ahead by the pilot of our aircraft. Range could

not be estimated. No evasive action was taken. No damage to enemy aircraft observed. D.R. compass and master unit hit, also mid-upper and rear turret and rear gunner wounded.

Second Combat:

1. Night 26/27 November 1943; Lancaster I, ZZ/166, DV365, Berlin.
2. 5017 North, 0425 East, 1935 hours, 19,000 feet.
3. Visibility hazy.   No cloud or moon.
4. No searchlights or ground activity observed.
5. No unusual phenomena.
6. FW.190 (one)
7. No lights carried.
8. Disposition of armament not observed.
9. Enemy aircraft was first seen by the mid-upper gunner on the port quarter at approximately 800 yards range.
10. One attack. Enemy aircraft attack from the port quarter up to dead astern, breaking away to port bow in shallow dive.
11. Our pilot corkscrewed to port as soon as enemy aircraft had committed himself to an attack at 600 yards range. Mid-upper gave the evasive orders 'corkscrew port', 'go'.
12. Enemy aircraft opened fire at 600 yards range, firing two short bursts until breakaway, scoring hits on starboard mainplane and tailplane.
13. Both mid-upper and rear gunners opened fire at 600 yards range, firing long bursts until breakaway. Port gun became unserviceable in mid-upper turret owing to being hit by cannon shell. Wireless operator and navigator injured, wireless operator in the back of the head, navigator in the left shoulder. Damage to enemy aircraft not observed.
14. Mid-upper fired 250 rounds. Stoppage in left-hand gun, due to damage by cannon shell. One of the left-hand guns in the rear turret was also hit and put out of action after the rear gunner had fired 150 rounds.
15. Mid-upper: 1615703 Sergeant Cushing. Rear gunner: R191205 Sergeant Meadows.
16. Monica fitted, warning received five minutes before attack. Pilot corkscrewed on warning but as no attack was made resumed course.
17. The enemy aircraft carried out a normal attack and the correct evasive action was carried out by our crew.
18. Enemy aircraft was first seen by mid-upper at 800 yards range. The combat manoeuvre ordered by the mid-upper was the corkscrew. Enemy aircraft opened fire at 600 yards range, firing long bursts until the breakaway. No damage to enemy aircraft observed.   Enemy aircraft scored several hits on our aircraft starboard mainplane and also tailplane. Wireless Operator and navigator wounded.

Third Combat:

1. Night 26/27 November 1943; Lancaster I, ZZ/166, DV365, Berlin.
2. Position between Charleroi and Caen. Time between 1935 and 2030 hours,
3. Visibility. Hazy no cloud.
4. No unusual phenomena.
5. (Space not used)
6. Ju.88 (one)
7. No lights carried.
8. Armament situated in nose of aircraft.
9. Mid-upper first sighted enemy aircraft at 400 yards on the starboard quarter, slightly up.
10. One attack. Enemy aircraft attacked from the starboard quarter up, breaking away to starboard beam level.
11. Mid-upper gave the evasive order 'corkscrew starboard', 'go' on first sighting enemy aircraft.
12. Enemy aircraft opened fire at 400 yards, firing one continuous burst until the breakaway. Mid-upper opened fire until ammo in the right hand gun was expended. Left hand gun was out of action due to being hit. The crew is not certain if the rear gunner [George Meadows] opened fire on this attack or not as he is now in hospital wounded, no information can be obtained at the present time.
13. No claims of damage to enemy aircraft. No hits occurred to our aircraft.
14. 100 rounds from the mid-upper. Unknown, from the rear turret.
15. Mid-upper: 1615703 Sergeant Cushing. Rear gunner: R191205 Sergeant Meadows.
16. Monica fitted. No warning given.
17. Enemy aircraft carried out a normal attack and the correct evasive action was taken. The gunners were rather handicapped in the shooting, having had some of their guns put out of action and also servo ducts damaged.
18. Enemy aircraft was first sighted by the mid-upper at 400 yards range on the starboard quarter, slightly up. The combat manoeuvre given was 'corkscrew starboard'. Enemy aircraft opened fire at 400 yards range; Mid-upper opened fire with one gun firing until he ran out of ammo. No damage to enemy aircraft observed and no damage to our aircraft.

Two days after the raid, once the intelligence summary had been completed and submitted, George was recommended for the Conspicuous Gallantry Medal. The recommendation read as follows:

This airman was the rear gunner of a bomber detailed to attack Berlin one night in November 1943. During the operation the aircraft was attacked by a fighter. Bullets from the enemy aircraft hit and damaged the mid-upper and rear turrets, one bullet struck Sergeant Meadows in the back, which was deflected by the wiring in his electrically heated clothing, and came out in the groin. Another attack developed, and the mid-upper gunner, the wireless operator and navigator were wounded. Despite his injury, Sergeant Meadows remained in his turret and by his excellent co-operation with the pilot, together with his good shooting, beat off a further eight attacks by fighters. This airman showed skill, courage and fortitude of a high order.

Following the events of 26-27 November and having landed at the aerodrome at Ford, West Sussex, George was immediately taken to the St Richards Hospital in nearby Chichester. A month later he returned to 166 Squadron arriving on 28 December 1943. He was greeted with the tragic news that Charles Cushing, his mid-upper gunner, had failed to return from a raid on 16 December 1943. His fellow air gunner, who had experienced that amazing episode of combat had lost his life in the dark skies over Berlin, and he now lies in the Hanover War Cemetery, cared for by the Commonwealth War Graves Commission.

George Meadows CGM returned to operational fitness on 27 April 1944. He continued with his tour of duty and was later commissioned and repatriated to Canada in late November 1944. His survival as a rear gunner had clearly been against the odds and the award of the CGM acknowledged his immense bravery over Berlin.

14

Corkscrewing

'Corkscrew to port' – these were words that rear gunners hoped that they would never have to shout into their microphones. When these words were heard, everybody in the aircraft knew exactly what was about to happen and why the rear gunner had uttered the emergency call. The corkscrew was a manoeuvre taught at operational training units, and seen as the recognised way to try and avoid an imminent or active attack by night fighters. All pilots acted instinctively to the utterance of those words from their rear gunner, and when a bomber corkscrewed, the worst place to be was in the rear turret. The pilot, who would have been flying at between 200 and 225 mph, would immediately open the engine throttles, banking 45 degrees to make a diving turn to port and descending some 1,000 feet in just five or six seconds, whilst reaching airspeeds of nearly 300 mph. After the descent, the pilot would pull the aircraft into a climbing turn, still to port. As the wings went down, the tail would come hurling up resulting in the gunner who was facing backwards going skyward incredibly fast, and then the tail section was plunged back down as the pilot pulled back on the controls, causing the plane to climb steeply in the opposite direction. The G-force pressure on the rear gunner's head would have felt like a ton of concrete with their chin pressed hard into their chest. The rise and falls were initially in thousands of feet, reducing to around 500 feet per corkscrew. While the corkscrew was initially being undertaken, the gunner would attempt to fire at the enemy fighter who would have been attempting to maintain contact on the tail turret. The flight path taken in the sky would replicate a coiling corkscrew configuration hence the name of the manoeuvre.

It goes without saying that a corkscrew could be replicated by turning to either the port or starboard but regardless the stresses imposed on the bombers airframe were intense and these manoeuvres were known to induce structural collapses, most probably failures connected to combat or flak damage. The weight of the laden bomber with thousands of gallons of fuel, oil and the heavy bomb loads was significant and pilots required a lot of strength to complete the corkscrew effectively. The corkscrew had three primary features built into the manoeuvre that were of benefit. It created an excellent chance of throwing off the night-fighter's attack, and even if they were not thrown off, the bomber represented a seriously difficult target to follow. Finally, as the manoeuvre was most probably executed along the main heading, towards or away from the target it created the minimum deviation from the bomber's intended direction. Without any doubt, this manoeuvre saved a great many bombers from destruction but ultimately the success or failure of these emergencies rested solely on the shoulders of the rear gunner's alertness in shouting the words, 'Corkscrew to port!'

Early Halifax aircraft were powered by Rolls-Royce Merlin engines, similar to the ones in the Hurricane and Spitfire. In 1943 these were changed to the air-cooled Hercules engine. This change made the aircraft much easier to corkscrew when attacked by a German night fighter, not to mention creating better handling conditions on take-off. The photograph illustrates a Merlin equipped Mk.I Halifax with an interesting camouflage configuration.

15

Prisoners of War

The percentage of air gunners held in prisoner of war camps was high due to the fact that they always outnumbered the other aircrew trades. That said, rear gunners faced difficulties when escaping from their turrets and the unique enclosed environment was just as likely to cause their death. Those men that were successful in escaping from an airborne incident inevitably had to engage the use of a parachute and hope for a safe descent to earth suspended below their silken canopies. Having executed a safe escape, there were two possible outcomes: immediate capture or, if lucky, an opportunity to evade capture and commence a treacherous journey to safety through enemy held territory. Without question, an evasion was attempted if at all possible, but the odds of success were always stacked against them. The unfortunate individuals that fell into central Germany were always likely to face the experience of reprisals against them with beatings and even death being inflicted on them. Lucjan Klucha, a rear gunner from 300 (Polish) Squadron suffered at the hands of the German police who located him whilst he was in hiding, having being shot down from his Lancaster whilst bombing Gelsenkirchen on 13 June 1944. He was the only survivor from his crew but his life was also taken when the police transported him to a pre-arranged location and executed him. This was not an exceptional case by any means and many of these atrocities were investigated post-war. In this particular instance, one of the guilty parties was identified and, after a trial in 1948, he received a sentence of life imprisonment.

For those aviators who were lawfully detained, they were sent under guard to the Luftwaffe's interrogation centre known as Dulag Luft, a name derived from *durchgangslager* or entrance camp. The German processing of RAF prisoners of war commenced at Dulag Luft surprisingly early on 15 December 1939, and continued throughout the entire war. Pilots and aircrew were initially detained in single cells and interviewed by specialist interrogators all of whom spoke excellent English. As the war waged on, the intelligence centre developed rapidly and the Germans mastered many ways of gathering and collating evidence. All Allied aircrew were interrogated but the Luftwaffe prioritised the aircrew personnel that were likely to be in possession of the knowledge of technical applications, as

Stalag Luft III PoW camp. Five of the prisoners are wearing the half brevet, no doubt several are most likely to be gunners. A pilot wearing the full wings sits alongside a man still wearing his flying boots. Red Cross food parcel boxes are stacked upon the cupboard. Within any camp, there was likely to be men who had a trade or skill that could be adapted to the industry of escape. In Stalag Luft III, there was a problem to be solved for the escape committee and a rear gunner from 78 Squadron named D. W. Lusty solved it. Essential escape documentation was needed for the 'great escape' and stiff linen covers were required to contain some of the particular documents. Lusty had some previous experience in the publishing trade and using tracing paper, cardboard, and other handicraft supplies provided by the YMCA. He created superb linen replicas which were used by the escapees.

opposed to tasks such as manning the Browning machine guns. All Allied airmen who went through this process and were later destined to spend the rest of the war behind barbed wire in the various PoW camps that were sprawled across occupied Europe.

Life and companionship for the rear gunners within the various PoW camps was a sharp contrast from the solitude of serving in their isolated turrets. Even within what should have been the safe confinement of a camp, chances of seeing the end of the war and the much hoped-for Allied victory, were slim for some whose captivity ended in tragedy. The following account secured from official records and personal PoW records bears witness to events that took the lives of two Bomber Command rear gunners whilst held behind the wire.

Sergeant Percy Crosswell, a Canadian was serving in the Canadian 429 Squadron. His crew was made up with men from the USA, Canada and Great Britain and they regularly flew within Halifax LK802. On the night of 22 April 1944 whilst progressing towards Dusseldorf, enemy anti-aircraft flak hit the aircraft as they flew over Holland. Having sustained serious damage reports indicated that their aircraft appeared to have purposely ditched into the 'St Elizabeth Polder' in order to avoid a Dutch residential area of occupied houses. The Polder was an area of ground reclaimed from the sea and protected by a system of water dykes. The Germans forbade the recovery of two of the aircrew who had died – their remains were known to be in the crumpled wreckage. It was not until June 1945 that the area was drained and the two unfortunate crewmembers' bodies were finally and respectfully recovered.

The four other crewmembers survived the crash. One of them was Percy Crosswell. He managed to make contact with the Dutch underground operatives and was sheltered by them to avoid capture. At this time in mid-1944, the Germans were utilising various means to both infiltrate and frustrate the underground movements and they achieved a measure of success during late 1944 and early 1945. Percy was arrested by the German police while in hiding and became a prisoner of war where he was later to be incarcerated in Luckenwalde PoW camp. Percy became good friends with a fellow prisoner and Halifax rear gunner, Sergeant Geoffrey Johnson.

Geoffrey was a young 19-year-old who had been serving in the RAF with 158 Squadron and who had bailed out from his rear gunner's turret of Halifax MZ737 during a raid that took place on Essen in October 1944. Luckenwalde camp was always short of food but as the war progressed into 1945, conditions became extremely difficult for the huge numbers of men confined there. The Germans started the movement of men from Luckenwalde camp on 13 April 1945 and although not confirmed, it is possible that Percy and Geoffrey were included in the first group of men taken from the camp. However they were all later returned, as the goods train they were being loaded onto had been unable to depart, probably as a result of Allied bombing. Both of these young air gunners appear to have acted completely spontaneously in an escape attempt on that night. It transpired that in desperation they bravely tried to climb or cut through the barbed wire fence in an effort to escape. It must be said, that little hope would have existed for such a plan. At 2300 hours, four rifle shots were heard by the prisoners in their bunks. Geoffrey Johnson had been killed instantly at the wire, shot by a bullet fired from a guard's rifle. Percy Crosswell was also struck by the rifle fire, but he clung to life for 14 hours before he died at 1300 the following day. These two fellow rear gunners, Percy Crosswell and Geoffrey Johnson were both buried in the prison camp cemetery at 1030 on Monday 16 April 1945. As a result of post war evidence supplied by their fellow prisoners of war from Luckenwalde camp, both men were awarded a posthumous mention in dispatches award, recognising the escape attempt which had cost them their lives. The award was published on 13 June 1946.

The Royal Air Force Missing Research and Enquiry Services (MRES) was set up in an attempt to investigate the circumstances and deaths of all Allied casualties. In a vast number of incidents, either the Germans or other local authorities had interred casualties in graveyards close to the scene of their death or, in the case of PoW camps, close by. The MRES arranged for proper exhumation and formal identification wherever possible and in many cases, identity discs or dog tags and scraps of uniforms with the various brevets assisted greatly. At Luckenwalde there were no official records in existence to assist with the recovery of the victims buried there and a great many of the temporary grave markers were removed or destroyed. In addition the area was subjected to serious flooding which inevitably destroyed a lot of evidence. The Royal Canadian Air Force engaged in specific exhumations at the Luckenwald prisoner of war camp cemetery during May 1947, but despite exhaustive efforts, Percy Crosswell's body could not be located. In these dreadful circumstances where no remains were recovered, his life was commemorated on panel 279 at the Runnymede War Memorial. It should be noted that the authorities made further concerted efforts to locate the grave of Percy, but those efforts additionally failed to locate any trace of his body. Geoffrey Johnsons' remains were however recovered and he was later re-buried in the Berlin War Cemetery where the Commonwealth War Graves Commission tends his grave in perpetuity.

16

Sergeant Neil Stockdale

Rear Gunner, 102 Squadron

Squadron Leader George Geoffrey Davies was a most respected and talented pilot serving in 102 Squadron. He commenced his training in the Royal Air Force on 13 September 1939, war having been declared just ten days previously. Sergeant Neil Stockton became his regular and reliable rear gunner when he was posted to 102 (Ceylon) Squadron in January 1941. The operational duties commenced with a sortie to Rotterdam on 10 February where George flew as the second pilot in one of the squadron's Whitley bombers. Unfortunately the Whitley suffered a port engine failure on the return journey, which resulted in a forced-landing at Buckenham in Norwich. It proved to be a bumpy start to the tour of duty, which was followed by a crash landing at Sedgefield after his very next sortie to Cologne, and a through-the-hedge landing following a raid on Lorient in late March. These experiences in the Whitley's exceptionally low positioned rear gunner's turret, created by the rear wheel being positioned further forward from the tail would have been most disconcerting for Neil. Another one of the peculiarities of the Whitley was its wing design, which induced the aircraft in level flight to adopt a nose-down attitude, creating the unusual situation of the rear gunners' position being elevated.

For Neil, April 1941 started with sorties to the German target of Kiel. This port was a major target for the RAF – it had huge berthing facilities capable of holding the largest of Germany's naval vessels and some berths were more than nine metres deep which was particularly noteworthy. In addition, the 5th U-boat flotilla was based at Kiel and the harbour complex had upwards of twenty floating dry docks; it represented a target of some significance to Bomber Command. Following the attack on Kiel, Emden was bombed and in May a brace of outings to Hamburg and Bremen. In addition they struck the German battleships *Scharnhorst* and *Gneisenau* at Brest on the night of 11 May, and their Whitley Z 6576 was 'shot up very badly'. Despite the damage, the pilot was able to return to base, and manage a respectable safe landing. Their aircraft was repaired, but later failed to return from an operation to Hanover in July. Brest once again became the selected target for Neil and his crew on 10 June, where once again they tried to bomb Germany's three large warships. The 104

A full complement of ground crew undertaking various repair and maintenance duties on this Whitley bomber. Many of these duties were carried out in terribly harsh weather conditions across the open and windswept airfields. Aircrews were very understanding and appreciative of the dedication of their ground crews. (*Squadron Leader Davies*)

aircraft that attacked the target all returned safely, many bombs had landed within the docks but the ships remained intact and undamaged. With luck having appeared to have eluded Neil for quite some time, the subsequent operations to Aachen, Brest, Dortmund, Essen and Osnabruck proved successful, and thoughts of a smoother ride through the remaining operations occupied his mind. Once more however, his Whitley was shot up by a night-fighter on a raid to bomb the railway yards at Schwerte and Neil witnessed one of the accompanying Whitley bombers being shot down on this operation. The searchlights were particularly effective, regarded as beams of death waiting to locate and snuff out the life of the bombers. Plus, the flak gunners were getting very good at predicting the height of the Whitley aircraft.

Bremen was the next operational target, taking place during the night of the 14 July in Whitley Z 6820. The crew was Pilot Officer E. Anderson, Pilot Officer N. Bennett, Sergeant W. Swain and Neil in the rear turret. This return raid to Bremen was to be a most significant operation for the pilots and crew of Whitley Z 6820. The events that night are portrayed in the recommendation for the Distinguished Service Order. The recommendation provides an excellent statement of events.

The immediate award recommendation published in the *London Gazette*, 8 August 1941, states:

This officer was Captain of Whitley aircraft Z 6572 [6820] detailed to carry out a bombing sortie against Bremen on the night of 14-15 July 1941. At about 0215 hours, when over the target area, the aircraft was held in

RAF daylight bombing raid upon Brest, the targets were the Nazi battleships *Scharnhorst* and *Gneisenau* in dry docks and the cruiser *Prinz Eugen*, protected by anti-submarine nets in the harbour basin. Brest was a regular target for Bomber Command and significant effort was deployed to bomb these particular battleships over many months.

a concentration of searchlights and was heavily fired on by flak. The flak ceased suddenly while the aircraft was making its run on to the target, and although this indicated the immediate presence of enemy fighters, the captain continued on his bombing run and warned the rear gunner to keep a very sharp look out for enemy aircraft.

Very shortly afterwards, the captain saw tracer and cannon shell passing very closely on both sides of the fuselage of his aircraft and felt considerable movement on the control column, indicating that the control surfaces had been hit. At the same time the rear gunner called out to him that he had been hit by bullets from the enemy aircraft. The gunner was in fact killed in this first attack, and the rear turret rendered useless. The aircraft then went out of control; the nose going up until it stalled and went into a left hand spin at a height of 10,500 feet. The captain wound the tail-adjusting gear well forward to try to gain control by using the elevator trimming tabs, as the elevator control wires to the control column had been shot away. He found however, that the stop on the tail-adjusting wheel prevented it from being moved forward for more than half a turn, and with great presence of mind the captain instructed the navigator to get the axe and hack away the stop. The navigator did this and by winding the wheel fully forward and by skillful use of rudder and engines, the captain succeeded in righting the aircraft after having lost 7,000 feet. However, it was only by skillful use of engines and elevator tabs that the captain was able to maintain the aircraft in level flight, and soon after coming out of the spin the aircraft was again attacked by enemy fighters and later by light flak.

During the whole of this most hazardous experience the captain showed the utmost determination and coolness and was alone responsible for extricating the aircraft and the remainder of the crew from almost certain destruction. He continued to fly the badly damaged aircraft, still exercising exceptional control, until he reached Driffield, to which airfield he had been diverted owing to fog at Topcliffe. Knowing that his elevator controls were shot away and only a few weeks before having seen an aircraft stall and crash at Topcliffe while trying to land in the same position, this officer still stuck to his post and gave no thought whatever of abandoning the aircraft. With great skill and care he succeeded in landing at Driffield with no further damage to aircraft or crew than that sustained over enemy territory.

I cannot speak too highly of this most marvellous effort on the part of an officer who has already done exceptionally good work during a number of previous sorties. His coolness, courage and devotion to duty saved the lives of the remainder of his crew, and brought back to this country a valuable aircraft. I strongly recommend him for the immediate award of the Distinguished Service Order.

In the words of the Air-Vice Marshal who approved the recommendation. It was, 'One of the best shows of the war by a captain of an aircraft in his group'. His group captain wrote that the pilot displayed 'almost miraculous airmanship in bringing his aircraft and crew safely back to this country'. This was probably no understatement when one considers the damage inflicted on his Whitley which included over forty large holes, including those that punctured the petrol and oil tanks, two tyres shot through by cannon fire and the elevators clean shot away from the wings. The rear gunner's turret had suffered intense damage to the starboard side, which was where Neil had traversed the turret, no doubt indicating that he had engaged the night fighter with some ferocity.

The pilot wrote the following entry into his pilot's flying logbook:

Operations Bremen MLR 719. [Reference for operational record book entry] Camera. [Reference to camera used to record operational dropping of bomb load.] Hell of a time over target. Clamped in searchlights, fighter attacked and killed air gunner Sergeant Neil Stockdale. R.I.P. Elevator shot away. A.S.I. useless BXF Driffield. Port & rear wheels punctured. Good write up Awarded DSO.

Several newspapers carried accounts of the Distinguished Service Order awarded to George Davies, with one of these providing further details upon the night fighter attack upon his aircraft. Additionally the cutting provides further information on the circumstances that befell Neil Stockdale sitting in his Rear Gunners' turret.

Suddenly all the anti-aircraft fire stopped and he [the pilot] knew that fighters must be about. He had scarcely had time to warn the rear gunner when he saw tracer bullets coming at him from the front, while cannon shells seemed to be coming from below and up from the rear. The navigator sat unperturbed at his bomb sight with bullets and shells crashing past him and released the bombs on to the target. The captain heard the Rear Gunner call out – 'I'm hit'. He answered. 'Stick [with] it'. Then again he heard the Rear Gunner say, 'They've got me,' and that was the last he heard of him.

The turret has several penetrations where the metal skin surface has lost the paint finish and the Browning gun barrel has itself been struck by the enemy night fighters' rounds. The Whitley tail unit appears intact which indicates that the enemy fighter was only just off centre to the starboard side of the bomber when it discharged its fatal rounds into the rear turret.

Upon returning to base Sergeant Neil Stockdale's body was removed from the rear turret and taken to the station mortuary. These were grim circumstances for those involved in such duties and it was not uncommon for the deceased's own crewmembers to have to undertake such tasks. The confinement of the rear turret created difficult circumstances for such extractions and little imagination is

Above and below: Two photographs from the collection of Squadron Leader Davies. The rear gunner's turret in detail, illustrating the damage sustained in the attack – of note are the Browning gun barrel casings which has been torn back by the enemy gunfire. (*Squadron Leader Davies*)

required to understand how traumatic it must have been. The formality of writing to Neil Stockdale's parents in Huddersfield fell to the Commanding Officer and following arrangements with his family, Neil was later buried with full military honours at the town cemetery in Driffield, situated thirty miles East of York.

Following repair, Sergeant Neil Stockdale's rear turret was soon to be manned by another volunteer, but within a matter of weeks the aircraft and crew failed to return from a raid to Berlin on 8 November 1941. The squadron records indicate that a wireless message was picked up alerting others that the crew required assistance but nothing further was received. It was presumed that the aircraft was lost at sea whilst returning from Berlin, a fate that befell three Whitley aircraft from 102 Squadron that same night. Those fifteen crew names are now commemorated on the Runnymede Memorial as they have no known graves.

102 Squadron Whitley N1386 being loaded with propaganda leaflets to be dropped during a raid over occupied France. A member of the flight crew is in the access door which would be used by the rear gunner, his guns can just be seen in this image. Whitley N1386 served in Sergeant Stockdale's squadron for some considerable time before it transferred to a training role. Remarkably the aircraft was still in service in June 1945.

17

Sergeant Eric Marvin DFM

Rear Gunner, 76 Squadron

Eric Marvin enlisted into the Royal Air Force during June 1940. He was 24 years of age and had lived and worked as an electrician in the Poole area of Dorset all of his life. His grandfather had served in the Royal Flying Corps in a ground duty capacity and this had been a deciding factor for Eric in volunteering for service in the RAF. Eric was appointed for ground trade duties as an electrician and provided with the lowest rank – Aircraftsman Second Class. He was posted to RAF Calshot, No. 3 Wing, School of Technical Training in Hampshire.

Working hard, he qualified and received a posting to serve with the newly formed 91 Squadron at RAF Hawkinge in February 1941. This squadron was being re-equipped with the latest MKV Spitfires, flying tactical reconnaissance sorties as singletons or in pairs. The Spitfires flew over the French coast into France, reporting back on enemy shipping and aircraft movements and only after completing their primary duty were they permitted to engage the enemy taking advantage of any opportune targets.

In early 1942, Eric responded to the request for ground crews to apply for aircrew duty in the RAF. Feeling comfortable with service life and having gained in confidence, Eric presented himself as an ideal candidate to the selection board. On 29 September 1942, he was accepted as an 'under training' air gunner and reported the news back to his parents who lived at 212 Bournemouth Road, Branksome, Bournemouth.

Eric completed his initial air gunner training during October 1942, and in November 1942 he moved to the No. 9 Air Gunner School at Llandwrog. Here he was issued with his personal observers and air gunners' flying logbook which was immediately rubber stamped with his course assessment. On 21 November he placed the first entry into his logbook, recording an hour in a Blenheim aircraft and performing a camera gun exercise. This set a precedent for an intense training period which concluded on 22 December 1942. Eric had fired a total of 3,100 rounds of ammunition and shot over 8 feet of camera gun film. All of his flying experience was within the Bristol Blenheim aircraft and his logbook recorded that the course had been achieved with just over 12 hours flying time. He achieved a pass mark of 76 per cent in his examination and was promoted to the rank of sergeant on 31 December 1942. A most chilling experience occurred for Eric during a firing exercise – shooting at the target drogue his guns jammed solidly. In combat, such circumstances if not immediately rectified would have serious consequences, and so being able to clear the jam provided great confidence to him.

In February 1943, Sergeant Eric Marvin joined other aircrew personnel at No. 10 Operational Training Unit. His air gunner training continued with additional camera gun exercises and some general flying. It was here that he was to form a crew. The process of forming a crew was far removed from the orders and directions that normally surrounded the life of these service men and it was left entirely to those young men who were put in one of the large aircraft hangers to sort out. Eric was invited to join as the rear gunner in Sergeant Arthur Thorp's crew as they had already flown together on 18 February 1943 when Thorp captained his first solo on a Whitley bomber. Eric happily took his place in the rear gunner's turret, flying on night training sorties and several bombing exercises. At the end of April 1943, Eric had reached a total of 114 hours and 25 minutes flying time recorded in his logbook, but this had all been within two-engined aircraft. Bomber Command had by now seen the development of larger four-engined aircraft and in order to operate the Lancaster or Halifax types, new crews were required to attend a conversion course.

Arriving at 1663 Conversion Unit RAF Rufforth, the exhilarating experience of climbing into the large Halifax bomber presented itself to Eric. At last he was going to fly in one of the command's heavy bombers. The Halifax had a Boulton-Paul gun turret in the tail and the controls were like a fighter pilot's control column; if you move the control to the right, the gun's turret will turn to the right, hold it back and the guns elevated upwards – the gun control replicated a modern computer games joy stick. It extended through a diamond shaped central cut out panel. The controls were swift in operation and the firing button was incorporated on that same central control, sitting above the central control was the reflector gun site. The conversion course was naturally designed for all crew positions to gain experience but the pilot was required to undertake a number of exercises learning to fly on three engine configurations. Eric had the opportunity to fire his guns but it was an infrequent event. These exercises did however provide opportunities to practice his escape procedures and emergency manual operation of the turret. The large turning handle sat conveniently to his left side, and enabled the turret to be manually turned in order to locate the access doors to face into the aircrafts fuselage, or for direct escape out of the turret into the slipstream.

The Halifax was a shapely aircraft, its wings spanning approximately 99 feet and with a length of 70 feet. The top line of its fuselage was straight with the lower line slightly curved and this design created the easily identifiable profile of the Halifax. The aircraft had the ability to fly higher than the Stirling even, it was accepted that aircrews could work at up to 10,000 feet with only a slight decrease

A Halifax bomber on the apron of an airfield. Both gunners' turrets have the Browning machine guns in place. The original Handley Page tail fin rudder design dates this to be an early model, the bulbous 'C' type mid-upper gunners' turrets were later replaced with the lower profile 'A' type of Boulton Paul design.

in efficiency created by a reduced oxygen supply. Over 10,000 feet, oxygen is required for efficiency and agility of mind, but at a height of over 15,000 feet oxygen is also required for safety. Any lack of oxygen supplied to aircrews increased the sensation of feeling cold and vision was most likely to be impaired this could lead to an inability to perform any task and for the member of crew to become sleepy. Breathing oxygen and communicating with the full facemask, whilst listening to the microphones fitted in your flying helmet, were experiences that required time to become competent at. In cases where sickness overtook them, efforts to avoid the mask becoming the receptacle for vomit needed to be immediately taken. Such an event would render communication and breathing oxygen almost impossible. Eric wore electrically heated clothing, fitted into his Irvin jacket and trousers, as no heating was provided to the rear of the Halifax. In addition, he would generally wear a Brynzie vest made of silk netting in a mesh configuration, a forerunner of the string vest.

The eventual and long awaited operational posting arrived for Eric and his crew to join 76 Squadron at RAF Sywell where during the first week in June, they flew on three cross-country exercises which were designed to allow the crew to gain a good orientation of the land. The squadron then moved station to Holme on Spalding Moor just north of the Humber and close to the towns of Beverley and Hull. It was not a welcome move for the squadron as they were leaving the comforts provided by the pre-war aerodrome at Sywell. On 16 June, Sergeant Marvin recorded in his logbook 'on station' and within two days, he had undertaken two air gunnery exercises and simulated fighter attacks. Sergeant Thorp was allocated Halifax P aircraft, the serial number was DK 201. This aircraft became the crews regular aircraft and one in which Eric flew the majority of his operational bombing sorties, having been manufactured by Rootes and allocated to 76 Squadron in June 1943.

The crew's thorough training was about to reap rewards when they received a briefing for an operation to Kreffeld. Pre-flight checks and personal tasks were completed. In common with all crews about to undertake their first operation into Germany, nerves and the harsh reality of becoming another of the endless crews that failed to return to base, filled their inner thoughts. Eric would have ensured his guns were in the best possible condition and that the Perspex was as clean as it could possibly be, alongside a few glances at the recognition models that abounded in crew rooms. For this operation, a total of 700 bombers were going to converge over Krefeld all with instructions to bomb on the pathfinder markings and respond to the instructions of the master bomber.

A few minutes short of midnight on 21 June 1943, Eric's tour of duty in Bomber Command commenced. Carrying a full load of fuel and bombs, the four Rolls-Royce Merlin engines strained at full capacity in an effort to try and lift the weight of the aircraft into the air. Eventually, DK 201 overcame the forces of gravity and the airframe entered the state of flight. Eric was enveloped in darkness looking back towards the airfield and naturally relieved to be safely airborne on the way to Germany. The moon was clear and in the knowledge that twenty Halifax bombers were all departing from Holme within a few minutes of each other, he kept a good look out. The target was reached and the bomb aimer was able to drop the bombs onto the clearly visible red target markers. The load was dropped successfully from 19,000 feet and as the aircraft left the area Eric could see smoke rising up some 8,000 to 9,000 feet. Sergeant Thorp landed DK 201 back at Holme at just past 0400. The raid had been a success for this novice crew. Not so for Bomber Command as it had cost an estimated 308 lives and forty-four aircraft failed to return – casualties from the inevitable night fighters and anti-aircraft flak defences. As always, hope existed that a large proportion of those men would survive and become prisoners of war.

Eric recorded in his flying logbook, the red ink entry, 'Ops Kreffeld'. The following night he simply entered 'Mulheim' and two nights later 'Wuppertal'. In just four days he had experienced three major raids upon Germany and completed nearly 15 hours' duty encased within his rear gunner's turret. The squadron experienced the loss of a most experienced crew captained by Pilot Officer J. Carrie and Group Captain D. Wilson RAAF. This most high-ranking officer had gone along as his second pilot and observer during the raid to Mulheim. Targets in the Ruhr were of utmost importance and the concentrated efforts of Bomber Command at this time became known as the Battle of the Ruhr. The expectations

Three heavy bombers can be seen overflying this heavily defended target. Flak is all around in the sky and below pathfinder marking flares illuminate the area. The sheer enormity of the task of bombing the well-defended targets over Germany could not be better illustrated than in this Air Ministry photograph retained by Eric Marvin.

imposed upon Bomber Command by the directives of the Casablanca summit earlier that year had been 'the progressive destruction and dislocation of the German military, industrial and economic system and the undermining of the moral of the German people where their capacity for armed resistance was fatally weakened.' Operations to achieve the directives of that summit lasted for nearly five months and 76 Squadron pursued in its objectives consistently.

In 1943, the squadron operated on 104 nights and lost fifty-nine crews to enemy action – some crews were almost reaching the end of their tour whilst others were no more than in single numbers of completed operations.

Surprisingly, Eric was selected for an additional gunnery course at No. 1484 Gunnery School at Driffield which necessitated him departing from the squadron on 26 June. This particular gunnery school was No. 4 Group's target-towing, refresher training unit and Eric operated the Frazer Nash FN4 turret in various ground exercises as well as enjoying the opportunity to partake in clay pigeon shooting. He consumed over 3,000 rounds of ammunition and fifty clays during the five-day course. The gunnery officer recorded the results in Eric's flying logbook classing him as 'A superior type of gunner who did exceptionally well by finishing top of his course.'

Returning to the station at Holme, Eric immediately re-joined his crew who were flying air to sea firing range exercises. Frequently such exercises were combined to provide the pilot with flying experience on two and three engines, and the flight engineers were actively engaged in such practices. Returning to the

A rather unorthodox way of exiting the Halifax rear gunner's turret, this may well be a posed press release photograph. Eric Marvin would normally leave his turret by simply exiting the twin doors and join his crew in the aircraft. (*Eric Marvin collection*)

airfield after these training sorties was always a pleasant experience for any crew because inevitably plans would have been made for that evening's entertainment at one of their regular pubs.

The Rear Gunner is shown climbing from his rear gun turret by the back doors, the turret having been swung around to expose the pair of exit doors. This method of extraction would normally have been used in any emergency escape from the aircraft. In normal circumstances the turret would be in its 'in line' position and with the doors open, the air gunner could leave the aircraft through the body of the aircraft. The ground crew aircraftsman is seen holding the gunner's parachute whilst the remaining crewmembers are seen to be climbing into the vehicle for transporting back to the airfields for their de-briefing.

Eric's navigator, Joseph Philippe Suzor, was the only officer in the crew but despite this, he was very much one of the men. This may possibly be explained by the fact that he was himself a minority, having volunteered to serve in the RAF from the former British colony of Mauritius. He was a most popular member of the crew and together they were subsequently tasked with a raid to Gelsenkirchen on 9 July. It was to be one of the first attacks against Hitler's oil stocks. The objective was to disable the oil supply, particularly the coal liquefaction plants which were necessary for fuel production. Following the raid, the refinery at Scholven was partially damaged resulting in the operation being regarded as

The normal crew access door to enter or depart the Halifax was much smaller than that of the Lancaster; it was an opening that included a section of the side fuselage and floor panel. The actual door lifted up and folded upwards into the aircraft, it was an easy procedure to lift oneself into the fuselage from the ground. This air gunner's half brevet can just be seen behind the life preserver, his parachute having been thrown into the aircraft prior to climbing in himself. (*Norman Hood*)

unsuccessful. Four hundred and eighteen aircraft had taken part in the attack and twelve had failed to return. The next raid to take place was on 17 July, and it too had a similar result in respect of limited damage being inflicted. This mission was to be a longer period of confinement for Eric as the target was the Peugeot motor factory at Montbeliard in the suburbs of the French town of Sochaux, close to the Swiss border. The factory was producing tanks and goods vehicles and had never previously been attacked by the RAF. Eric suffered from the exceptional cold and cramps during this operation which lasted just under eight hours. It was by far the longest and most uncomfortable period of time he had ever experienced to date.

The long high altitude operations exposed rear gunners to the dangers of frostbite. One particular danger was wearing any article of clothing that may be damp. This included the electrically heated outer clothing. All underclothing, socks and gloves needed to be thoroughly dried and warm, and in particular rear gunners were advised to avoid rushing in the heavy flight clothing to alleviate any tendencies to perspire. In wet weather they were told to ensure that their flying boots remained dry, as once the gunner has slid himself into the turret he had very little ability to move or reach anywhere close to his feet. In the circumstances of damp or wet feet, frostbite was almost inevitable. Skin damage could be caused within minutes because airman had to remove their gloves to make necessary adjustments to the equipment in the turret. This may only require a minute or two, however, during this brief time, fingers would become painfully cold and numb. Frostbite causes the skin surface to adopt a waxy white appearance, becoming completely insensitive to touch. Fingers were likely to go rigid and often became so stiff that they could not be moved with the other hand. Recovery from this condition could be quite slow, even after removal to a warmer environment, and quite often hours elapsed before the tips of the fingers began to soften. Even after the tissues had become less hard and were approaching normality, the waxy or ashen white ischemic appearance would persist for several more hours. Longer exposure would lead to permanent skin tissue damage and possible amputation. Eric made every effort to avoid the possibility of sustaining these types of injuries but the intense cold of the rear turret often created the impression that he was suffering from the condition.

Emergencies in the air sometimes subjected the crew to unavoidable exposure to frostbite. Such instances were acts of bravery of a most specific kind but the resulting injuries were terrible and frequently the loss of tissue required amputations and reconstructive surgery. The Guinea Pig Club was founded in 1941, and is now well associated with pioneering reconstructive plastic surgery that took place at the Queen Victoria Hospital in East Grinstead. The New Zealand surgeon, Archibald McIndoe, became the consultant surgeon to the Royal Air Force, specialising in plastic surgery. Although plastic surgery was established during the First World War, McIndoe was one of only three experienced plastic surgeons in Britain when war was declared against Germany in 1939. He carried out ground-breaking reconstructive surgery techniques on pilots and aircrew who had suffered serious burns or significant disfigurement whilst serving within the Commonwealth air forces. A lesser-known fact is that among the patients that he operated on were a significant number of casualties who had suffered from severe frostbite. The term 'guinea pig' indicated the experimental nature of the reconstructive work carried out on the club's members, and the new equipment and procedures designed specifically to treat these terrible injuries.

Membership was open to all Allied air forces servicemen who underwent surgery by Archibald McIndoe, primarily as a result of fire, but other injuries were included. Inevitably aircrews suffered considerably from explosions and fire eruptions when involved in crashes. However ground crew personnel often risked their lives in rescue attempts, resulting in similar injuries. Reconstructive surgery operations at East Grinstead conducted by McIndoe automatically entitled the patient to Guinea Pig Club membership. The types of injuries requiring his attention frequently entailed significant numbers of operations and the piece-by-piece rebuilding of damaged skin tissue over weeks, months, and years. Unlike many military hospitals at the time or since, patients at East Grinstead were encouraged to lead as normal a life as possible. They could wear their usual clothes or service uniforms instead of convalescent blues, and were encouraged to socialise as much as possible.

The emblem of the club became a guinea pig with RAF wings, to signify they were McIndoe's Guinea Pigs. The guinea pigs had their own particular style of black humour. If patients had fractures or lacerations the club members referred to them as 'mashed', and if they had severe burns they were 'fried' or 'hash-browned'. None of the patients came direct to the Queen Victoria Hospital, but were sent to general air force hospitals first. McIndoe then handpicked a selection of cases, by referral or personal intervention, from across the country. Initially most were British, casualties from Fighter Command during the Battle of Britain, but representatives from Canada, Australia and New Zealand were also present. The entire Commonwealth and Allied forces were eventually represented, however a total of around 80 per cent of the Guinea Pig Club membership originated from crews from within Bomber Command.

Air Chief Marshal Sir Arthur Harris directed Bomber Command to undertake four major raids against Hamburg in the space of ten nights, commencing on 24 July 1943. The planning of the operations took place under the name 'Operation Gommorah'. Many factors made Hamburg the focus of attention; it was an industrial city, home to the famous Blohm & Voss shipyards and hundreds of other small manufacturers grouped around and within the city. To reach Hamburg, the bomber stream could fly eastward over the North Sea, to avoid as far as possible, the anti-aircraft guns and night fighters in occupied Holland and reach Hamburg without having to fly over large swathes of Germany. Another route was to proceed towards Lubek and redirect from Ratzeburg to the port of Hamburg. These were clearly considerations included within the planning to attack Hamburg, but one of the biggest problems confronting Bomber Command at the time was the deadly combination of Luftwaffe night fighters and the radar warning system that controlled them. The Luftwaffe controllers had devised a grid box system that covered occupied Europe and each box contained a night fighter capability, typically a Bf109 or Bf110 equipped with its own short-range cockpit radar. Antennae projected out from the noses of the night fighters and gave their radars a range of about four miles in a 70-degree cone. This was an effective means to attack Bomber Command and the long-range Freya radar system was able to pick up bombers at their assembly points about 80 miles from the British coast. The Luftwaffe also had a dense line of Wurzburg radars that gave ground controllers accurate vectors to the bomber. In addition, these radar units also assisted flak gun laying by communicating information relative to height and direction.

To counteract the Luftwaffe's radar capabilities, the RAF had developed window, foil strips designed to swamp the Luftwaffe radar systems with false readings. The RAF had kept this development a secret for over a year, not wishing to deploy it in case the enemy adopted it, however Sir Arthur Harris sanctioned the use of window strips for the first operational deployment during the raid to Hamburg.

Eric and his crew flew to Hamburg, leaving Holm at just past 2200 on 27 July. The success of the window deployment certainly provided a shield of protection against the night fighters. Hamburg was easy to find due to the firestorms created by warm conditions and accurate bombing which had engulfed the area, causing the most unexpected and extensive damage possible. The bomb loads on the raid combined high explosives and multiples of the 4-lb incendiary bomb containers. More than 700 aircraft of the main force dropped 2,326 tons of bombs into a concentrated area. The incendiaries caused thousands of fires to take hold. Eric had never witnessed such a sight before, gazing down at such a deep glow of carnage and destruction. Eric's crew were fortunate in that they never returned to Hamburg, but many bombers did return for the last raid that took place on the night of 2 August. Weather conditions were terrible with extensive thunderstorms raging and the Luftwaffe correctly predicted the target location. Thirty heavy bombers failed to return from the force of 740 which had departed that night. In total Operation Gommorah claimed over seventy bomber crews but despite this, it was regarded by the command as successful. Air Chief Marshal Harris had made his point. He had turned the tables on Germany itself and Bomber Command shook the Third Reich to its deepest foundations. For the aircrew of 76 Squadron the spectacle of Hamburg lived long in their conversation and subsequent memories. In reality, it was no more than one of the many raids, which ground on relentlessly. On 10 August, Eric climbed into Halifax 'N' Nancy, in preparation for his next raid. It was his first operation without their trusty Halifax 'P' Peter which, although they had air tested two days previously, was in need of attention from the protective ground crew who regarded her as 'their' aircraft. 'Nancy' the replacement was to carry them to Nuremberg. The seven and a half hour operation went well, despite the bomber stream suffering some losses from the night fighters.

After the crews safe return, they were informed that their own aircraft was repaired. On the morning of 12 August it was air tested, which included Eric doing some air to sea firing exercises to keep his eye in. Many hours had been spent on operations squeezed in the turret, yet no opportunity had presented itself to aggressively deploy his four Brownings against those that sought to shoot him down. Returning to the airfield, the crew were briefed for an operation that night. In the briefing room the target was revealed, when they saw the route to Milan, Italy. Immediately, Eric knew this was going to be the longest operation thus far as the Alps would need to be crossed twice. 76 Squadron were to send twenty-two aircraft to attack the Breda steel and locomotive plants. All of the crew saw operations as a challenge but for Eric, the thought of an estimated ten hours of entombment in his turret was truly daunting. It was a challenge however that he negotiated well. The operation went without a hitch and as far as could be seen, the bomb load was dropped precisely upon the green target markers. As was the norm, the cold was a constant enemy for Eric and he would have no doubt been longing to stretch his legs and move without restriction. Never before had he longed so much for the bumpy landing and the opportunity to relieve both his legs and bladder, however the report of fuel running low would have refocused his mind. Sergeant Thorp did manage to coax the aircraft back, landing at an airfield which was about an hour's journey short of Holm. Once refuelled, they departed from the temporary stopover and flew back to Holm very tired and longing to complete the debrief and sleep.

Life on any bomber aerodrome adopted a pattern of activity based upon a crew being on ops or resting. The news of not being scheduled for a raid on any night was always something that settled the nerves and allowed for the crew to enjoy time together in the local public house. On station, the bars were rank based and the crew's navigator, Pilot Officer Suzor was effectively separated from his crew. To complete a full tour of thirty operations must have seemed a lifetime away, as Eric and his crew were only just starting out. Their next sortie was to be one of utmost importance – a secret briefing was held on the afternoon of 17 August 1943. 76 Squadron was required to send twenty aircraft on one of the early wave of bombers from a force of nearly 600 to attack a small target on the Baltic. The name Peenemunde is now well known and immediately associated to Adolf Hitler's terror weapons the V1 and V2 rockets, but for Eric the name meant absolutely nothing until the briefing explained it was the enemy's most secret research establishment and the laboratories, workshops and staff quarters were to be destroyed. The target was to be located on the seaward end of a long peninsula of the southern Baltic shoreline. The moon was good and all 76 Squadron's aircraft were to drop their bombs after a timed run from the offshore island of Ruden to the actual target. The crews were advised that the raid was of huge significance and should the raid fail, without exception, they would be sent back until it was destroyed. This was like no other briefing they had experienced; the Pathfinder Force was going to be of ultimate importance – deploying primary green and yellow target indicators over the three separate aiming points with the bombing under the control of the master bomber. Eric was concerned as the moon would be high in the sky and the combination of moon and ground illumination would make them very susceptible to being picked off by night fighters.

At 2105 on 17 August, Eric moved away from the hard standing as the Halifax engines commenced the task of pulling the mighty aircraft towards the runway. Eric acknowledged the waving personnel who always supported the crews. The sudden lurch forward, which he had grown to expect, indicated that the pilot had tested the brakes. The Merlin engines roared loudly as the pilot and flight engineer called for more power. Even though Eric was at the furthest point from the engines, they were clearly audible and the airframe moved in anticipation of the inevitable release of brakes. It was almost an elegant manoeuvre as the aircraft gathered speed, and lifted off the ground. Having gained some height, the flight engineer responded to the situation and switched the undercarriage to fold and stow the gear. Immediately, the Halifax appeared to enjoy the fact that the drag in the air had reduced. Eric felt all of these aircraft responses and he had become a familiar sequence of events. Once the pilot had balanced all four propellers to run evenly, the scene was set for the long journey to the target.

The moon was bright enough for Eric to see the North Sea, which appeared calm and almost tranquil below him. Behind him, were hundreds of bombers all of which were to converge upon Peenemunde. The good fortune of being placed on the first bombing runs took advantage of the fact that the night fighters were

Date	Hour	Aircraft Type and No.	Pilot	Duty	Remarks (including results of bombing, gunnery, exercises, etc.)	Flying Times Day	Flying Times Night
					Time carried forward :— 155 / 125 / 44 / 45		
8.8.43	16.00	HALIFAX V " P "	Sgt. Thorp.	Air Gunner	Air Test	.35	
10 8 43	21.50	HALIFAX X N	"	"	OPS:- NÜRNBERG		7.30
12 8 43	10.30	P	"	"	AIR/SEA FIRING	1 .25	
12 8 43	21.05	P	"	"	OPS:- MILAN (LACK OF FUEL) LANDED AT WING. EX		
						9.15	
13 8 43	12.30	P	"	"	WING TO BASE	.55	
15 8 43	10.45	P	"	"	RDF PRACTICE & TEST	1.30	
17	21.05	P	"	"	OPS: PEENEMUNDE DIVERTED TO CASTLE DONNINGTON		7.30
18 8 43	06.10	P	"	"	CASTLE DONNINGTON TO BASE	.30	
20 8 43	16.00	P	"	"	RDF PRACTICE & TEST	1.00	
22.	20.55	P	"	"	OPS LEVERKUSEN. DCO.		5.20
23.	20.15	P	"	"	OPS BERLIN (LANDED AT CATFOSS) MET.		8.30
24 8 43	15.15	A	"	"	CATFOSS TO BASE	.30	
27.	21.00	P	"	"	OPS. NÜRNBERG		7.55

Signed :—

OC. 'B' Flt. 76 Sqdn

Summary for August. 1943

HALIFAX	DAY.	NIGHT	TOTAL
	6.25	46.00	52.25

Signed J Henderson. O/c

Total Time ... 141 / 150 / 140 / 55

Flying logbook entries written by Eric. Peenemunde is a location that is now immediately recognised in military history but when he wrote these records he had no idea how important that raid had been. Hitler's V2 rocket programme was deferred significantly as a result of this operation and without doubt it became a most important factor in the eventual conclusion to the war.

covering the options of other raids elsewhere. The targets were identified and the bomb loads dropped with accuracy.

Thankfully no night fighters were present and the defences were not particularly strong. The secret rocket establishment started to receive what proved to be a lethal bombardment by the RAF, and as Eric departed into safer skies, he watched the spectacle that continued over the target – an inferno of smoke and fire erupting on the ground. Within fifteen minutes of the raid commencing the Luftwaffe night fighters announced their arrival at the scene and tore into the bomber force. The moon and the fires raging fiercely on the ground illuminated easy targets for the fighters. Several bombers became casualties despite the valiant efforts by their air gunners to defend the aircraft. Bombers leaving the target area also became victims to the night fighters who stealthily approached from behind them in the hope of taking out the rear gunners with the result that they could rake the entire bomber with cannon fire. Fortunately, all twenty aircraft from 76 Squadron returned with no losses. They were the lucky ones, no doubt helped by the fact that they were deployed early over the target. But Bomber Command suffered the loss of forty aircraft – nearly 300 men never walked back into their mess rooms for the bacon and egg meal that would always greet the survivors on their return. Eric and his crew were diverted from returning to Holm and landed at Castle Donnington, a satellite airfield to nearby RAF Wymeswold. These were not unusual circumstances and they were required to remain at Wymeswold for two days whilst repairs were undertaken to their aircraft 'P' Peter, an aircraft which they were increasingly attached to and regarded as always providing them with good luck.

Eric was able to record yet another new target in his logbook; on the night of 22 August he flew to attack the chemical factories at Leverkusen. It was another operation that induced the tension and strain of searching for the enemy, but this time they managed to escape unmolested by the Luftwaffe. The weather had probably assisted that night, as thick cloud had enveloped them for much of the time spent in the air over Europe. The very next night it was Berlin, with over 700 aircraft scheduled to attack the primary target of the German capital. A full eight-and-a-half hours in the rear turret exposed Eric to terrible sights during this particular operation. The pathfinders were marking the route and turning points onto the target, to ensure the bomber stream was kept well on track, but Bomber Command again suffered terrible losses.

Initially Eric saw very heavy radar-assisted anti-aircraft fire penetrate into several bombers, which created catastrophic casualties. Then the night fighters exposed their lethal capabilities, resulting in fifty-six aircraft being lost. This was a terrible loss of aircrew personnel and a most significant loss of aircraft to Bomber Command. At the time, it was the heaviest loss to the command, thus far in the war. Several rear gunners had engagements with enemy aircraft and Eric saw some of those brief conflicts taking place in the skies around him, yet his guns remained silent. Eric had never had the opportunity to deploy his four Brownings against the apparently prolific Luftwaffe night fighters, and this raid to Berlin was not an exception to these circumstances. The Luftwaffe had correctly anticipated Berlin as the target and they had sufficient numbers to hunt with great efficiency, aided by the dropping of night fighter flares that floated down from a height well above the RAF bomber stream creating almost daylight conditions. The large black shapes of the bombers became easy prey in these circumstances. This was a spectacle not previously seen by Eric who quite correctly assessed his vulnerability as exceptionally high. Unscathed from this terrible experience, the Halifax returned the crew safely back towards their home aerodrome, but bad weather forced a diversion to RAF Catfoss. The following day, the crew finally arrived back at Holme where Eric provided a verbal debrief to the squadron's gunnery officer, Flight Lieutenant Ashton. All of 76 Squadron's aircraft had again returned safely with several of their rear gunners' submitting combat reports.

Four nights later, Eric was again provided with another opportunity to sit behind his guns and search for that elusive target. Nuremburg was the objective. It was another heavy raid to Germany which witnesses a tragic start when one of the Halifax bombers suffered a sudden and unexpected burst tyre during its take off. The undercarriage collapsed causing the wing to drop and rupture the fuel tanks. The inevitable ignition saw a fire ball which lit up the entire area. Despite this tragedy, the raid commenced and once over Germany, the squadron's rear gunners were in action once more. The aerial battles that ensued saw the demise of a several enemy fighters but once again Eric purely guarded their 'lucky' aircraft, which safely returned them to station. These were not exceptional circumstance for rear gunners – fate appears to have absolved many from actual engagements for an entire tour of duty whilst others were nowhere near as fortunate. Eric entered another red ink entry into his logbook operations to Nuremberg, 7 hours and 55 minutes operational hours, added to the 39 hours already completed that month. The rather chilling calculations also confirmed Eric had completed twelve operations, the next was to be unlucky 13.

Many men were able to divert their thoughts away from superstition but some found it impossible. This was entirely understandable when the terrifying odds were stacked against surviving a tour of duty in Bomber Command, and accounts abounded about crews having been lost on their thirteenth sortie. Eric had one pressing quest. He wanted to deploy his four Browning guns against the enemy with the skill he knew he had acquired. It was a double-edged sword because the crew had been fortunate in not having been singled out by a night fighter and that was always going to be the very best scenario to ensure survival. The dangers of being firmly caught in searchlight beams and the ever-present flak that exploded with lethal shards of white-hot metal seeking to penetrate both aircraft and the personnel within were more than enough to contend with on every operation.

Eric's thirteenth operation was in fact to change his life forever. The target was Mannheim and the important I. G. Farben chemical factory in Ludwigshafen. Ground markers were placed on the eastern side of Mannheim so that the main force could approach from the west and then overfly Ludwigshafen. Sergeant Thorp was able to identify the target easily due to fires having caught a good hold as the preceding bombers had dropped their bombs loads accurately. 76 Squadron provided twenty aircraft alongside the six hundred that attacked Mannheim. At a height of 18,500 feet and shortly after 2300, Halifax 'P' Peter dropped its bomb load on the target. The Luftwaffe night fighters were present and seen to be weaving through the bomber stream and using the cloud cover to their advantage. Eric was attempting to scan the sky from every perspective and in an instant, recognised a night fighter just below and behind them. He responded with the immediate discharge of his four guns towards the dark shape but as he did so a cannon shell from the night fighters powerful guns penetrated up from the floor of Eric's turret and exploded as it struck the control column of the Browning guns. The events that unfolded in the rear of the Halifax bomber were of the highest level of bravery. The secret recommendation for honours and awards written by the Commanding Officer of 76 Squadron, submitted to Sir Arthur Harris the Commander in Chief of Bomber Command, provides the background to why Sergeant Eric Marvin was awarded an Immediate Distinguished Flying Medal.

On the night of 5-6 September 1943, Sergeant Marvin was the rear gunner of a Halifax Bomber detailed to attack Mannheim. A few minutes after bombing the target, the aircraft was raked with cannon shell by an enemy night fighter. Handling his guns with cool determination, Sergeant Marvin returned the fire and probably destroyed the fighter. He did not see it crash, for simultaneously with his firing, an enemy cannon shell penetrated the floor of his turret and exploded as it struck the control column.

In spite of severe injuries to both hands, he showed a fine offensive spirit by continuing to fire until it was physically impossible for him to do so. His oxygen mask was torn away, so he opened the turret with his elbows and crawled in the dark to the rest room where he seized an oxygen tube in his teeth. The aircraft was flying at 19,000 feet and he was practically unconscious. He had also sustained a perforating wound of his left eye, on which account the eye was subsequently removed, and wounds of his leg. Two fingers were hanging from the right hand, and so, attracting the attention of the bomb aimer, Sergeant Marvin told him to take his pocket knife and cut them off. In spite of a three-hour journey home he maintained a cheerful attitude, and it is considered that his courage and endurance, merits the immediate award of the Distinguished Flying Medal.

Wing Commander, Commanding No. 76 Squadron RAF.
Date: 5 April 1944
Remarks by station commander:
Sgt. Marvin displayed extreme and outstanding courage. In the face of heavy odds, he continued to fire at the enemy, and although badly wounded, he did not leave his turret until the enemy fighter had disappeared. His cheerful courage throughout his trying ordeal was a fine example and inspiration to the rest of his crew and the other members of the squadron.

I consider his outstanding conduct fully deserves the Immediate Award of the Distinguishes Flying Cross.

Air Commodore, Commanding RAF Stn. Holme on Spalding Moor. Yorks.
Date: 8 April 1944.
Remarks by air officer commanding:
I strongly recommend the immediate award of the DFM.

Air Vice Marshal. Air Officer Commanding. No. 4 group. Royal Air Force.
Date: 10 April 1944
The situation within the bomber that night had reached a critical stage. Sergeant Thorp instructed the mid-upper gunner to pay particular attention towards the rear of the aircraft. The fact that Eric had probably destroyed the night fighter was a crucial factor in providing some assurance that the night fighter was no longer in a position to capitalise on his wounded prey.

Telegram sent to Eric Marvin from his Commanding Officer, postmarked 17 April 1944.

Eric was in a terrible state and his injuries were substantial and serious. Sergeant Thorp was well aware that his life was in danger and that they would need to seek out the closest possible safe landing in order that he received the urgent medical attention required. Blinded in one eye by shrapnel that had also penetrated his leg and tore the fingers from his hand, Eric endured the three hours required to reach the south coast of England. Permission was granted for the Halifax to land at the aerodrome at Ford near Littlehampton in Sussex. Shortly after 0300 on the morning of 6 September, Sergeant Thorp landed at RAF Ford but not without incident as he managed to collide with a Mosquito of the Fighter Interception Unit which was based at that station. (Mosquito serial DZ299 sustained damage but was successfully repaired for further operational service). Eric was immediately tended to by the qualified medical staff and removed by ambulance to St Richards Hospital in Chichester.

Sergeant Thorp's crew remained at Ford whilst arrangements were made for transit back to Holme up on Spalding Moor in Yorkshire. When they eventually arrived back at station, immediate efforts were made to secure a replacement rear gunner. The Canadian Wilkie Wanless volunteered to replace Eric. Wilkie had been slightly unfortunate in finding himself in the position of being a spare rear gunner and in being so, he had moved between several crews to replace tour expired, sick or deceased rear gunners. It was not uncommon for various aircrew personnel to find themselves in similar positions. He was a most experienced air gunner who was in fact nearing the completion of his first tour of duty, so in joining Eric's old crew, this was going to be an ideal way for him to acquire the

Right: Portrait image taken of Eric Marvin after his glass eye had been installed.

Below: Eric Marvin can be seen standing with his brother and parents outside Buckingham Palace after his medal presentation by the King. It is clearly a very proud mother who holds Eric's Distinguished Flying Medal. This photograph provides an opportunity to see Eric's right hand, showing the missing ring and little finger.

few remaining operations needed to qualify him to become 'screened' or retired from operations.

Flight Sergeant Thorp had recently gained a commission and captained his crew as a pilot officer. On 3 October he departed from Holm for a raid upon Kassel with his regular crew as well as Wilkie, the replacement rear gunner. Luck ran out that night when the crew fell to a preying night fighter near Detmold. Mortally injured, Arthur Thorp and his mid-upper gunner Sergeant Zuidmulder, both lost their lives in the initial incident. The remaining crewmembers survived but were all captured and incarcerated in various prisoner of war camps.

Unbeknown to Eric, he had received promotion from sergeant, to flight sergeant during his recuperation, but more importantly, the Commanding Officer of 76 Squadron dispatched a personal telegram to Eric to congratulate him upon the award of the Distinguished Flying Medal.

Eric had received surgery for his multiple wounds and following the total removal of his damaged eye, his left socket was fitted with a replacement prosthetic glass eyeball. His hands were found to contain multiple fragments of shell splinters, some of which gradually worked their way to the surface of the skin within just a few months of the injury, whilst others continued to do so for a great many years afterwards.

Eric Marvin reverted back to his trade of electrician, 2nd class on 31 July 1944, serving with 587 Squadron, an Anti-Aircraft Co-Operation unit based in the South West England. On 26 February 1945, Flight Sergeant Eric Marvin travelled to London for the investiture of his Distinguished Flying Medal which took place at Buckingham Palace on 2 March 1945.

It would appear that following his release from the Royal Air Force, Eric continued living in his home town, moving only a short distance from where he was born. Eric Marvin died there on 9 May 1976, aged just 60.

18

The Call of Nature

Bomber Command aircrews were frequently in the air for eight to ten hours and on some occasions even greater periods of time. Aircrew generally tried hard to resist the call of nature but sometimes this proved impossible. It became common place for the men to try and urinate immediately before taking off, resulting in a commonly seen routine of men emptying themselves on the tail wheel or if adjacent, any section of grass. Some of these practices for these men developed into good luck sequences that were routinely carried out before all operations.

With experience, some crewmembers adopted their own personal measures inside their aircraft, bringing bottles or other receptacles. The practice of actually using such receptacles could be fraught bearing in mind the dangers of exposing any skin to the potential of frost-bite when at certain altitudes. In addition, the need to move from their workstation would generally involve using independent oxygen supply bottles. This combined with the bulky clothing and difficult routes to negotiate within the aircraft all became problematical. A rear gunner was seriously restricted in movement and extracting himself from his turret would leave the aircraft vulnerable to attack during his absence. It was an extra burden upon these very special men. Clearly in some dire circumstances, the mid-upper gunner would be able to pay particular attention to the rear but his visibility was seriously restricted. Any rear gunner was more disadvantaged in this respect than his fellow crewmembers, particularly during air time over the occupied territories. Thankfully the rear gunner did have the opportunity to dispose of his urine receptacle simply by throwing it through the fixed Perspex opening, or if an early Frazer Nash turret, slide the side portion to the open position and toss it out into the passing slipstream.

However, in many operational instances it was impossible for rear gunners to do anything and the inevitable peeing into Long Johns underwear was an easy solution. Flight Sergeant Geoffrey Williams a Rear Gunner in 514 Squadron was not ashamed to admit such eventualities.

The official toilet looked like a waste bin and was known as the 'Elsan' which was fixed to the floor, towards the rear of the aircraft. The rear gunner was effectively the closest crewman to this rather crude and undesirable facility.

Left: The Frazer Nash turret illustrating the provision of the sliding Perspex panel.

Below: The interior view of a Wellington from the mid-section of the aircraft looking back towards the tail, illustrating the confined space and the position of the Elsan toilet, seen to the right of the crewmember. The receptacle being handled by the sergeant is a chute from which 'Nickle' leaflets or flares would be fed through.

The Elsan was nothing more than a large can with a lid which had a clip device to secure the top onto its base. It would have been an unpleasant experience to use. The wind would stream down the fuselage and clearly clothing needed to be removed to use the basic facilities. An added burden for the rear gunner was caused by the close proximity to the Elsan, as he had to endure the unpleasant smell and spillages that frequently occurred. Equally unpleasant was the duty of the ground crew who had to empty and clean the facility. Any insecure lid or faulty lid attached to an Elsan was always likely to allow its contents to spew out during violent manoeuvres conducted in battle.

The aircrews went through significant discomfort and pain to avoid using the Elsan. Flying at height on oxygen with a distended bladder became very painful and the body would obviously reach a point where over distension would likely lead to further medical symptoms. Unsurprisingly air combat frequently produced life-threatening situations and under such extreme stress the human body had no need for the Elsan device.

19

Army Rear Gunners

Various types of ordinance were deployed by the German Luftwaffe Flak units in an attempt to shoot down Allied bomber aircraft. The RAF intelligence services engaged in the cascade of information to the War Office and other services. In addition, damage assessments on returning aircraft provided vital intelligence. The Royal Artillery, with its knowledge and expertise in the world of ordinance, was a natural port of call to get such information. This inter-service liaison led to the unusual circumstances of Royal Artillery Anti-Aircraft Regiment Officers being seconded to the Royal Air Force. In many instances these officers were provided with training that enabled them to operate as air gunners within Bomber Command's operational aircraft. These secondments required the army officers to fly on multiple operations in order to gather their own intelligence within their specialist areas of expertise. In many instances it was possible to do their duties as an observer, but these men needed to have the best view possible of the German light and heavy flak ordinance trajectories, and ultimate detonations in the sky. The Perspex turrets were the ideal position to do their work and these men became integral crewmembers in a number of squadrons.

During late 1941 and early 1942 the selected volunteers left their Army colleagues and entered, no doubt apprehensively, the Royal Air Force. Most men were of Lieutenant or acting Captain Rank, and they naturally continued to wear their army uniforms whilst on station. However in the air, these men were unidentifiable by the generic flying clothing worn by aircrew personnel and in keeping with all aircrews, they were answerable to the pilot regardless of rank. Evidence suggests that sixteen or so of these men were seconded into the RAF for specialist duties during the first three years of the war. They were followed by others who served as 'flak liaison' officers. These men were not spared the lethal capabilities of flak, nor indeed did they have any greater chance of surviving the poor statistics of a tour of duty in Bomber Command. On 26 March 1942, Captain Alfred Mair Royal Artillery lost his life alongside his fellow five crewmembers in Wellington Z1143 during an operation to bomb Essen. Two days later on 28 March 1942, Captain Wyn Griffith Royal Artillery was also killed in a Stirling Bomber of 7 Squadron, his crew of six all perished with him on their raid to Lubeck.

The partial squadron lettering identifies this Stirling to be operational with 7 Squadron. The aircraft is undergoing repairs to the engines. One of the massive wings almost enables the adjacent Spitfire to sit beneath its span.

On 1 April 1942, Captain H. Tingle, Royal Artillery, was flying in Wellington X9979 attacking Hanau and the entire crew were all lost. On 10 April, Wellington HF856 departed from RAF Stradishall to bomb Essen with Captain H. Butterworth, Royal Artillery, in the rear turret. Tragically he and his fellow five crewmembers all added to the ever increasing fatalities suffered within Bomber Command.

Captain John Cecil Noel had been a pilot who had previously served in the RAF during the inter-war years and had subsequently transferred into the Royal Artillery. Qualified RAF pilots were permitted to wear their wings on army uniforms and he was one of a select few who did so during the Second World War. In company with 2nd Lieutenant E. H. G. Young and 2nd Lieutenant L. B. Murray of the Royal Artillery, these three volunteers undertook training and passed through No. 12 Operational Training Unit to be eventually attached to 15 Squadron with effect from 12 December 1941. John was to fly within Squadron Leader Sellicks crew and on 14 January 1942 embarked in Stirling N3674 for a raid to Hamburg. Of the five aircraft from 15 Squadron that departed only two reached the target area. John Noel experienced the situation of the rear turret oil pipe rupturing forcing an early return. A subsequent raid to Brest was not particularly eventful due to the bad weather conditions and on 25 February it was ice that caused squadron leader Sellick problems on a raid to Nordstrand. The Stirling bombers struggled for maximum height but with ice forming,

This is the stout figure of Squadron Leader Sellick, third from the right. Captain John Noel RA is third from the left, his 'Sam Brown' leather shoulder strap and RA Cap clearly identifying him, and fortunately the viewpoint illustrates his RAF wings worn on his army tunic. On the far left is Sergeant John Hart. This photograph is credited as having been provided by his son via the 15 Squadron archivist, Martyn Ford-Jones.

maintaining height was always difficult if not impossible. Engaged on that same raid was 2nd Lieutenant Murray, Royal Artillery, flying as a front air gunner in Squadron Leader Wilson's crew. They were required to divert and bombed Sylt, encountering flak whilst over the target. Running short of fuel they later crash-landed at Mildenhall where 2nd Lieutenant Murray was found to have died from flak injuries sustained over the target.

Essen was the target on 8 March and Captain John Noel Royal Artillery was to be provided the opportunity to see some significant flak whilst over this major target. Squadron Leader Sellick had the bomb load released at 15,500 feet and the raid was regarded as having been most successful. Twenty days later John Noel was to be provided with an even better spectacle, the weather was completely clear with a full moon. From a distance of 80 miles the target of Lubeck was clearly visible from the fires caused by previous bomb loads. One of the accompanying bombers fell to a night fighter but they returned completely unmolested by any enemy forces.

Stirling W7519 was captained by Pilot Officer Mackay on the night of 13 April 1942. The crew of eight men included Captain J. Noel, Royal Artillery, and their mission was to lay mines off of the island of Wangerooge, one of thirty-two Frisian Islands in the North Sea, close to the coasts of the Netherlands. This particular area was identified by the RAF with the code 'Nectarines'. Every sector of the sea allocated to receive mines was allocated a code, and some codes were associated to a term used by the RAF relating to planting or laying sea mines – 'planting vegetables'. The RAF had been long committed to offensive operations against sea warfare targets, which included ports, submarine bases and the prolific planting of sea mines. Some 12,000 operational sorties to such targets took place between April 1941 and March 1942. Amongst that figure 1,577 mines had been dropped, a figure that would see significant growth during the following months.

Captain Noel may well have assumed that the only possibility of assessing any enemy flak activity would have been from one of the many light flak ships that sat in wait for any low flying bombers attempting to drop mines in predictable locations. It appears however that their Stirling was in fact intercepted by a night fighter over the North Sea being flown by Hauptmann Hans-George Schutze of 4./NJG2 whilst over the North Sea at approximately 0109 hours on the morning of 14 April 1942. The New Zealand pilot was unable to avoid the inevitable onslaught from the enemy cannon fire and the Stirling crashed into the sea. The entire crew of eight men all died together, and their bodies were never to surface, presumably remaining together in their watery grave. In keeping with air force casualties that have no identifiable grave, the Runnymede Memorial records the seven aviators' names. Despite giving his life alongside his crew, Captain Noel's name was ineligible to be recorded on the memorial. His details are however duly imprinted on panel two, column two, of the Brookwood Memorial which commemorates 3,500 men and women of the forces of the British Commonwealth denied a known grave.

Five of the Royal Artillery officers were selected for the award of the Military Cross for their gallant and distinguished services during air operations whilst attached to the Royal Air Force. It appears that the recommendations were passed down the army channels despite the awards being won during flying operations within the RAF.

The following names were published in the *London Gazette* 9 July 1942:

Lieutenant (Temporary Major) John Hepburn 'Military Cross'
Lieutenant (Temporary Captain) John Mullock 'Military Cross'
Lieutenant (Temporary Captain) Terrance Southgate 'Military Cross'
Lieutenant (Temporary Captain) Howard Tingle 'Military Cross'
Second Lieutenant (Acting Captain) John Pullen 'Military Cross'

On 10 November 1942, the Royal Warrant was amended to include members of the army serving with air forces of the crown to be included in the award of the DFC. The author strongly suspects that this change in the criteria of awarding the Distinguished Flying Cross would, had it been actioned earlier, have resulted in these army officers being awarded the more appropriate awards. An example of the DFC being awarded to a member of the Royal

Captain Peter Varty, *c.* 1960, in army uniform with the RAF 'Half Brevet' and Path Finder Wing worn in contravention of the Air Ministry directive.

Artillery in similar circumstances would be that to Major Arthur Stephenson. He was serving as a Flak Liaison Officer and participated in 66 hours operational flying hours with the RAF, the National Archives document Air 2/916 illustrates his award on 6 July 1944:

> Since being attached to his present unit this officer has taken part in several operational sorties over some of the enemy's most heavily defended areas. He has also participated in shipping sweeps and night fighter patrols. During an attack on Munchen Gladbach in August 1943, the aircraft in which he was flying was attacked six times by enemy fighters and badly damaged but nevertheless the attack was pressed home. Throughout, Major Stephenson calmly made notes, bringing back valuable information. His conduct was an example of cool courage and devotion to duty and an inspiration to the other members of the crew. On another occasion, when his aircraft was attacked by enemy fighters and damaged, this officer's complete disregard for personal danger was instrumental in obtaining valuable information.

There was another anomaly associated with these army officers who served as rear gunners. The Air Ministry had expressly banned the wearing of RAF brevets except pilots on army uniform. These selected men from the Royal Artillery wore their air gunner brevets in defiance of that RAF order, a very select group of individuals to do so. Another and most probably, the unique individual, Peter Varty DFM, who served as a flight engineer in 35 Squadron and later served in the army wearing the flight engineer's brevet and the pathfinder wing on his army uniform for several years. He retired as a Captain having added a Territorial Decoration to his Distinguished Flying Medal.

20

Air Transport Auxiliary Rescue

The Air Transport Auxiliary (ATA), founded at the outbreak of the Second World War, was a civilian organisation whose headquarters was at White Waltham airfield from February 1940 until November 1945. The ATA made a significant contribution to the war effort with their primary task being to ferry aircraft between factories, maintenance units and front-line squadrons. The ATA employed both male and female pilots and ferried over 309,000 aircraft during the war. It was not only pilots that were needed. Flight engineers were also required to ferry the mighty four-engined bombers across the country. One of them, John Gulson, was awarded the George Medal for his part in the rescue of the crew of Halifax bomber which had crashed into the railway cutting at White Waltham in July 1944.

Halifax serial NA528 was in service with 420 RCAF Squadron and crewed primarily by Canadian personnel. The pilot, Flight Lieutenant Kalle had recently been awarded the Distinguished Flying Cross whilst another crewmember had been awarded a Distinguished Flying Medal. The experienced crew left Tholthorpe aerodrome, Yorkshire on 30 July 1944, tasked with a daylight mission to bomb a particularly strong area of German resistance entrenched in the Normandy battle area. The rear gunner's turret was occupied by the Canadian, Sergeant R. W. Wallace, who had an excellent view of the fifteen 420 Squadron bombers that were engaged in the operation. They all successfully bombed the target, dropping sixteen 500-lb bombs respectively from what was regarded as low level in order to gain the utmost accuracy. Halifax NA528 experienced some damage during the bombing run, probably from the light flak but in addition had the unfortunate experience of some bombs being hung-up and not releasing properly from within the bomb bay. In these instances the pilots would frequently attempt to jolt the bomb free but on this occasion the bombs remained stuck on their racks within the bomb bay. Leaving the target area of Amy-Sur-Seulles the crew of Halifax NA528 were anxious to return back to base as soon as possible and the navigator plotted the best options in the hope of reaching Tholthorpe.

The combination of damage by flak and the hung-up bombs presented them with serious concerns. The rear gunner was well aware that they were vulnerable

The Halifax bomber supporting the later modifications as seen in 1944, the rudder design has changed to a square construction and the mid-upper gunner's turret is the Boulton Paul low profile Type A with the fuselage fairing clearly visible.

and constantly kept a keen interest in the sky, comforted slightly that the daylight operations to France did allow for the RAF to provide fighter escort. Daylight operations were far removed from the inky conditions normally encountered at night. Sergeant Wallace was able to scan the sky at a distance instead of the close and inevitably low approach of night fighters. He was also provided with the rare luxury of having a mid-upper gunner's position. A number of Halifax's carried an additional crew gunner who manned the particular gun position, specifically designed and fitted to cover the vulnerable belly of their aircraft. As a result of the damage sustained to Wallace's Halifax it was becoming difficult to handle and the pilot made a decision to affect an emergency landing at White Waltham.

This was not an unusual set of circumstances and bombers returning from operations frequently faced similar issues. Landing ahead of them and also taking sanctuary at White Waltham was another Canadian Halifax flown by Pilot Officer Goldstraw of 425 Squadron. The weather conditions were not particularly good as low cloud had started to form so the crew within Halifax NA528 were braced to experience an emergency landing on an airfield that they had no knowledge of, but more worryingly, one they were unable to view properly. Dropping through the cloud with the undercarriage down, the aircraft approached one of the runways. Unfortunately it was the section of runway that was preceded by the Great Western Railway cutting. In ideal circumstances this would not have been a problem, but when exceptionally low and with a damaged aircraft to control, no pilot would chose to approach with that landscape to negotiate. The railway cutting was fairly deep and any aircraft struggling to maintain height was more than likely to enter and strike the banking.

From their quarters the ATA Pilots had heard the struggling bomber and saw it appear as it dropped into view. The station fire and crash tenders anticipating tragedy were already making to the area, as were personnel from the ATA quarters.

Sergeant Wallace opened his rear gunner's doors in an effort to extract himself from the turret and the dangers from being thrown about in such a confined space with metal structures either side. Accounts on station abounded of rear gunners suffering serious facial injuries from smashing into the control columns and sighting equipment, so Wallace was hoping to avoid this in the last critical minute of the pending crash landing. The inevitable crash occurred causing the starboard wing fuel tanks to immediately explode in flames, but due to their quick response, the fire unit was fortunately in a position to spray foam and control the fire before it escalated. The following extract has been taken from the joint citation where five medals including a George Medal were awarded for bravery in the exceptional rescue of the crew.

An aircraft crashed on landing and burst into flames. Despite the fire and the bombs on board, which subsequently exploded, the crew, five of whom were seriously injured in the crash, were extricated … Third Officer Gulson ATA, on being informed that there were still some injured crew on board, climbed into the fuselage through the cockpit escape hatch, in spite of the fact that the starboard wing was by this time a mass of flames. He found one of the crew unconscious on the floor beside the pilot's seat and with great difficulty managed to drag this man through the pilot's escape hatch and lower him to the ground. He was then joined by Second Officer Lees ATA and they entered the blazing aircraft but the fuselage was full of smoke and they were unable to see anything. When told that another member of the crew was still in the aircraft in the rest bay area, Gulson and Lees immediately re-entered the machine to search. The missing man was located, huddled up against the rear spar and after a struggle over the front spar and through the flames, they were able to pull him through the cockpit hatch and lower him to safety. First Officer Cotter gave invaluable help in getting the rear gunner out of his turret which had become jammed. The gunner was unconscious, lying partly in the turret and partly in the rear of the fuselage. While others worked on the turret from the outside, First Officer Cotter ATA and Pilot

Officer Goldstraw RCAF finding the turret could not be swung back, entered the fuselage after forcing the normal entrance hatch. The starboard wing was blazing fiercely and the heat was so intense that the starboard elevator burst into flames. It was then found necessary to remove the gunner's flying equipment before putting him back into the turret which could then be swung, thereby enabling helpers outside to extricate him safely. This gallant rescue was successfully accomplished in circumstances of great danger. Despite the flames and smoke, there was risk of the petrol tanks, bombs and ammunition exploding and, when the rear turret had been swung and the gunner passed to safety, exit was only possible through smoke and fumes. Second Officer Lees, Third Officer Gulson, Pilot Officer Goldstraw, First Officer Cotter and Fire Officer Baldwin showed courage and self-sacrifice in an action which undoubtedly was responsible for saving the lives of at least two comrades.

Fire Officer Baldwin was made aware of a bomb that had fallen from the aircraft and come to rest on the nearby railway line. Fortunately, the accident occurred on a long straight section of track, and an approaching train from Maidenhead had sufficient space to safely stop and reverse away from the danger. The rescued crewmembers were all suffering from injuries but the wireless operator, more seriously so. Once they had been safely removed the fire officer withdrew the personnel from the scene. Within a short period of time, one bomb exploded, completely disintegrating the remains of the Halifax. Flight Sergeant Cussack the wireless operator later died as a result of his injuries whilst the survivors lived in the knowledge that their lives had been saved from the horrors of being burned alive, a fate that the unconscious rear gunner would without doubt have been subjected to and one that befell many others in similar events throughout the war.

21

Emergency Landings

Bomber Command had several overall commanders during the war, however in February 1942, Air Marshal Sir Arthur Harris took control. He was nicknamed by Winston Churchill 'Bomber Harris'. It was a name that thereafter lived with him, and he remained as commander-in-chief, Bomber Command from 1942-1945. Prior to taking over as commander-in-chief, Bomber Harris had voiced his concerns over what he considered to be the unnecessary loss of aircrews in the early years of conflict. He felt too many were lost due to forced landings when it would be safer for the crew to bale out. Harris took the view that the pilots and crews were far more valuable than the actual aircraft, and although the risk of an abandoned aircraft subsequently killing civilians was a concern, it was regarded as remote enough to be an acceptable risk. Harris put forward that pilots should assess a situation and not attempt a forced landing unless there was a 75 per cent chance of succeeding. In addition, he suggested that the pilot should not retain his crew on board any distressed aircraft unless it was assessed that the landing would have as 99 per cent certain of being successful. Clearly this last statistic indicates that aircrew personnel were to be ordered to jump from the aircraft far more frequently than had been previously been experienced.

There were two primary reasons to abandon an aircraft. Firstly, catastrophic damage received whilst flying over enemy-held territory by anti-aircraft gunfire, securing a hit which resulted in the inability for the aircraft to continue flying. Secondly, a culmination of events, possibly as a result of engine failures, fuel shortage or battle damage, which then rendered the aircraft unsafe to attempt a landing. Many differing circumstances existed during the Second World War where pilots or aircrew leapt from an aircraft and entrusted their lives to the fragility of a parachute thus becoming eligible to join the 'Caterpillar Club' – their lives having been saved by the silk parachute. But the losses of men and machines by Bomber Command continued to accumulate as the war progressed. In many instances, pilots were bringing back their damaged aircraft with injured crew on board, in particular rear gunners. Insufficient ability to gain height to deploy parachutes, or crewmembers not being able to parachute out due to injuries sustained, left the pilot with no options other than to reach the first available aerodrome to land.

Frequently the runways were too short to facilitate the requirement of aircraft with defective brakes, flaps or landing gear and crashes occurred. These blocked the runways and created additional hazards to other crews needing to use the airfield. Previously in 1941 the concept of building an emergency runway had been put forward and on 5 August 1942 the Air Ministry works department which operated within the ministry's aerodromes board, decided to build three emergency runways, geographically separated to provide a spread of capability to distressed aircraft returning from operations over occupied Europe. These were at RAF Woodbridge in Suffolk, RAF Carnaby in Yorkshire and RAF Manston in Kent. Due to the runways being designed to be extraordinary long and wide, the construction programme was considerably problematic and they fell behind on anticipated completion dates.

RAF Woodbridge was opened on 15 November 1943, and was situated just east of Ipswich. It was no more than one massive runway encompassing a width of three normal runways and extending in length for some 3,000 yards long. From the air it looked like a huge slab which had fifteen large hoops, also known as loops running along the southern side of the runway. These facilitated hard-standings for heavy bombers, should they be capable of taxi-ing to them. Aircraft that were unable to land in any conventional way, or simply crashed onto the runway, were attended to immediately with the intention to save lives. Frequently returning aircraft on heavy landings suffered undercarriage collapses. Once any life saving measures had been accomplished, these aircraft were simply bulldozed off the runway. The width of the runway was such that other aircraft were able to land despite the presence of a crashed bomber. But efforts were always made to clear the runways as soon as possible. At night, the runway was illuminated by three sets of lights, creating three individual runways, with the most southerly runway prioritised as always available for any emergency. Pilots required no communication or authority to use it, in effect, making it a non-regulated facility. The main runway had a 500-yard grass run-off and approach areas situated at each end, an additional safety facility for aircraft falling short, or running long on their approach and landings, a facility of great importance to those aircraft that had failed brakes and damaged flaps.

It would be entirely inappropriate to let the reader think that these emergency landing grounds solely managed everyday emergencies. RAF Tangmere for instance provided the first point of refuge for Lancaster JA922 operating with 300 (Polish) Squadron in July 1944. The rear gunner of that aircraft, Franciszek Zenta had the misfortune of having his Frazer Nash turret torn past its normal traversing limits, by the sheer force of a blast from an exploding flak shell. The twin rear doors from his turret ripped from their mountings and tore away exposing the surrounding sky. The force of the slipstream immediately sucked him backwards, out of the opening and only his left foot saved him from being completely drawn out from the turret as it became jammed. It would appear that his simple lapbelt had failed to restrain him and he was perilously close

An aerial photograph or RAF Woodbridge illustrating the massive concrete structure and the loop standings constructed along the length of the main runway. (*Air Ministry*)

to falling thousands of feet to his death. The mid-upper gunner and the flight engineer responded to the plight of the rear gunner. Desperate measures to reach him failed until the flight engineer, Jozef Pialucha, squeezed himself through the narrow opening between the fuselage and the turret. Clinging on with just one hand and with his feet on a tiny ledge, Pialucha saw his friend Zenta flailing in the terrifying slipstream. A rope was eventually passed around the main body of the rear gunner and secured to the turret seat. It was however impossible to actually recover him from the precarious situation in flight. The flight engineer had risked his life in the most extreme set of circumstances but in addition to the terror engulfing the rear turret, the Lancaster had been unable to drop its bomb load and the bombs remained on board in a precarious condition. The rear

A Lancaster seen landing with FIDO in full operation. The heat haze accounts for the poor quality of this picture, which was transmitted over a cable system for publication in newspapers in the United States of America. (*Wirephoto, Wide World Photos*)

gunner remained hanging from the turret flying over the English Channel until reaching RAF Tangmere, the first airfield available to them. The danger of the rear gunner's head striking the runway were obvious and only averted by Zenta, who managed to swing his torso to the side in the lessoning slipstream. Suffering from shock and bleeding from his ears, his life was saved and the bomb load remained secure. Most appropriately the flight engineer Pialucha, was rewarded with a well-deserved Conspicuous Gallantry Medal, but his life was later lost on 1 September 1944, whilst serving with the Polish Special Duties Squadron.

The emergency landing ground at RAF Carnaby was opened in 1944. It was of similar dimensions to RAF Woodgate but had only one large dispersal loop to facilitate an aircraft hardstanding area. In common with the design of all emergency aerodromes, the runway was only about a mile from the sea providing pilots with an uninterrupted approach from the east. RAF Manston was an almost identical facility, which had been constructed on the grounds of an existent aerodrome, long associated with the Royal Air Force. These emergency airfields were responsible for saving many airmen's lives, and a significant number of aircraft which might otherwise have been completely lost to the Allied air forces. In 1944, the addition of FIDO, Fog Investigation and Dispersal Operation, at the emergency landing stations provided even greater safety measures. Fog frequently enveloped the bomber aerodromes, and as it was difficult to predict, it occasionally completely shut down the availability of several bases. Bombers returning from Germany were faced with searching for a safe aerodrome at a time when they would be low on fuel. FIDO created a controlled burning of petrol, along lengths of pipes running along the runways. The immense heat dissipated the fog creating a corridor of vision that enabled the bombers to land safely. Prodigious quantities of fuel were required to operate FIDO. At Woodbridge, four, huge storage tanks each holding approximately 350,000 gallons had been installed, and a railway cutting was built to enable the delivery of such large quantities of petrol into the storage tanks, which were fed by underground pipes. These enormous quantities of fuel were replicated across some fifteen airfields that were equipped with FIDO. The Ministry of Petroleum organised a huge logistical system of fuel management to support the FIDO airfields, but this has to be balanced against the monumental regular petrol supplies required to service Bomber Command. Each heavy raid conducted by Bomber Command upon Germany was likely to consume an estimated two million gallons alone.

During the Second World War, the Air Historical Branch estimated that there were some 4,270 emergency landings at Woodbridge. The first operational deployment of FIDO took place on 23 June 1944. Lancaster JA911 was returning from operations and being flown by Flight Lieutenant Brian Frow. He landed safely at Woodbridge, his rear gunner was Ernest Wharton, a man who had experienced a most extraordinary and lengthy war. The story of that emergency landing at RAF Woodbridge is included within the account of this very long serving recipient of multiple gallantry awards.

22

Sergeant Ernest Wharton DFC, DFM

Rear Gunner, 97 Squadron

When war with Germany was declared, Ernest Wharton wasted no time in volunteering to serve, committing himself to taking up arms in the Royal Air Force for his king and country. Ernest, known to his friends and family as Harry, had been a gamekeeper in peace time and was an excellent shot with a rifle, a skill that was to serve him well in his military service.

Ernest was gallantly to serve in a rear gunner's position within Bomber Command and became one of only 335 men in the RAF to be awarded the coveted DFC – DFM combination of awards. These impressive awards were awarded when aircrew had completed around eighty operational sorties. The likelihood of any air gunner surviving such a monumental accumulation of operations was truly remarkable given the dangers that existed for them in their vulnerable Perspex turrets.

Military service started for Ernest in November 1939 when he commenced initial training. However, amazingly, it was to be 13 July 1941 before he climbed into an aircraft. On that important day Ernest recorded his first trip into the air, in a Whitley K7237 for a training sortie which saw Ernest fire 300 rounds of ammunition on an air to sea exercise. On the completion of his training Ernest was graded as an 'above average' air gunner. He had fired a total of 2,650 rounds during his 13 hours and 15 minutes in the air.

Ernest joined other students at RAF Finningley where No. 25 Operational Training Unit was based. Here he commenced training in the Wellington bomber, an aircraft fitted with the same Frazer Nash rear turret as in the Whitley. It was a home from home for him. Ernest was introduced to night flying sorties and managed to fire off a great many rounds of ammunition on various exercises. On 13 September 1941 the crew were excited to engage with fighter interceptions. It was Ernest's first opportunity to use the cine camera gun equipment and the fighter squadron that engaged them in the mock attacks came from the well-known Eagle Squadron with Spitfires flown by American RAF Pilots.

At that time in the war, it was illegal for any United States citizens to join any foreign nation's armed forces and to do so would mean that they would potentially lose their country's citizenship. Disregarding this concern, many

The classic image of the unsuccessful Avro Manchester banking in the air, this aircraft deserves the credit of paving the way for the development of the incredibly successful Avro Lancaster.

hundreds of American citizens volunteered to fly with the Royal Air Force well before America officially entered the war in December 1941. In recognition of their bravery, in 1944 the American Congress passed a pardon to all those early volunteers. Without doubt, the RAF American Eagle Squadrons are an important part of Second World War aviation history.

Ernest also became engaged in another historic and important development in RAF history. He gained operational experience flying in the new Manchester Bomber. This aircraft proved to be flawed but what was important was that it provided the footprint for the Lancaster, which was a truly iconic aircraft for Bomber Command. Of the 1,200 Manchester aircraft ordered from Avro, only 200 were eventually produced. Fortunately this meant that very few squadrons were equipped with this troublesome aircraft. However, one of the squadrons was No. 97 and Ernest found himself posted into that particular squadron in late October 1941. Ernest was made aware of the squadron's historic connection with the Straits Settlements, a group of British territories located in Southeast Asia. Those territories had provided funds to purchase aircraft for the RAF and this resulted in his squadron being known as 97 (Straits Settlements) Squadron. The unit was supported by a group training flight at RAF Scampton and prior to operations on the Manchester, Ernest flew several additional training sorties. His captain was to be Pilot Officer Keir, later they would fly together regularly on operations. For Ernest, the novel experience of a full operational briefing took place on the afternoon of 15 November with the target identified as Emden, which meant Ernest was sitting in his rear turret for an estimated five hours.

The crew comprised the following personnel: Pilot Officer Keir, Pilot Officer Whamond (2nd pilot) seen sporting the Rhodesian Pilots' Wings, Pilot Officer Hallom, Sergeant Shepherd, Sergeant Jenkins, Sergeant Saw, Sergeant Canning and Sergeant Ernest Wharton standing far right.

Due to the casualty statistics in relation to the Manchester aircraft being so appalling, the Air Ministry took great strides to limit its deployment in the operational arena. Therefore 97 Squadron was earmarked to receive the Avro Lancaster at the earliest opportunity. Ernest did however fly in Manchester R5792 to attack Emden, and L7475 to attack both Aachen and Wilhelmshaven. Those operations would have been some of the most anxious hours spent in the air for Ernest and his crew due to the unreliability of the aircraft. With great relief, on 22 February 1942, Ernest commenced flights in the Lancaster. This aircraft flew higher, faster and remained in the air with far greater reliability than the Manchester. His first operational duty in the Lancaster was carrying a 6,000-lb bomb load to Warnemunde on 8 May 1942. Ernest was encased in his Perspex turret for just less than seven hours during that first operation and witnessed the demise of a Lancaster which had become consumed in flames and the crew who were tragically falling to earth with no possibility of escape. He went on to complete an eventful tour of thirty-seven sorties enduring some 200 hours operational flying. The daylight sorties to Danzig, Le Creusot and Milan were no doubt, among the highlights. The latter saw his aircraft return on three engines although spirits would have been high with two enemy trains having been shot up with his guns in lieu of the bombing run, which had to be aborted. He also found himself on the sharp end of enemy fire on at least two further occasions, namely on the night of 16 March 1942 when his aircraft was engaged by a flak ship while returning from a 'gardening' or mine dropping raid, then again on the night of 29 May 1942, in a raid on Gennevilliers. The crew's second pilot was killed by flak, an incident described within the No. 97 Squadron Operational Records.

> Impossible to identify target owing to searchlights and heavy concentration of flak, made four attempts to identify target and then outboard starboard engine was hit and failed. Sergeant Bond, second pilot, was hit in the thigh and died on the return journey.

Exploding flak shrapnel was an ever-present danger to both aircraft and crew. Small pieces of flak had the ability to pierce or fracture oil and fuel lines and other vital components, which resulted in aircraft failing to reach their home airfield. White-hot fragments of shrapnel frequently tore through the aircraft fuselage entering one side and exiting the other, with fate being the decider as to whether it would strike anyone during its rapid journey. Sergeant James Alfred Bond lost his life at the age of 21, when a small piece of shrapnel tore into his thigh. His family in Stanford Le Hope had the benefit of knowing the crew in which he had served and the untimely and unlucky circumstances of his death. Such facts were sadly denied for so many other casualties where parents, wives, families and friends were unable to know how they had died and the fate of their loved ones stated simply as 'failed to return'.

The operational targets for 97 Squadron target, tended to be major German towns and cities – Bremen, Cologne, Dusseldorf, Essen, Frankfurt and Hamburg being among the more heavily defended areas visited by Ernest and his crew. Ernest would have spent many anxious hours anticipating the heavy flak and night fighter defences, with casualty rates at a frightfully high level. Ernest was a witness to tragedy on a raid to Essen on the night of 25 June, one of the famous 1,000 strength raids. It was a raid where fifty aircraft failed to return and from his turret position, Ernest saw at close hand, the demise of two of these aircraft – a bomber tumbling down and out of control with just five small white parachutes escaping, followed by the sight of an aggressive night fighter carrying out a sustained attack on a lowly Wellington which was eventually consumed in flames. The sky was even more threatening than usual that night and Ernest would have been covering every possible sector of the sky with his turret movements, his pilot well aware of the constant turning of his turret, as it always created a slight but tangible effect upon his controls. Danger always lurked on any operation and in July 1942, during a raid to Saarbrucken their Lancaster's trailing aerial was shot away by flak. They were then pursued by a tenacious enemy fighter. Skilful piloting by the captain, who would have been provided with a running commentary from Ernest in the rear turret, saw their Lancaster go into a rapid dive from 12,000 feet to 7,000 feet which eventually shook the enemy fighter off. The rapid emergency dive pushed Ernest onto the Perspex roof, his lap belt straining to hold his body. Terrified, he knew only too well that his turret was a prime target of the enemy fighter pilot. With relief, Lancaster R5548 survived the attack and brought her crew home safely.

A further test came on 11 July. Ernest was provided with an opportunity to be part of a formation of Lancasters that were commencing an operation in daylight. Taking off at just prior to 1700, forty-four aircraft took part in an experimental semi-daylight operation. The evening was delightful and having formed up, the stream of Lancasters crossed the North Sea at a low level. Rarely had Ernest seen such an impressive sight. The Lancasters then gained height and entered cloud over the Danish coast. The target was the Danzig U-boat yards and the force of Lancasters independently progressed towards the target. Ernest was well aware that this sortie was a long-range effort of some 1,500 miles, and without doubt it would be the longest duration of time spent in his lonesome turret.

The operation was designed to thwart the Luftwaffe night fighters, and it succeeded in that objective. However Ernest's Lancaster R5572 was located and held by searchlights as it approached Danzig. The pilot was forced to evade the incessant lights but unfortunately needed to make a further run upon the target. This time they were met with heavy flak but the 4,000-lb cookie was dropped amongst the buildings within the dock complex. The enemy's coastal batteries troubled several of the Lancasters; the flak units were very proficient and had destroyed two Lancasters over the target area already.

Ernest had survived yet another shaky operation. He arrived back on station having been in his turret for 9 hours and 40 minutes. The fatigue was all consuming but he knew this particular raid would need to be debriefed in great detail before he could take a much needed rest.

During September 1942, in the midst of an attack on Essen, another encounter with an enemy fighter took place. Sufficient damage was sustained to their aircraft that the operation had to be abandoned. Ernest was rapidly approaching the end of his tour and raids to Krefeld, Osnabruck, Wismar, Kiel and Cologne reached a total in excess of a tour requirement. He had already reached thirty-three but an additional six operations were to be scheduled for him and his crew, two of which were to see him restricted in his turret position for 10 and 11-hour periods. These would have felt incredibly long and the stress of such concentration and responsibility are without doubt worthy of recognition, in addition to the fact that he had completed his tour, yet was still being allocated operational raids. Ernest sat in the briefing for a raid to Le Creusot and the crews were made aware of the importance of this particular operation. It was to be a deep raid into France, to the Schneider factory which was producing railway engines, heavy guns and other large industrial wares for the Third Reich. It was to be another raid similar to that upon Danzig, leaving in daylight with ninety-plus Lancasters engaged in the raid. They were instructed to fly at tree top height across hundreds of miles of occupied France – Ernest was in disbelief. He couldn't help thinking that he had already

The type of view Ernest Wharton experienced whilst flying low level across France to attack Le Creusot. This photograph appears to have been retained by several aircrews engaged upon this famous operation. It was presumably printed and distributed after it was used for publicity purposes in various newspapers.

completed sufficient operations to be regarded as tour expired. Once again his pilot, Flying Officer Keir, demonstrated his abilities to his crew. Lancaster R5538 departed at five minutes past midday on 17 October 1942, flown impeccably by Keir. Ernest was treated to a ride which was unique – at low level the visibility was excellent. French people were seen waving from the streets and villages as the aircraft progressed to the target.

It was an exhilarating experience for Ernest, the raid was successful, and once again the Luftwaffe fighters were negated. Only one Lancaster failed to return and for Ernest, he extracted himself from his turret shortly after 2200 hour. He had taken part in one of the most extraordinary raids of the war, and one which still ranks highly among Bomber Commands achievements during the Second World War.

The other remaining endurance raid for Ernest took place in daylight operation on 24 October, when they were tasked with flying to Italy to bomb Milan with a 4,000-lb cookie. Leaving at midday, the flight progressed well until the starboard inner engine became unserviceable four hours into the sortie. The weather was getting worse and the captain decided to abandon the operation. The cookie was dropped at a target point estimated by the navigator, and the return journey was completed on three engines. At Montlucon, two trains were identified and Ernest used his gunnery skills in shooting up the steam engine using the train's fire-box illumination as his target area. Very few Bomber Command air gunners had such an opportunity. These trains were generally the targets for the Mosquito night fighters of the RAF who preyed upon such opportunities. It had been of great compensation to Ernest that the 11 hours and 20 minutes encased in his turret had at least brought some results.

His final sortie with 97 Squadron was to Genoa on 15 November 1942. It was his 37th operation, an incredible accumulation of raids for which he was deservedly awarded the Distinguished Flying Medal. His recommendation reflected upon the end-of-tour standard type of text for a non-immediate award.

This NCO has completed thirty-six [error of calculation] operational sorties against the enemy. His targets have included many of the cities of western Germany, Gydnia and Genoa. He also participated in the daylight attacks on Danzig and Le Creusot. Throughout his operational tour his example has been of a high standard.

Ernest Wharton DFM subsequently received a commission as a pilot officer and was rested from operations with an appointment at a gunnery school. He served as an instructor at No. 14 Operational Training Unit, followed by a move to the Central Gunnery School at Sutton Bridge.

Ernest returned to operational flying in early 1944, appointed to 7 Squadron, one of the original pathfinder squadrons operating within the Pathfinder Force (PFF). Newly promoted to Flight Lieutenant, Ernest joined the squadron alongside his new skipper, Flight Lieutenant Brian Frow, DFC. They were to become a significantly effective crew within the PFF – Brian Frow was the officer commanding A Flight and like Ernest, a seriously experienced individual. The new crew flew several training sorties during March, and on the fifteenth of that month, they flew their first operation in Lancaster M 643, to Stuttgart. Ernest was to perform a tour consisting of an additional thirty-nine sorties with this squadron, and to gain the award of the immediate Distinguished Flying Cross in a multiple award citation to his crew. In addition he was to become the gunnery leader, responsible for all air gunners on the station.

Returning to March 1944, Ernest flew to attack Frankfurt on the 18th and the 22nd of that month. The crew were settled and consisted primarily of very experienced officers. That factor was however insufficient to reduce losses in the air. In some instances, service in the pathfinders increased vulnerability by being over and around the target area for greater periods of time. Ernest was in his turret for just over 10 hours during April, covering raids to Tergnier, Dusseldorf and Aulnoye. He chose to record his second listing of operations in his flying logbook numerically, by starting at No. 1 again, this being slightly unusual as it was common for the aircrews to complete a running total of entire operations completed. Much of his initial second tour of operational duty was based around strikes on mainland France, at that time the Command was bombing main railway and communication targets. For example, in May, Ernest conducted

PFF duties over the extensive railway network at Chambly, Paris, Nantes, the aerodrome at Château Bougon, and Le Mans. These operations were in support of the Allied landings in Normandy both prior to and post D-Day. On the evening of 5 June 1944 he attacked the Gun Battery at Longues as well as many other similar targets. With his pilot having been promoted to squadron leader, the crew acted as Deputy Master Bomber or on occasions as the Master Bomber crew attacking V1 rocket sites and railway yards.

A new terror had been unleashed by Germany with the first flying bomb exploding on the United Kingdom, at Swanscombe, near Gravesend on 13 June 1944. V1 flying rocket bombs launch and storage sites became a primary target for Bomber Command, second in importance to the absolute needs of Operation Overlord, the invasion of France. As most of the flying bomb sites were only lightly defended and situated fairly close to the coast, Luftwaffe fighters had few opportunities to intercept the Allied bombers. Initially losses were low, but that changed on 23 June when five selected V1 sites were attacked. The previous activity to these rocket sites had allowed the German aerial controllers to predict the raid to be in the Pas de Calais area and they mustered their fighter strength accordingly.

Ernest Wharton vividly recalls this raid.

Our crew, piloted by Flight Lieutenant Frow DFC who had recently been promoted to the role of Master Bomber in the Pathfinder Force, a highly prized position in the force, the members of which were chosen carefully and have to pass stringent tests before being accepted by the founder of the group. And Wing Commander D. C. T. Bennett, soon to become an Air Vice Marshal, and generously decorated for his war effort, and destined to become a legend among airmen throughout the Royal Air Force.

Our crew had been granted the honour of leading the attack on the L'Hey V1 site situated on the edge of the forest, not many miles inland and Brian did not disguise the fact that he intended this trip to be a success. With all our preliminary duty completed, our Lancaster took off at approximately 0030 hours and headed for the target. The outward flight was uneventful, only sporadic anti-aircraft fire was directed at us as we crossed the French coast, and soon we were approaching the target. We found the site very well camouflaged but as we had special equipment, coupled with radar co-ordinates which gave our navigator pin-point accuracy. We quickly found our marking point and dropped our bomber markers.

These were special, multi coloured bombs which on exploding marked the target with the chosen colour of the day. The colour was not disclosed to crews until just before take-off in order to ensure that the enemy did not have the opportunity to duplicate the colour before the main attack began, or even during it. Jerry quite frequently did just that, much to our discomfort, for that meant we had to go in once again to re-mark. It also meant that the following bomber force was torn between choices of two targets, ours and Jerry's which were always well away from the real target area.

However, on this occasion the main force bombers arrived precisely on time and began their bombing. A couple of aircraft passed over our marker when suddenly there was an almighty bang, followed by a display of pyrotechnics that was a joy to behold, at least it was for us, for it told us that the raid had been successful. The whole scene convinced us that a fuel dump or maybe an ammunition dump had been hit, as shell bursts were taking place hundreds of feet in the air and in all directions. We, at 5000 feet, were being rocked by the successive explosions.

This was providing a grandstand view until Brian's voice came over the intercom. 'There is a Lancaster being attacked by a Junkers 88,' and he ordered our bomb aimer [Flying Officer Milligan] in the front turret to open fire on the attacker. After a short burst from his two Brownings, everything went quiet when the bomb aimer reported a stoppage. Whereupon Brian manoeuvred the Lancaster to provide the rear turret and mid-upper turret a field of fire at the attacker, the mid-upper gunner [Warrant Officer Erasmus] had chosen that moment to visit the Elsan, so it was down to me to deal with the situation. Immediately I got the enemy aircraft in my sights I opened fire with a five-second burst, and that was sufficient. I hit the Junkers on the starboard side engine. He dived steeply away and down, exploding just before he entered the clouds. The rear turret is fitted with four Brownings which are capable of firing 1,000 rounds per minute from each gun, a very formidable hail of bullets to encounter.

There was a certain amount of excitement on board, and I think that contributed to our lapse of concentration, which is oh so necessary to maintain at all times, particularly over enemy territory. For we failed to spot another Me210 that was positioning himself for an attack on us and as he straightened up, I called on the mid-upper gunner to his whereabouts and to open fire. Our combined power proved too much for him and he broke off the engagement. We learned later that we had scored hits and he had force-landed in a field quite near to some resistance fighters, who at the first opportunity set the aircraft on fire. We had hardly regained our breath however, when we were hit. The tailplane received a large hole on the starboard side and the line of fire continued up along the side of the fuselage, then tearing an even larger hole in the mainplane. In fact, it shot away a petrol tank situated in the wing clear out, leaving a gaping hole. As the enemy aircraft broke away to reposition itself for another attack, I recognised it as another Me210. It was equipped with the fixed-angled firing cannon, placed on top of the fuselage to position itself well down under its target, adjusting itself to the direction and speed of its prey, then drifting slowly upwards and slightly astern making its attack. I lost no time opening fire on the attacker at the first sighting. I was lucky for I definitely scored hits. The tracer bullets that I used were obviously hitting him, for there were no ricochets and my bullets were not going past him. Soon I had verification, for he too suddenly dived and through the clouds we observed a brilliant and widespread flash of light from the ground.

Brian was by then wrestling with the controls attempting to keep the Lancaster flying. Gradually he was able to steer a course home. Bloodied but unbowed we made a more detailed assessment of the damage. To put it in the words of the flight engineer, [Flight Sergeant Morrison], 'a bloody great hole in the tailplane, with the attendant damage to the tail-fin, part shrapnel holes in the fuselage all the way from the rear turret up to the main wing member in the fuselage. Then there's another bloody great hole in the starboard wing that you could drop a piano through. Other than that I cannot possibly see why we are still flying.' I dare not add, that I had nowhere to rest my feet for there was nothing but a gaping hole when I looked down, also my guns were useless for the hydraulics had been shot away. I reckoned that Brian had enough on his mind concentrating on getting home.

He asked for a course for Woodbridge which was a recognised emergency landing site and asked for silence on the intercom allowing him to nurse out faithful 'F' for Freddie home. Lurching, swaying, crabbing sideways but always fighting to reach home. Brian at last crossed the English coastline practically in line for landing at Woodbridge. On asking to land we were asked to identify ourselves before they would switch on the landing lights flare path. Brian was livid, but all to no avail we had to obey regulations. This meant we had to fire flares, which were the colour of the day, and we landed not knowing if the wheels had locked as there was no pressure indicated on the instruments in the cockpit. The flight engineer had fired all six of the remaining flare cartridges. We gently rolled to a stop and a second or two later the Lancaster slowly tilted, quite gently onto the starboard side where the wing just settled down on the grass. Then slowly the port wing gently dropped down as well, and I swear I heard a sound, very similar to a sigh, as if to say, 'well I managed it lads, I got you home'.

For myself, I manually wound the rear turret to astern, preparatory to opening the two small doors to enable me to evacuate the turret. Then I just placed my head on my clasped hands, resting on the gunsight, and in addition to saying a little prayer, just relaxed.

Ernest later used his red crayon and entered the fact that he had destroyed one fighter, and damaged two further fighters, adding a swastika symbol which was in keeping with gunners who had such a confirmed kill. His entry concluded with the fact that his trusty Lancaster was 'written off'. This had been his fifty-sixth operational sortie. Brian and Ernest counted up a total of 182 holes inflicted upon that Lancaster and the ground crew were amazed that it had reached Woodbridge.

The entire crew were lucky to have survived, a fitting testimony to the amazing strength of the Avro Lancaster and those men and women who had built Ernest's aircraft.

Just four nights later, Ernest and his crew returned to mark another raid on the Pas de Calais V1 rocket sites and then on 29 June 1944, the eventful and traumatic month was completed with a daylight operation to another V1 site at Siracourt. His crew were to act as the Deputy Master Bomber. However when the Master Bomber, Flight Lieutenant Clarke, went below cloud to access the target indicators, his Lancaster was immediately shot down by flak. Flight Lieutenant Frow, the deputy, assessed that something was wrong. Penetrating the cloud to inspect the target indicators, he took command directing the bombers onto the correct target as some of the main force had dropped their bomb loads in error.

Ernest's pilot was promoted to the rank of Squadron Leader, but the incessant daylight operations to the V1 sites continued unabated. On 4 July it was their turn to be hit by flak whilst acting as Master Bomber, flying too close to the target at Neufchâtel. However they completed their duties before returning to base where they landed on three engines in Lancaster V956. This had been Ernest's 60th operation and although these raids to the Pas de Calais were fairly short in duration, his time in the turret was becoming fraught with the dangers associated with the duties of Master Bomber status.

Another encounter with enemy fighters took place on the night of 19 July 1944, during the raid upon the oil plant at Homberg. His logbook quotes '1 destroyed, 1 probable'. The Bomber Command diaries provide us with the following details concerning this target.

> HOMBERG – 147 Lancasters and eleven Mosquitoes of 1, 3 and 8 Group attacked the oil plant and caused severe damage. German documents show that production of aviation fuel, which had stood at nearly 6,000 tons per day at the end of April, was now fluctuating between 120 and 970 tons per day, following the Bomber Command and American raids. However German night fighters caught the Homberg bomber force and twenty Lancaster's were lost.

Research into the fighter attacks has proved difficult; no combat reports exist but clearly from other records, the German night fighters heavily attacked them. For Ernest Wharton to have claimed a fighter as destroyed and another probably destroyed, it had clearly been a sustained attack upon his Lancaster. Very few rear gunners accumulated such statistics against enemy fighters. With one probably destroyed and two damaged, he had been engaged in exceptional events and demonstrated his ability as an excellent rear gunner.

The events in July had resulted in the Commanding Officer of 7 Squadron submitting recommendations for immediate awards and these appeared as published in the *London Gazette*, 1 August 1944.

The intense and concentrated bombing of the VI rocket sites could not be better illustrated than in this Air Ministry example taken of the Siracourt target. Complete obliteration was always desired in order to prevent these sites from being able to continue in sending the deadly unmanned flying bombs onto London and the South Coast of England.

Immediate award of the bar to the Distinguished Flying Cross

Flight Lieutenant Brian George FROW, DFC (100087), RAFVR, 7 Sqn.
Immediate Distinguished Flying Cross
Acting Flight Lieutenant Ernest WHARTON, DFM (135017), RAFVR, 7 Sqn.
Acting Warrant Officer Owen Glyndwa ERASMUS (1314546), RAFVR, 7 Sqn.

One night in June, 1944, these officers and warrant officer were captain, rear gunner and mid-upper gunner respectively of an aircraft detailed to attack an enemy target. When nearing the enemy coast on the return flight, Flight Lieutenant Frow saw a Junkers 88 about to attack another aircraft of the bomber force. He immediately ordered his gunners to open fire. Flight Lieutenant Wharton and Warrant Officer Erasmus promptly delivered bursts of fire, which struck the enemy aircraft, causing it to dive to the ground where it exploded. A few minutes later, Flight Lieutenant Wharton sighted another fighter coming in to attack. He quickly warned his captain who manoeuvred to a good position from which Flight Lieutenant Wharton delivered a long burst of fire. His bullets struck the attacker, which caught fire and dived earthwards. In the meantime, Warrant Officer Erasmus had sighted yet a third fighter on the starboard quarter. Although the inter-communication system was defective he managed to warn his captain and co-gunner, and the latter drove off the attacker which had closed in. These members of aircraft crew displayed great skill, coolness and co-operation throughout this notable action. They have completed many sorties against dangerous and difficult targets.

On 6 August a 'Special Operation' took place and a crew was formed around Flying Officer Mccarthy who piloted Lancaster C PB148 to Cabourg, in Normandy. The Lancaster carried no bomb load and the only indication of its nature is the reference: 'experimental target reconnaissance flight, considered successful'. Ernest appears to have been especially selected to fly this rather intriguing and unexplained duty. It was a break for him from the continuing daylight operations around France.

There was a frequent addition to Ernest's crew, an additional member who was known as the specialist visual bomb aimer. These were men with extensive PFF primary visual marker experience. They were being carried by the marker crews for attacks requiring the utmost precision, their duties were to pinpoint the target and advise which markers to back up, in effect advisers to the Master Bombers. The raid on 12 August up on the battlefront at Calais, required just such precision. Cloud conditions made the task of Squadron Leader Frow very difficult when a mixed force of 175 Lancasters, Halifaxes and Stirlings attacked the road junction north of Falaise. Because Flight Lieutenant Crutchley, the crew's specialist visual aimer performed his duty so proficiently that night, there was always a plentiful supply of closely grouped ground-markers. This allowed Frow to concentrate on giving directions to the bombing force and they in turn followed his instructions. He was able to report several large explosions, followed by fires and a mushroom of smoke billowing through the cloud tops, as indicators to a very successful attack. These extended durations over the target required Ernest to be extra vigilant. The Luftwaffe took every opportunity to claim a leading pathfinder Lancaster as a prize of great worth.

Flight Lieutenant Ernest Wharton is standing second from the left. The aircraft bomb doors are seen in the open position. This tended to be the normal procedure even once 'bombed up' as any complication with loss of power to the engines would require some 15 to 20 minutes hand cranking to open the massive twin doors. The photograph was taken at RAF Oakington showing Lancaster 'F' of 7 Squadron. The aircraft serial was ND 744, and known to Ernest and his crew as 'Freddie'. It is possible to date this photograph to around June 1944, as it was lost on 15 June during a raid upon one of the many French railway targets in support of D Day, whilst being flown by another 7 Squadron crew.

Squadron Leader Frow and his crew had adopted a Cocker Spaniel dog as their mascot. The photograph of the crew with the dog has a few scant details written on the back indicating that the dog had flown on a minimum of eight operations with them.

Warrant Officer Roy Claridge was the crew's wireless operator and he took responsibility for looking after the dog's welfare. The dog was a firm favourite with both the air and ground crew personnel. Named Pirate by Roy, he developed a close relationship with the dog. Squadron Leader Frow was tolerant of the dog but drew the line over certain issues, never knowingly authorising Pirate to fly with them. Unbeknown to Roy, there were other pilots who quite happily allowed him on board, and only later was he to find out that Pirate had accumulated a few additional hours in the air when a Lancaster landed behind them and Pirate appeared from the aircraft with the crew. The dog was registered with the Kennel Club and proudly carried the full title of Pirate Maroy of Ware. Pirate was actually given a coveted Pathfinder Wing by the crew, which was attached to his collar and worn by him at all times.

Air Vice Marshal Bennett, the officer in command of the Pathfinder Force, was insistent on the pathfinder badge being acknowledged and respected. Bennett

'PIRATE' A TRUE WAR
DOG 1944 - 1953

Watercolour sketch of 'Pirate'
painted by Roy Claridge.

personally issued the authority for personnel to wear the badge once qualified
to do so. It was the tradition to attach the small authorising letter slip signed by
Bennett into the recipient's flying logbook. Ernest had received his authorisation
letter on 15 May 1944.

The Pathfinder Wing was instantly recognisable to all aircrews and was a
unique and enormously respected symbol normally worn within the pleat of the
left breast pocket. Operationally, the badge was removed as any unfortunate
individual falling into enemy hands would be instantly recognised by their
interrogators as a member of this elite group of airmen. Such recognition would
clearly result in additional interrogation at the Luftwaffe *Dulag Luft* intelligence
gathering camp.

The last operational entry written in Flight Lieutenant Wharton's flying
logbook related to the attack upon the Soesteburg Airfield in Holland. The crew
knew this was to be their last operation and the aerodrome staff also recognised
the extraordinary achievement of this Master Crew becoming tour expired. The
target was an enemy airfield which was a base for Luftwaffe fighters. Ernest
found it pleasing to be attacking those that had attacked him whilst encased in
his Perspex turret. This particular operation had the provision of an American
escort of Mustang fighters, always a heart-warming sight for any bomber crew.
The master bomber was known as the 'master of ceremonies' among the men,
and this last operation was completed with ease, achieving excellent bombing
accuracy by the bomber stream. The crew were excited as they left the target area
in full power, the Rolls-Royce engines straining to get back to base as soon as
possible. Flight Lieutenant Ernest Wharton DFC DFM had completed his 76th

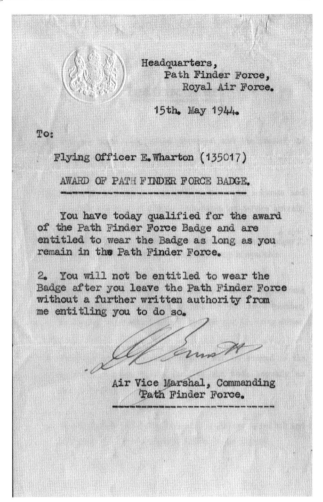

Personal letter from AVM Bennett authorising the wearing of the coveted Pathfinder Force badge. The badge was frequently worn on the left hand pocket flap underneath the Pilot's Wings or crew brevet. (*Air Ministry Order A1244/42*)

operation, which was the combined accumulation of operations completed. This was an exceptional personal tally.

The crew were tour expired and for the second time Ernest was posted to an instructional duty. In November 1944 he was posted to the Pathfinder Navigators Training Unit at RAF Warboys where he was engaged in the development of the new Automatic Gun Laying Turret (AGLT). The Automatic Gun Laying Turret, code named 'village inn', was a radar controlled turret. The device consisted of the standard four 303 machine guns in the rear gunner's turret, below which was mounted a small parabolic radar scanner. The gunner was provided with a method of tracking an enemy night fighter without necessarily seeing it. A total of only nine aircraft were fitted with this device during 1944, this clearly indicates the high level of confidence placed upon the exceptionally experienced, Ernest Wharton. Testing was carried out by the Telecommunications Research Establishment at Defford, a venue known within the RAF simply as the TRE.

Ernest Wharton is standing third from the right in this crew photograph.

Training Unit RAF Warboys (AGLT). Ernest Wharton is centre row sixth from left.

Flight Lieutenant Ernest Wharton DFC DFM was demobilised from the RAF in June 1946. Without doubt he was one of the most experienced rear gunners to have been serving within The Royal Air Force at the time. By his very survival through two full tours of duty, he was an inspiration to his crews. The value of a competent rear gunner could rarely be better evidenced, his skills accounting for three Luftwaffe aircraft destroyed and a further two damaged.

The crew's mascot, Pirate, remained with Roy Claridge, and followed him into civilian life. Pirate lived a long life and it was a sad day in 1953 when Roy buried him in his garden. Very few dogs had experienced service in a pathfinder squadron. He had worn his pathfinder badge on his collar for all of those years and it remains with him to this day.

WWII - R.A.F. PATHFINDER FORCE BADGE.
(Air Ministry Order No. A. 1244/42).
Worn on left hand pocket flap underneath Pilot's Wing or Aircrew Brevet. This coveted wing was permitted to be worn only by personnel holding the Pathfinder Certificate.

The RAF 8 Group 'Path Finder Force' badge.

23

Sergeant Charles Boyce
Rear Gunner, 207 Squadron

This Canadian born gunner experienced the excitement of training in his home country under the Empire Air Training Scheme prior to a convoy passage to the United Kingdom where he had aspirations to fly in one of the named Royal Canadian Air Force Squadrons. Known as Article XV or 400 Series Squadrons, these units were raised by the RAF with their nationality officially recognised – for instance 408 RCAF Squadron, the eighth 400 Series Squadron to be formed. This unit had the Canadian goose emblem approved by the King for its badge.

The volunteers from Canada, New Zealand and Australia were all likely to harbour the desire to serve alongside their compatriots in these named squadrons. Unfortunately, such hopes were frequently dashed as the associated squadrons were in the minority when compared to the entire strength of squadrons within Bomber Command. That said there were Commonwealth aircrew personnel serving in the vast majority of squadrons and it was common for many crews to have such men within them.

Charles joined 207 Squadron, a squadron with a long history within the Royal Air Force and one that had struggled in the early years of the Second World War due to operational flying taking place in the unreliable Manchester bomber. Fortunately, 207 Squadron was able to develop a long and heroic association with the Avro Lancaster and in common with a great many squadrons, the strength of aircrew reflected personnel from across the Commonwealth. Charles's crewmembers included British and Australian personnel.

Flying Officer 123026 Denys Oliver Street, had been serving on the squadron's strength of pilots. He was the son of Sir Arthur Street, GCB, KBE, CMG, CIE, MC, a most important figure within the Air Ministry. During the Second World War, Sir Arthur was appointed as permanent Under Secretary of the Air Ministry, a post which he occupied throughout the war. The substantial and consistent casualty rates within Bomber Command would have been most prominent in Sir Arthur's mind. On 29 March 1943, Denys and his crew attended a Squadron briefing, the target being Berlin. Any crew seeing the long taped route across Germany to Berlin would have become filled with thoughts of flak, searchlights, night fighters and the many hours that would be spent in the air. From that moment onwards

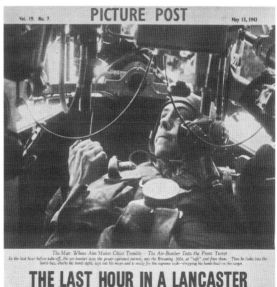

This page: The popular *Picture Post* magazine featured a front cover and photo-captioned article on a Lancaster crew from 207 Squadron in 1943. The magazine article provided the public with clear and detailed illustrations of where the Lancaster crew operational positions were within the aircraft. The article provided the opportunity to see where Charles squeezed into his rear turret, and the claustrophobic environment he and other rear gunners were to endure for hours on end.

it was difficult to think of little else. The gunnery leader held a separate briefing for all the gunners. Lancaster W4931 had been allocated to Flying Officer Street's crew, a fairly new airframe which had only arrived on station on 14 March. This particular aircraft had participated in one previous raid and coincidently it had been to Berlin just two nights previously.

Bomber Command had committed a total of 329 aircraft to undertake the raid upon Berlin that night. The time was just past nine thirty in the evening, when Lancaster W4931 lifted off the runway and the skipper requested the testing of all guns whilst the crew settled into the dangerous business of carrying the bomb load to Berlin. When almost upon the actual target area, and flying at a height of around 15,000 feet, Lancaster W4931 was struck by flak. Flying Officer Street fought hard to keep control over the aircraft. They initially lost a lot of height but Street managed to stabilise at around 8,000 feet. Almost immediately a night fighter attack took place as no doubt Lancaster W4931 was by then regarded as a lame duck. This time there was to be no escape, so the skipper immediately instructed all crew to bail out, shouting his instructions over the microphone fitted within his oxygen mask. No crew ever wanted to hear such instructions, least of all when almost directly over Berlin.

Flying Officer Street explains the events over Berlin in a letter sent to his father from a prisoner of war camp in late 1943.

> I cannot obviously tell you the story of how I became a prisoner of war until later, but we were shot up, and despite all our efforts I had to give the order to bail out. I saw all the crew go out, then jumped myself, and you will be pleased to hear that they are all safe and well. They were all glorious and behaved with great fortitude. I wonder if you would be so kind as to write a letter to their next of kin on my behalf saying they are OK and were absolutely grand.

Sir Arthur Street was able to rest easy with the news that his son was safe, as was his entire crew, all of whom were to spend the rest of the war in a German prison camp. Denys Street's incarceration as a prisoner of war was to become truly historical, and it was to have a tangible impact upon his squadron, touching upon a young Canadian, rear gunner Charles Boyce and his crew. On 19 May 1944, news arrived at 207 Squadron that Denys Street had taken part in the Great Escape from Stalag Luft III, and that he had been one of the fifty escapees to have been murdered upon the direct orders of Adolf Hitler. The impact of this news was palpable, and the immediate response from within the squadron was that the popular Flying Officers life would be avenged. The official news of Denys' murder had originated from an announcement in the House of Commons that morning.

The following day, rear gunner Charles Boyce and his crew were amongst eighteen Lancasters from 207 Squadron that were detailed to bomb the railways

The mangled wreckage of the rear gunner's turret sustained during the aerial collision with another bomber. Incredibly the rear gunner survived.

at Amiens in France. The fresh and painful news of Denys murder would have provided stiff resolve to the crews taking part. Charles's pilot, Flying Officer Trevor Smart, approached the target in the darkened sky. It was only his fourth operation, but his crew were confident that they would plant their bomb load directly on the pathfinder markers. The large network of railway junctions which lay just ahead of them was a specific communications related objective chosen to support the impending D Day invasion. Charles was monitoring the sky from his rear turret but as he did so another bomber traversing port to starboard and slightly behind them collided with his turret and the port wing tip. The collision was immense, almost ripping the rear turret from its mountings. Half of the turret was torn away leaving jagged metal, smashed Perspex and ammunition belts flailing in the slipstream. In all probability the fact that Charles had traversed his turret away from the direction of the impacting bombers trajectory saved him from a grizzly death. The impact was completely unexpected and it would have created sheer terror for Charles, with only his lap belt holding him back from falling into the darkness. Wearing no parachute, the thoughts of such a death would have been impossible to avoid and with the rear doors to his turret torn away, there was no possibility of reaching for his parachute. Charles was unable to do anything and unbeknown to him, the pilot had issued orders for the crew to don their parachutes as the situation looked dire.

Incredibly, the pilot was able to maintain control and having being committed on the bombing run he continued, almost immediately dropping the bomb load onto the target. Charles realised that the Lancaster was once again under control and the sudden lift into the air created by the loss of the bomb load signalled that the odds of surviving were better than he could have expected. The official recommendation for the award of the Distinguished Flying Cross to the pilot explains further:

> Whilst over the target, his aircraft sustained severe damage. In spite of this, Flying Officer Smart maintained his bombing run and executed his attack. The aircraft was now becoming well nigh uncontrollable but, although he ordered his crew to don their parachutes, this resolute pilot decided to attempt to reach home. Twice, when crossing the English Channel, the aircraft went into spiral dives but by skilful manipulation of the engines' throttles, Flying Officer Smart recovered control. Finally he affected a safe landing at an airfield near the coast. An inspection of the aircraft then revealed that the tip of the port wing and parts of the port aileron, rudder and fin had been torn away, a part of the port tailplane was also missing … Flying Officer Smart displayed noteworthy skill, great courage and tenacity, setting a fine example.

The historical records associated to this incredible feat do not explain the ultimate survival of rear gunner Charles Boyce. It is possible that the crash axes were used by crewmembers to force an entry into the turret to enable his escape from the wreckage. It is just as likely that he would have remained clinging on as best possible in the remains of his turret enclosure until the emergency landing took place after they crossed the Channel. Regardless of which, it was nothing short of a miracle that Charles had survived at all.

One Lancaster is recorded as failing to return from the raid to Amiens. This casualty was Lancaster ND689, operating with 44 Squadron and captained by the Rhodesian, Pilot Officer Hobbs. This aircraft was suspected to have been the Lancaster that collided with the rear turret section of Lancaster LM535. The aircraft crashed at a location known as Long, near Amiens, claiming four crewmembers' lives whilst the remaining three became prisoners of war.

The remarkable survival of Charles from the remnants of his rear turret was unfortunately short lived. Exactly one month later, on the night of 21 June, he once again took the responsibility of guarding his crew in the rear gunner's position in Lancaster LM578. The crew had survived previously together despite the odds stacked against them over Amiens, and the raid to bomb the synthetic oil plant at Wesseling should have been relatively routine. Taking off from RAF Spilsby, Lancaster LM578 joined the force of 132 bombers that set off, intent to drop their bombs on the pathfinder markers. The German defences were helped by clear weather conditions, which enabled their night fighters to successfully engage the Lancasters. Thirty-seven Lancaster crews never returned, signifying a devastating loss of aircrew from Bomber Command, and amongst them was the Canadian rear gunner, Charles Boyce and his crew.

The fate of Charles and his crew is unknown, but it is suspected that their Lancaster was badly mauled by the German defences and they were unable to cross the English Channel and had ditched off the Dutch Coast. Four bodies were either washed up or recovered from the sea following the ditching. Three men, Sergeant Sansom the mid-upper gunner, Sergeant Shaw the wireless operator and Sergeant Mcarthur the Flight Engineer were buried at different cemeteries in Holland, a factor that reflects that they were found at different geographical locations. The body of Flying Officer Bowes, the bomb aimer came ashore on the English coast and he now lies in the cemetery in Cambridge, far away from his home in Australia. The four remaining men who perished were never found, Flying Officer Smart who was denied the opportunity to receive his DFC, his navigator, Flying Officer Faires, the second bomb aimer, Flight Sergeant Jackson and of course the man who sat right at the back of the Lancaster on his own, the recently promoted and commissioned Charles Boyce from Canada.

Historical records do not disclose if Charles lost his life engaging in an aerial fight using his four Browning machine guns against the Luftwaffe, or if he was unable to escape from his Perspex capsule that sank to the sea bed. There are 232,931 military personnel from the Second World War who are, like Charles Boyce registered as still missing, and have no known grave. The son of Eva Boyce from Toronto, Pilot Officer Charles David Boyce RCAF has his name precisely chiselled and displayed on panel 249, at the Runnymede Memorial which overlooks the River Thames on Cooper's Hill at Englefield Green, between Windsor and Egham.

24

Pilot Officer William Davies
Rear Gunner, 630 Squadron

Pilot Officer William Davies was another rear gunner who found himself *en route* to Wesseling on 21 June 1944. Bomber Command had the target of Wesseling firmly in its sight as Germany had developed and refined a method to synthesize oil from coal. The production of this oil which was being created in the factories at Wesseling, it was one of the most important ingredients for the mighty machinery of war. The Allied blockades had successfully prevented fuel imports into Germany and the fuel resources secured from conquered countries was insufficient for their needs resulting in them having to rely on coal-to-oil conversion. Synthetic oil production capabilities within Germany were able to create significant quantities of fuel thus making them targets of prime importance for the Allied forces.

One Lancaster ME795 from 630 Squadron was amongst the force of Lancasters briefed to bomb Wesseling on that summer night in June and the importance of the targeting of the synthetic plants had been emphasised in the operational briefing. The aircraft took off from East Kirkby with the Australian pilot Lionel Rackley at the controls. Beneath him in the combined bomb aimer – front gunners' section, was his fellow Australian crewmember Douglas Morgan. The remaining crew were all members of the Royal Air Force, amongst them the rear gunner Pilot Officer William Davies.

The crew were as engrossed as anyone at that time with the invasion of France having taken place just fifteen days earlier. The news was carrying positive reports with casualties lower than had been expected, which caused spirits to rise as this was seen by most to be the turning point in the war. On this operation, William in the rear gunner's turret, was well aware that the factories were most likely going to be well defended and additionally that the Luftwaffe night fighter controllers were capable of directing their fighters into the bomber stream. Those fears proved to be well founded, as the raid was to cost the RAF thirty-seven aircraft – 259 men failed to return to various airfields that night. In all probability the casualty numbers were higher than that figure as many aircraft carried additional crew acting as second observers or bomb aimers.

Lancaster ME795 was not within those terrifying fatal statistics, but it had been subjected to a violent attack by the Luftwaffe night fighters that utilised their

A typical crew briefing conducted by their pilot prior to operations, one shoulder flash identifying membership of the Royal Australian Air Force within this particular crew.

The mighty Avro Lancaster illuminated in a bright beam of light, with all engines running – probably a last minute engine check prior to an operational flight. The three self-sealing fuel tanks fitted in each wing carrying 1,077 gallons each and the combined maximum fuel load of 2,154 gallons would provide for one of the deepest penetrations into Germany.

newly deployed upward firing guns. This was a new attack measure that enabled the fighter to side slip or gradually come upon the bombers from below, thus avoiding conflict with the rear gunners who were more than capable of shooting them down. On this occasion, when the night fighter approached, they were over the target area. Cannon shells ripped into the underside of their Lancaster causing some serious but not terminal damage. For the rear gunner, he was lucky that the cannon shells entered the aircraft just aft of his position. The bomb aimer and flight engineer were both needed to help the pilot keep the aircraft under control and a course was set and followed for an immediate return back to base. The pilot, Lionel Rackley, had already endured a previous operation which had ended with an emergency landing of his aircraft where the rear gunner in his crew had lost his life. His sole objective this time was to get back to base and avoid such similar losses.

When England was reached, all efforts to turn the Lancaster onto a course for their base proved impossible. It became obvious that any form of controlled landing was going to be futile so the pilot advised the crew that they were going to have to abandon the aircraft. It was at this point, that the rear gunner looked for his parachute which was stored in the fuselage behind his turret. To his horror, the parachute had been damaged by the enemy gunfire, making it incapable of working. Worse still, the Lancaster carried no spare parachutes. With consideration only for his fellow crewmember and demonstrating selfless bravery, Flight Sergeant Morgan, the Australian bomb aimer immediately volunteered to jump from the Lancaster with the rear gunner tied to him.

The parachute worn by Flight Sergeant Morgan was an RAF Observer parachute assembly. Manufactured by Irvin, the personal harness was worn at all times whilst in the air with no actual parachute attached. The parachute pack was stowed and accessible at all times. Fitted with metal loops, it was a simple requirement to clip the parachute pack onto the harness hooks. This Irvin assembly was well liked by the vast majority of aircrews, and in emergency situations, the parachute could be attached with no regard to its position. Whichever way up, the D ring or ripcord could be pulled by the left or right hand. The observer parachute assembly became the most commonly used harness used by aircrews across all commands of the Royal Air Force. The key to its success was the way in which the parachute pack simply attached to the two chest mounted fasteners. The parachute pack itself was a rectangular shaped brown coloured canvas envelope, fitted with four carrying handles, one to each side. It closed centrally, secured with a flap and had three metal clips. The metal D ring and ripcord directly connects to the parachute canopy, normally located in a fabric pocket. Fitted to the reverse, are a pair of metal buckles with spring clips for attaching onto the hooks fitted to the observers parachute assembly harness. Once attached, the parachute sits upon the wearers chest but when deployed the harness strapping becomes detached by the stitching to rise from the wearers shoulders. This design meant that the rear gunner William Davies would need to be carried on the back of the bomb aimer

Example of the Irvin parachute manufacturer's advertisements for the 'Caterpillar Club' as published in the wartime *Flight Magazine*.

IRVIN AIR CHUTES
make the world a safer place

THE IRVINC AIR CHUTE OF CREAT BRITAIN LTD, LETCHWORTH, HERTS, ENGLAND
Telephone : Letchworth 888.   *Telegrams : " Irvin, Letchworth."*

Douglas Morgan because the parachute would, upon deployment be pulled up above their heads from the carried chest position.

Efforts were made to attach the rear gunner onto the gallant volunteer and with limited resources available. This was done as best possible. Obviously, both men needed to jump together and the floor escape hatch was designed for single manned exits. The aft access door was much larger, so in all probability, the two men would have been deployed from the aircraft with assistance from the remaining crew from that entrance, making sure they cleared the tail configuration which was likely to strike anyone who did not dive purposely or tumble downwards from the doorway. Clearly, the effectiveness of the single parachute was compromised and at this stage, whether it would support them both was an unknown commodity. The fall away from the Lancaster was without injury. Douglas Morgan reached across for the D ring and pulled it sharply as required. The parachute operated correctly with its canopy eventually being pulled from the parachute pack, but on opening the rapid deceleration of falling through the air, forced the rear gunner William Davies to lose his grip and the bindings proved insufficient to hold the two men together. At that terrible moment, the two men parted; William fell to his death but Douglas managed to stay attached and descend to safety under the control of his parachute.

Pilot Officer William Davies' body was later located and recovered. He was buried in his hometown cemetery at Templeton, Narberth, Pembrokeshire. All of his remaining crewmembers survived their parachute escape from the stricken Lancaster which itself crashed in Barton with no civilian loss of life.

Flight Sergeant Douglas Morgan RAAF and his fellow crewmembers had saved their lives by using an Irvin parachute and as such they were able to apply to become members of the Caterpillar Club. At the end of the Second World War, the number of members who had joined the club and who were able to proudly display the tiny gold caterpillar membership pins had grown to over 34,000 although the total of people saved by Irvin parachutes was estimated to be 100,000. Each recipient of the Caterpillar Pin is living testimony to the lifesaving ability of the Irvin Type Air Chute. In addition to the membership pin, Irvin's issued a membership card. At least two variants exist; one is the European Division, which has an illustration of a large caterpillar upon the card. The more commonly seen membership card depicts two parachutes. Both variants were hand signed by Leslie Irvin and heat sealed within plastic. Some examples exist where Mrs Leslie Irvin has applied her signature.

Flight Sergeant Douglas Morgan's membership must stand out as being a truly exceptional one. He had displayed a complete disregard for his own safety knowing that he faced the risk of serious injury or death in his gallant attempt to save the life of his rear gunner. His actions were to be recognised by the award of the British Empire Medal in 1946. The BEM was a typical award for gallant action, not in the face of the enemy.

Pilot Officer William Davies requires a different form of recognition. By consistently occupying his rear gunner's turret, he displayed personal courage on every individual operation. On 21 February 1944, luck had been more on his side, when he had been the sole survivor from another incident when his Lancaster crashed on take-off carrying a full bomb load to Stuttgart, the aircraft slewed across the runway and onto the roadway which triggered the explosion of the bomb load, killing all of his remaining crewmembers. His tragic fall to earth and ultimate death on 21 June 1944 would have been unimaginable – a sad conclusion to an incredible and unique bond of trust that existed within the crews of Bomber Command during the Second World War.

25

Sergeant Alexander Barrie BEM
Rear Gunner, 51 Squadron

At the age of 33, Alexander Barrie was regarded as an elder statesman to his crew. He came from Cupar in Scotland where he was a master baker, married with two young children. Alexander was well grounded and a reliable pair of hands occupying the rear turret to the crew's Halifax bomber piloted by the 21 year old, Bruce Brett from Ferndown, Dorset.

Operating within Bomber Command's 51 Squadron, Alexander's crew initially comprised entirely of men holding the rank of sergeant, not a particularly unusual occurrence in Bomber Command. In 1943, the crew were engaged in the bombing of German U-boat pens and carried out two sorties flying to Berlin, on 1 and 27 of March. That same month, Alexander's crew had also engaged in raids to Frankfurt, Stuttgart and the Skoda armaments factory at Pilsen. Halifax DT628 had become his crew's regular aircraft.

On 14 April Alexander Barrie was required to attend a medical board at nearby RAF Rauceby. His journey took him along a public footpath near Grantham. At around midday, he witnessed a Blenheim aircraft making fairly low circuits in his vicinity. As it passed overhead, one engine failed and the aircraft went into a dive, crashing some three quarters of a mile away. Alexander ran through the fields to reach the crash scene, which was he couldn't see but smoke was visible. He saw that the Blenheim had crashed onto a railway line situated at the bottom of a very steep cutting and the aircraft was burning fiercely. He could see a train that had stopped a short way up the line but nobody from the train was making any attempt to approach the scene.

Alexander negotiated the embankment half scrambling and half tumbling down the steep terrain. At that time an explosion occurred causing the aircraft to break apart. The pilot was visible in the wreckage which remained blazing, so Alexander wrapped his flying tunic around his head to protect himself from the flames. He gestured towards the train for someone to help him and entered the aircraft where he managed to release the pilot and drag him clear. Nobody from the train came to assist Alexander and he was fearful that there were others trapped in the aircraft. However the rescued pilot was too badly injured to answer any questions in relation to any other crew being present. Alexander returned to

The very blunt cockpit nose can be appreciated in this view of an early Mk.I Blenheim, the type being flown by Flying Officer Sprinkle on 14 April 1943. Group Captain T. Arbuthnot is seen standing in the RAF great coat. The pilot is sporting a shoulder badge with his country embroidered on the badge and below his wings the medal ribbon of a Distinguished Flying Cross. (*Robin Arbuthnot*)

the burning aircraft to search for any other survivors, and satisfied himself that no others could have survived due to the fierceness of the fire he was forced away. His clothing was itself badly burned but his jacket had protected his face. He attended to the pilot who had sustained burn injuries and was seriously injured. It was quite apparent that both legs of the pilot had been badly broken. This was not unsurprising as the early Blenheim aircraft had an unusual cockpit, with the pilot sitting exceptionally close to its blunt nose design.

The pilot was Flying Officer William Sprinkle, an American serving in the RCAF, and attached at that time to the No. 12 Pilot Advance Flying Unit at Harlaxton. It was in effect a relief landing ground to nearby RAF Spitalgate, a very busy location for air traffic. The pilot was in fact the only occupant of the Blenheim serial number L1508, the aircraft had suffered an engine failure, leaving the pilot with no control at a low height, therefore crashing into the ground. The steep cutting, which Alexander negotiated to reach the crash scene, was the railway cutting for the London North Eastern Railway main line into Grantham. The crash-scene created difficulties for the subsequent rescue of the badly injured pilot. The RAF Grantham ambulance arrived shortly after midday, manned by Flying Officer Turner and Corporal Hukon, but the cutting, which was some 125 foot deep, prevented them from recovering the pilot to their ambulance. The train was commandeered and the injured pilot was conveyed to Grantham Railway Station where the ambulance was then able to transport him to the nearby hospital in Grantham.

Unbeknown to Alexander, Flying Officer Sprinkle was attended to by the mobile surgical team from the RAF Hospital at Rauceby. They successfully operated on the compound fractures to both shattered legs, and he received treatment for his burns. After a period of recovery and once fit enough, he was shipped back to his home country, his life having been saved by a gallant Scottish rear gunner from Bomber Command, a man whom he would forever be grateful to, for the rest of his life.

For Alexander, it was just six days between the rescue of the pilot and the final raid which was imposed upon him at the end of the month. No doubt Alexander had advised his wife of his exploits in rescuing Flying Officer Sprinkle, facts that she would no doubt treasure when the official announcement of his British Empire Medal was published. However Alexander's commanding officer, Wing Commander Pawyer, recommended for him to be awarded the George Medal, and that recommendation was submitted on 18 April.

On 20 April, Stettin was to be the target, and once again Alexander was to occupy the familiar rear turret of Halifax DT628. Stettin was an industrial province with substantial chemical production capability and a direct supply route from Germany, to the Eastern Front. This target was in the depths of the Reich and it would represent for Alexander, an extensive period of time to be spent scanning the skies over the highly defended areas of Germany, and her occupied territories. Flak belts and searchlight activity, combined with night fighters would mean little, if any time to relax. Despite this, thoughts of his wife and his two young children who were living in Highbury, London, must have been very much present in his mind. The squadron records advise that at 2123 hours, Halifax DT628 received the signal to take off from their base at Snaith. Alexander would have pre-checked his turret as would his friend, Sergeant Clifford Vandy, sitting above him in the mid-upper turret. Clifford was a full thirteen years younger than himself. Together these two air gunners were a close team who complimented each other's abilities and provided the best possible aerial defences for their crew.

The next official record concerning Halifax DT628 record the words 'failed to return' with no evidence forthcoming in relation to the crews status. Hope existed that the crew may have become prisoners of war, but that proved to be a false hope as no news was received through the Red Cross communication channels. The official letters sent by the Air Ministry, left eight families with little if any explanation of events other than their loved ones were lost on operations. Alexander died before receiving recognition for his bravery in saving the life of Flying Officer Sprinkle. His actions were recognised posthumously with the announcement in the *London Gazette* of the British Empire Medal being awarded on 27 July 1943. He was one of only 679 Sergeants in the Royal Air Force to receive such a medal during the Second World War. It is worthy to note that Air Vice Marshal Roderick Carr, the Officer Commanding 4 Group RAF, had strongly endorsed the recommendation for the award of the George Medal

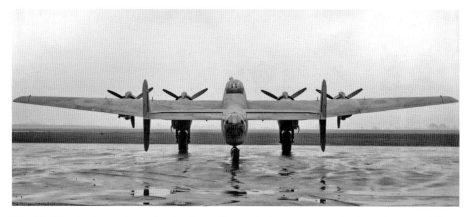

The Halifax looking along the fuselage. Alexander's rear turret displays the curved lines of the shaped Perspex, whilst the large bubble shape of the C Type mid-upper turret sits mid-way along the upper fuselage.

for Sergeant Barrie. Despite this, the award recommendation was downgraded to that of the BEM, a fact most probably unknown to his family. Unbeknown to the board who downgraded the award, they made that decision six days after he had been reported missing.

Alexander Barrie BEM and his fellow crewmembers were officially recorded as having lost their lives, and that they had no known graves. Post war, the crew names were carved onto the large panels at the impressive Runnymede Memorial.

Seven decades later, seven unidentified airmen's graves in the Bisperbjerg Cemetery Denmark, were subsequently thought to be the crew of Halifax DT628. Research identified that on 21 April 1943, a four-engined RAF bomber had been struck by flak whilst crossing the Danish coastline. The aircraft crashed at Halskov, causing a massive crater from which the Germans buried what was thought to have been seven remains of the aircrew. At that time, the crew's remains were unidentifiable, and the fire created by the incendiary load in the bomb bay had caused total obliteration of the aircrafts identity.

Sufficient evidence existed for the Commonwealth War Graves Commission to strongly suspect that the grave of Alexander and his crew had finally been located. Due to the publicity, a number of locally taken photographs from the crash scene surfaced. The massive crater clearly evidenced that the impact of the aircraft had been immense, but the examiners at the Air Historical Branch identified a more significant piece of evidence. In one photograph, there is a piece of machinery that was connected the crash scene, but that is part of an Avro Lancaster. Thus without any doubt whatsoever, it was not related to Halifax DT628 and sadly the grave of Alexander Barrie BEM had not been discovered. He and his crewmembers lives remain commemorated on the memorial at Runnymede. These unfortunate circumstances dictate that the original crew recovered from the crashed Lancaster also remain as unidentified and continue resting in the cemetery in Denmark.

26

Sergeant Vaclav Spitz

Rear Gunner, 311 (Czech) Squadron

Vaclav Spitz was born on 21 September 1921, in the small town of Curcovice in Czechoslovakia. He was a technical clerk in civilian life. The escalation of Germany's aggression towards his home country saw Vaclav enlist into the Czechoslovak Army, intending to bear arms and fight. Following the invasion of Poland by Germany, Vaclav escaped to France where he intended to fight in the defence of Europe. Not expecting France to fall, he managed to escape once again. This time he reached England, maintaining his strong ambition to fight for freedom. Many men like Vaclav endured great hardship, but even greater hardship fell to the families of those left behind.

On 24 July 1940 Vaclav enlisted into the Royal Air Force. Allocated the service number 787249, Vaclav commenced training and immediately volunteered for aircrew duties. There were many Czech and Polish men who made it very clear that the opportunity to fight in the Royal Air Force was their first and primary objective. In August l940, it was estimated that 932 Czechoslovak airmen had come to Britain with the direct intention of flying in the RAF. Communication barriers created some issues but language classes were eagerly undertaken by men like Vaclav who consistently their desires to take to the sky known. Vaclav passed the aircrew selection process and duly commenced training as an air gunner within the Royal Air Force Volunteer Reserve. Qualification to become an air gunner was the shortest possible course one could undertake to become an aircrew member within the RAF. On 19 July 1941, Vaclav commenced an initial gunnery course at RAF West Freugh. The course was completed on 16 August and he achieved an examination pass mark of 71.5 per cent, and had accumulated eight hours and forty minutes flying time within his personal flying logbook.

311 Squadron was formed from a nucleus of Czech Air Force personnel in July 1940 when it became operational, undertaking Bomber Command operations over Germany and occupied Western Europe. The training of Czechoslovak airmen proceeded as fast as possible and men like Vaclav were posted to serve in these dedicated Squadrons.

During the Battle of Britain, 310 and 312 Squadrons were manned by Czech fighter Pilots and they gained an excellent reputation for their courage and ability.

A 311 Squadron Czech bomber crew illustrating the early Irvin combined flying suit. In all probability this posed publication photograph was taken during the 1940-41 period. (*Vaclav Spitz*)

It must be remembered that should Czechoslovak pilots or aircrew ever be shot down in combat over occupied Europe and later captured by the Germans, they potentially faced the most serious consequences under interrogation. This danger extended to their entire families, and for that reason many of these men operated with false identities. On 23 September 1940, 311 Squadron attacked Berlin for the first time. In the first months of 1941, prior to Vaclav joining the squadron, the bombers were involved in operational flights to the centres of industry in Bremen, Wilhelmshaven as well as attacking targets in the occupied countries of France, Belgium and the Netherlands.

Having received promotion to Sergeant, Vaclav was considered to be a competent air gunner but required the operational and competency training to operate the rear turret of the Wellington Bomber. Within the Czechoslovak structures these areas of training were undertaken within the squadron's 'training flight'. Following completion of their training, students would then progress onto the 'advanced training flight' in preparation for full operational status. Vaclav successfully completed the comprehensive training schedule towards the end of February 1942, his flying logbook recording a grand total of just over 80 hours in duration, 46 hours and 15 minutes of training within 311 Squadron. As a fully qualified air gunner and ready to commence his operational tour of duty Vaclav was posted into a crew captained by Sergeant Doktor.

Early in the Second World War, the Butt Report of 1941 concluded that less than one in three of all Allied bombers had actually got within five miles of their appointed target. In the industrial smoky and densely populated Ruhr valley this figure dropped to one in ten, sometimes closer to one in fifteen on moonless nights. These statistics did not improved greatly when Vaclav commenced operations, the first of which was to Wilhelmshaven on 22 February 1942. Vaclav was a tall man of just over six feet in height, which was unusual as it was fairly common to see rear gunners of a much lower height due to the space restrictions within the rear gunnery turret. This appeared to be of no consequence to him, as the opportunity to partake in the retribution for the occupation of his homelands by flying to Germany to drop bombs was of superior importance. At this time the morale and spirit in 311 Squadron was exceptionally high, despite their quite appalling and consistent losses.

In the spring of 1942, 311 Squadron operated over France and Germany, their objective being to bomb industry centres in Paris, Essen, Kiel and Essen. One of the youngest gunners to lose their lives in 311 Squadron and probably from within Bomber Command was Frantisek Janca at just 19 years-old. His Wellington failed to return from a raid upon Paris after it was forced to ditch into the English Channel. The rear gunners turret in the Wellington was rather unique in that the gunner accessed it by walking along a narrow walkway whilst holding onto the geodetic aluminium fuselage. The fuselage was built up from a number of metal channel-beams that were formed into a large network. This construction designed by Sir Barnes Wallis gave the plane tremendous strength because any one of the 'stringers', as the beams were called, could support some of the weight from the opposite side of the fuselage. Despite flak damage the aircraft would generally remain intact and Wellingtons with large holes blown out of them continued to return home when other aircraft with similar damage were likely not to have survived.

In April 1942, Vaclav was crewed with a new pilot, Sergeant Zezulka. This pilot was lucky to be alive, having survived a mauling by a night fighter over Emden during March. He adopted Vaclav as his rear gunner for seven raids undertaken against Cologne, Essen, Hamburg, Essen (twice), Dortmund and Hamburg. The first three raids took place on consecutive nights with Essen being visited on three individual occasions. This was a target of utmost importance. The steel works and the extensive workforce engaged in the factories were targeted by Bomber Command on many occasions. As such, it was well defended by both heavy and light anti-aircraft guns so the rear gunners were always exposed to a display of pyrotechnics exploding around them with trails of coloured tracer fire arching up from the ground. The operation on 12 April, over Essen, also brought with it the first attack upon Vaclav's aircraft. An enemy Me110 night fighter singled out Wellington 9880 as a likely kill. The aircraft was subjected to a sustained

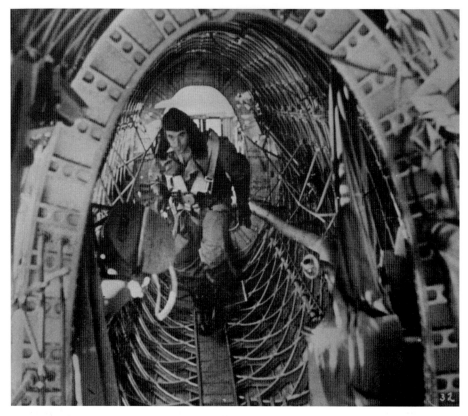

Photograph taken from within the fuselage of a very early Wellington bomber, the geodetic construction method of the fuselage as designed by Sir Barnes Wallis is clearly illustrated. (*Vaclav Spitz*)

attack that prevented them reaching their target area. The first interception took place near Lille, and the pilot's evasive action instigated by the air gunners was sufficient to avoid any damage being inflicted. A further attack took place south of Aachen resulting in both air gunners using their guns against the persistant night fighter. Two attacks were pressed home from below and towards both quarters of the Wellington. The crew presumed it to have been the same aircraft but the possibility exists that it had been two seperate night fighters. Sergeant Zezulka decided to drop the bomb load to enable greater manoeuvrability in an effort to escape the clutches of the Me110. This was a typical example of a situation where remaining alert and instantly firing a defensive volley of fire from the browning guns, reaped the reward of survival. Vaclav climbed out from his turret after five hours in the air, following the long encounter with the night fighter but he had done precisely what he was charged with doing – protecting his crew. Two days later, seven aircraft from the squadron were detailed to join Bomber Command's operation to bomb Dortmund with Vaclav once again, the rear gunner to his regular crew. The squadron suffered its last loss that night whilst still operating with Bomber Command. Wellington Z1098 flown by Sergeant V. Para met a fate experienced by several crews during the war: his aircraft was at first hit by flak in one of its engines and then seized upon by a night fighter as an easy kill over the Dutch village of Boshoven.

311 Squadron suffered exceptionally heavy losses and the training units were unable to keep pace with the required replacement of men lost in action. On 21 April, Vaclav was given the opportunity to hone his gun-skills on an air to sea training sortie flying to Kings Lynn. It was a relaxed trip but the crew were well aware that rumours abounded within the base that 311 Squadron was going to be stood down by Bomber Command as their losses were unsustainable. The squadron had accomplished 1029 sorties and attacked seventy-seven different targets during its service in Bomber Command. In total, out of fifty-three operational crews comprising 318 aircrew and pilots, 128 men were lost on operations, tragically representing an estimated 40.25 per cent loss rate. Vaclav grew accustomed to saying 'one more means one less' after his safe return from an operation.

Having left Bomber Command, 311 Squadron was one of several squadrons that were transferred to Coastal Command where operational flying continued. The German U-boats had been claiming significant and costly shipping losses against the allies and Coastal Command needed strengthening to mount patrols to combat the threat. Winston Churchill was seriously concerned by the enemy's submarine capabilities, decisions to weaken the strength of Bomber Command were not taken lightly. 311 Squadron moved to RAF Aldegrove in Northern Ireland on 30 April 1942, an area known by its nick name 'Nutts Corner', simply because Aldergrove was in close proximity to Nutts Corner airfield, near Belfast.

Vaclav and his crew were given lectures and study notes on the organisation of Coastal Command, understanding convoy procedures, escort duties, depth charging and low level bombing. Attacking a submarine, or just its periscope, were techniques far removed from those of bombing Essen or any other prime target in Germany. Once again, Vaclav changed crews. He was allocated Flying Officer Jaroslav Bala as his captain to patrol and attack ships and submarines in the Bay of Biscay, the North Sea and the Baltic Sea. The additional dangers of long-range Luftwaffe Ju88 fighters stalked the skies over Biscay. Vaclav played a vital role in scanning the miles of sea for elusive U-boats in addition to monitoring the sky. The first daylight operation commenced on 22 May 1942 and no doubt the experience of flying over miles of open sea took a little getting used to. Vaclav would have been slightly nervous of this new type of operational flying especially in the knowledge that it was his thirteenth operation. The six hours and twenty minutes in the air were completed without incident, as was the eight-hour operation undertaken four days later. The crew's navigator was tasked with even greater responsibilities, negotiating the masses of vast sea with patrols flown at an altitude of around a thousand feet above the waves. If a Luftwaffe fighter was sighted, it was common to climb into the cloud base that frequently sat above the aircraft, however the cloud also provided an ideal place for the enemy long-range fighters to stalk and strike from. In those conditions it was indeed a dangerous place and the thought of ditching into the sea was something to be dreaded and avoided at all costs.

In June, the Squadron departed from Aldergrove and moved to Talbenny, Wales, one of the most westerly positioned airfields within Coastal Command, with a classic wartime three runway layout encompassing a central intersection providing for what proved to be an excellent operational station. Several men, including Valclav departed Talbenny, were flown to RAF Bircham Newton on 24 June as Bomber Command had requested support from all commands to enhance its third maximum effort raid upon Bremen. 311 Squadron had responded to the request and supplied fourteen Wellingtons with full crews. Vaclav had never seen so many aircrews together at the operational briefing. The reality of so many aircraft converging over Bremen in a small time frame would have been daunting. At just past eleven on the evening of 25 June 1942, Vaclav found himself once again alone in the darkness and bound for Germany. Luck held for his crew and indeed everyone else from 311 Squadron as they suffered no fatal casualties, but not so for others as a total of forty-eight aircraft failed to return home from Bremen, five of which were from the 102 aircraft committed to Bomber Command from Coastal Command. Interestingly, Coastal Command aircraft were allocated the specific target area of the Weser shipyards during that particular raid. For Vaclav having safely returned to Bircham in the early hours of the following day, he later returned to Talbenny on 27 June where he rejoined the strength of 311 Squadron.

The next dramatic event for the squadron was the transformation of the Wellingtons from their dark Bomber Command camouflage exterior into the light colours of Coastal Command. The linen covering that stretched over the metal framework took the paint well and it was a task that completed their arrival into the command. In the first full month of operations conducting anti-submarine patrols, Vaclav was encased within his rear turret for 45 hours and 25 minutes. During that time he experienced the squadron's first attack on a target which occurred on 15 July 1942. This certainly provided the encouragement needed after spending so many hours isolated in the tail end of the Wellington. Vaclav was a most unassuming man who was dedicated to his crew and country, an indication of this is the fact that he chose to make no specific reference to the U-boat attack in his flying logbook. However, the squadron operational record book (accessible at the National Archives), provides a descriptive account recorded by the pilot Captain Bala:

This aircraft (Wellington T 2564) was at 1449 hours, on course 326 degrees flying just below cloud base at 2000 feet, when a U-boat was sighted on surface 15-20 miles on starboard beam in position LG BQ 55. 00. U-boat was on course 250 degrees, speed 8 knots. Little or no super structure was noticed, but wake was clearly defined. Aircraft altered course to starboard, and arrived over position of U-boat three-four minutes later when pilot could see nothing, but rear gunner [Vaclav] stated that he definitely saw a black speck travelling through the water, leaving feather, which he took to be periscope. An aluminium sea marker was dropped at U-boat position and aircraft climbed again to 2000 feet so that an attack could be made out of the sun if the U-boat resurfaced. When aircraft returned to position seven minutes later, U-boat had resurfaced on same course as before and aircraft attacked after a few minutes of re-sighting. As aircraft was diving from 2,000 feet at 220 mph, six depth charges were released from a height of fifty feet from ahead of the U-boat, and at angle of 15 degrees to her track. The U-boat conning tower and stern were visible, and all six explosions of depth charges were seen by the rear gunner. Owing to the speed of the attack (220mls/191 knots), the spacing which was set for 36 feet at 150 knots, would have been increased to 45 feet. The first three depth charges undershot, but the remaining three depth charges straddled the U-boat. Immediately after the attack, the aircraft altered the course to port, and thirty seconds after the depth charge explosions, the pilot and rear gunner both saw clearly, from a distance of 200 yards, two underwater explosions producing a red glow under water, and spray on the surface. Aircraft circled position for twenty minutes, dropping second sea marker. During that time, air bubbles rose to the surface intermittently, and ten minutes after the attack, a series of large spouts of oil, some three yards in diameter rose to the surface and burst forming a circle of oil patch which when last seen was 60 yards in diameter. Twenty minutes after attack, the aircraft went away for five minutes and then returned to scene of attack but noticed no new developments. Aircraft then set course for base.

The elation of probably having destroyed their first submarine was tinged with the confirmed loss of a Wellington with its crew, whist on a similar anti-submarine sweep that same day. The following month saw an increase in flying time spent over the sea for Vaclav – 68 hours on anti-submarine duties and seven hours providing escort to a convoy. Every solitary hour was uneventful, yet the necessity to maintain an alert guard remained. Some respite came to Vaclav in the form of manning the front gunner's turret on occasions. These two positions were of such stark contrast and the front gunner's position enabled him to interact with the forward crewmembers. It was also much warmer – a much improved situation.

From the middle of 1942 the RAF Coastal Command had concentrated a considerable part of its capabilities over the Bay of Biscay. It was simply referred to as 'the bay' and everybody knew it as the 300 miles long and 120 miles wide section of sea off the north-west coast of France and the north coast of Spain. The German Atlantic submarine fleet were based in the chain of U-boat bases at Brest, Lorient, St Nazaire. La Pallice, better known as La Rochelle and Bordeaux, all had to pass through the bay on their way to and from patrols. By covering this transit route with long-range aerial patrols, Coastal Command hoped either to destroy a significant number of submarines, or force them to remain submerged for longer periods, which significantly affected their operational capability. On 25 August an opportunity came to bomb the submarine pens at La Rochelle, providing an interesting change to the mundane anti-submarine sweeps and a reminder that Coastal Command was proactive in its overall campaign against the U-boat threat to Allied forces. Flying Officer Bala took the crew's regular Wellington on the raid with Vaclav who once again adopted his night-time role of protecting the aircraft's rear quarters. It has to be assumed that Bala had reached the required number of hours to be regarded as tour expired as this was the last time that his name was recorded within Vaclav's flying logbook.

A few new names were to appear in Vaclav's flying logbook during the next three months. Sergeants Petrasek, Vycha and Horak all captained Wellingtons on a high number of anti-submarine operations undertaken between September, October and November 1942. Vaclav amassed an impressive 130 hours in his gunner's turret, but those months had once again claimed many lives from the squadron's personnel. Flying Officer J. Nyvtl failed to return from an anti-submarine patrol over the Bay of Biscay on 15 September, most probably having become a casualty of a prowling Ju88. On 27 September Flight Lieutenant V. Student attacked a U-boat which replied with accurate anti-aircraft fire, badly damaging their Wellington which managed to limp back, but crash-landed at St Eval with all of its crewmembers wounded. The principal weapon employed in the air attacks on U-boats was the 250-lb explosive depth-charge device set to explode at around twenty-five feet below the surface. Aircraft carried between four and eight of these according to their type and the length of their patrol. Although aimed visually by the pilot, they were released by an electrical distributor so that they fell in an evenly spaced stick, the idea being to straddle the U-boat so that one depth-charge fell near enough to cause lethal damage. Aircraft usually patrolled at heights between 1,000 feet to 5,000 feet according to cloud cover but the actual attack was made from the amazingly low level of approximately 50 feet.

On 29 September Wellington DV886 flown by Flying Officer V. Nedved was engaged by three Ju88s but his skill and some good fortune saw him survive. Wellington HF921 flown by the Squadron Leader J. Sejbl was not so lucky, and was attacked by a Do17 which seriously damaged the Wellington. A further aerial fight ensued with three Ju88s and during the sustained attack all of the crew received some injuries, but Squadron Leader Sejbl suffered serious wounds to his head and back. He continued to stay at his controls displaying the utmost gallantry in endeavouring to reach the English coast and the first available airfield. He never reached such safety as the Wellington, short of fuel, was forced to ditch into the sea off Land's End. The automatic release mechanisms operated the inflation of the dinghy correctly and the crew managed to climb aboard despite their injuries. Fortunately being relatively close to landfall, they were rescued during the following day. Squadron Leader Sejbl was subsequently awarded the Distinguished Flying Cross for this action and the surviving crewmembers all gained entitlement to apply for membership of the 'Goldfish Club', having saved their lives by the use of the rubber life rafts after the ditching.

October 1942 became a most tragic month for 311 Squadron. Wellington DV716 was carrying out a training bombing mission over the sea on the thirteenth of that month. This was just one of the many training sorties flown but the aircraft suffered engine failure. The pilot, Flying Officer Kozelka managed to return over the coast but crashed in a field near Pembroke, with four crewmembers injured. Just five days later on 18 October, Wellington T2564 carrying 311 Squadron personnel crashed on its way from Talbenny to Northolt. All of the men on board were killed: Pilot Officer Bulis, Flight Sergeant Blaha, Flight Lieutenant Hanka, Pilot Officer Gissubel, Flight Sergeant Dolezal, Pilot Officer Jebacek, Sergeant Svec, Pilot Officer Bunzl, Sergeant Rajecki, Sergeant Cech, Flight Sergeant Stoklasek, Sergeant Gotzlinger, Pilot Officer Leemans and Corporal Paclik. In addition to these losses two adult females and a number of children also lost their lives when the Wellington crashed onto grasslands just short of Northolt. The majority of these Czech service casualties now rest in the Brookwood Military Cemetery, which is the largest Commonwealth war cemetery in the United Kingdom. There is a large Royal Air Forces section in the south-east corner of the cemetery which also contains the graves of Czech and American airmen who served with the Royal Air Force.

The bad news continued to cascade upon 311 Squadron but Vaclav maintained his personal trust in his captain and his own ability in the gunners' turret during his operations. A lucky escape involved the crew of Wellington DV779 on nineteen of November when Flight Lieutenant Liska crashed just after takeoff. The aircraft erupted into flames although fortunately the crew suffered only slight burns. Two further serious attacks by Luftwaffe fighters upon patrolling Wellingtons completed the events that befell 311 Squadron at the conclusion of November 1942.

Sergeant Vaclav Spitz had endured great hardship and a monumental number of hours encased within the Perspex and metal dome that sat precariously on the end of the Wellington bomber. He had experienced flying over vast expanses of sea, squinted into bright sunlit skies and endured the inky black night sky with the wide eyed anticipation of engaging with the sudden and unexpected night fighters. Like many rear gunners from the Second World War he would had counted the operations whilst accumulating the operational flying hours required to reach the end of his tour. Vaclav had achieved fifty-six operational raids on 1 December 1942. The Flight Commander and Squadron Commander of 311 Squadron applied their signatures to the hefty red rubber stamp that had been applied to his logbook. It marked the completion of his first tour of duty. On 11 December the Wing Commander of the squadron endorsed his logbook: 'Sgt Vaclav has completed fifty-six operational flights with outstanding courage and

Date	Hour	Aircraft Type and No.	Pilot	Duty	Remarks (including results of bombing, gunnery, exercises, etc.)	Flying Times Day	Night
					Time carried forward :— 382.15		75.55
1-12-42	13.14	988	*Sgt. Sotola *Sgt. Vycha	A.G.	Operation A/s sweep	7.50	

311 (CZECHOSLOVAK) SQUADRON

SUMMARY FOR DECEMBER 1942	AIRCRAFT TYPES	HOURS DAY	NIGHT
FLYING CATEGORY — REAR GUNNER	WELLINGTON		
FLIER — SPITZ VACLAV	OTHER AIRCRAFT		
FLIGHT COMMANDER — [signature]	MONTH'S TOTAL	07.50	
SQUADRON COMMANDER — [signature]	GRAND TOTAL	390.05	75.55
	DATE	31.-12.-1942	

First operational tour finished

Total of operation hours:

Night raids Bomber Command 68.50
A/s patrols Coastal Command 268.40

Total Time ... 390.05 | 75.55

Sgt Vaclav's flying Log Book entries recording the completion of a full tour of duty.

ability – recommended for the DFM.'

Vaclav was rested with much needed leave, after which he departed on a troop ship to the United States of America for 'Special Duties' with 63 Group USAAF in Florida. In all probability he was performing a training role, instructing student air gunners. The six-month posting was a normal resting period after completing a tour of duty. He returned to the United Kingdom and re-joined his Czechoslovak friends in his old squadron. In his absence, the Commanding Officer's recommendation for a Distinguished Flying Medal to be awarded to Vaclav had been turned down. In this particular instance exhaustive investigation has failed to locate any evidence for the justification of such a decision.

Back at 311 Squadron the personnel were preparing for a transfer from Talbenny to Beaulieu in Hampshire. At the same time, No. 1 Coastal Operation Training Unit was itself transferred to Beaulieu to undertake the conversion training onto the newly acquired Liberator aircraft allocated to 311 Squadron. The long awaited upgrade from the Wellington aircraft finally happened and training flights commenced as soon as was possible, these proceeded throughout June and July and continued into the beginning of August.

The Coastal Command Liberator aircraft were externally similar to USAAF B24 but were fitted with British equipment required to meet the specific Royal Air Force specifications. The aircraft were equipped with standard browning machine guns despite being delivered with American Consolidated A-6 rear turrets. Almost without exception the Liberators had the rear turrets replaced by the four-gun Boulton Paul tail turret. This meant that the conversion onto the new aircraft was fairly simple for Vaclav – it was the same turret that he squeezed his large frame into. The Liberator had a tricycle undercarriage configuration and so Vaclav found himself sitting high up off the ground with no landing wheel underneath him. The take-off and landing were much more comfortable and a very different experience from the old Wellington bomber. After the conversion training, the squadron gained its operational status once more and the first operational duty undertaken in the Liberator was on 21 August 1943.

Vaclav had flown several exercises with Squadron Leader Korda DFC during the conversion course and Vaclav was selected by Korda to fly on the first anti-submarine sweep patrol. It must be remembered that by this time he was a most experienced rear gunner. Very few men had completed and survived a previous full tour of operations. Two 311 Squadron Liberators were to commence that first deployment. The second aircraft was led by the Commanding Officer, Wing Commander Breitcetl DFC. Vaclav enjoyed the experience of operational duty in the new Liberator but the average time of each sortie in this new type of aircraft had increased to nine or ten hours, with even longer hours to follow. It is difficult to imagine how such isolation and confinement affected men like Vaclav, the personal discipline required to endure that solitude and concentration is hard to comprehend. Whilst Squadron Leader Korda returned the new Liberator back at Beaulieu, it was a very different experience for Vaclav, landing without the feeling he was almost in contact with the concrete runway. The crew was greeted with the news that their Commanding Officer and crew had not returned – nothing further was known of Liberator BZ780. It became apparent that converting to the Liberators did nothing to lessen the odds of being killed on 311 Squadron.

During 1943, the primary operational U-boats used by the Germans were very efficient vessels of between 500 and 700 tonnes, carrying crews of 45-55 men respectively. The Germans constructed the submarines to withstand the underwater blast of the RAF depth-charges, constructing an extra pressure hull of high tensile steel in their designs. The submarines had two means of propulsion: diesel engines on the surface and electric motors for use when submerged (the former also re-charging batteries on the surface). When on patrol the U-boat's lookout was always manned with four men on duty at a time standing back to back in the conning tower. They were supplied with quality binoculars supplied by the Leitz Company, who were regarded as the best optical makers in that industry. The lookout watches were changed frequently to avoid fatigue. In clear weather they would sight an aircraft at such a range that the boat could dive in ample time to avoid any attack. It was of utmost importance for Vaclav and his crew to maintain a similar vigilant watch for the potentially surfaced U-boats, but unlike the mariners who had short watches, the aircraft crews were expected to carry out that task over many hours. As evidenced with the U-boat attack on 15 July however, when Vaclav spotted the tiniest wake of a periscope, it confirmed

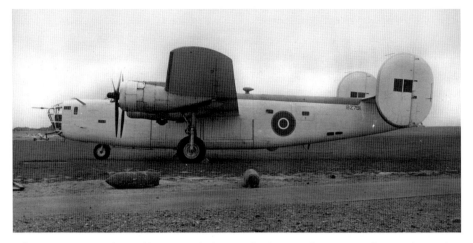

Liberator BZ791 side profile seen with the standard camouflage paint of matt white sides, glossy white undersides and dark grey upper surfaces. The rear gunner's turret is obscured by the rudder tail fin and two abandoned munitions appear to have been left alongside this aircraft. The photograph is dated 1943 and taken at an unknown location by the Ministry of Aircraft production. (*MAP*)

The rear turret of the Liberator was just as liable to become the focus of attention to enemy fighters or susceptible to being torn away from the fuselage by collision or impact. This example from the USAAF archives illustrates the demise of its rear gunner and the entire turret assembly.

that the aircraft did have the potential of using the sun to their advantage. The pilots were also aware that in a heavy sea, the U-boat watch could never be fully efficient because of the spray and ships motion on the surface of the water. In the squadron's new aircraft, the onerous task of spending longer periods of time in the rear turret position fell upon Vaclav with occasional sorties taking 12 hours or more to complete. Vaclav became well established in the crew captained by Flying Officer Irvin and between September and December 1943 he accumulated a total of nearly 160 hours within his turret. Another one of 311 Squadron's youngest volunteer air gunners, Felix Heller, aged just nineteen, lost his life alongside his crew when they were forced to ditch in the Bay of Biscay on 18 November. The casualty statistics had no respect for age or experience and Vaclav entered his turret knowing that death potentially awaited on every single operation.

A level of normality set in from the beginning of 1944. The regular crews were briefed for the standard anti-submarine patrols which appeared to get even longer in duration. Between January and May 1944 Vaclav completed a further thirteen operations which represented some 155 hours in his turret. One of the tasks that he did engage upon which provided a little respite from the monotony and sheer boredom of screening the sea and sky, was assisting the navigator. The rear turret was fitted with a simple device at the top of the turret at dead centre, a pointed marker which protruded over the turret top for about six inches. On the inside of the turret roof starting from the centre at zero and graduating to about 25 degrees was a scale. This was to enable the gunner to inform the navigator how many degrees of drift the aircraft had, and in which direction it was drifting. The pilot

Left to right: Navigator Shaw, Wireless Operator Polak, Rear Gunner Vaclav Spitz, Pilot Irvin, Air Gunner Hajek, Engineer Sedlak. (*Czech Association, Mr Polak*)

would drop a flame float which provided a point of reference for Vaclav to centre his turret, look through his gun sight at the float and keep the object in his sight for three or four minutes whilst looking up to see where the indicator was pointing. For example a few degrees left would translate to the identified degrees starboard of the aircraft's position. It has to be noted that Vaclav's left is everyone else's right as he sat facing rearwards everyone else within the fuselage faced forwards.

The squadron moved once more, this time a little westerly along the south coast to Predannack, Cornwall. The move took place in late February 1944 and the personnel found the station to be very cold and exposed. 311 Squadron were in the optimum position to fly to the U-boat patrol sectors and at the same time provide cover to the English Channel if required. On 1 June 1944 Air Vice Marshal Baker CB, DSO, MC, AFC visited the station. The build-up of military strength on the south coast had brought speculation of an imminent invasion of France, which subsequently took place on 6 June. This influenced some of the operational patrols but the squadron remained focused upon its primary role of anti-submarine sweeps.

In June 1944 Vaclav flew eight daylight operations with Flying Officer Irvin and his crew. After an incredible accumulation of hours spent encased in his rear gunner's turret the sudden reality of a confirmed sighting of three U-boats, or at least their periscopes, occurred on 24 June. His Liberator BZ745 'E' had taken off from Predannack at 0526 hours and whilst on patrol the captain reported sighting the multiple targets. Vaclav swung his turret to gain a sighting and anticipated the possibility of using his guns against the target if at all possible. As with all submarine attacks, the aircraft needed to get as close as possible in the shortest time. Plunging towards the sea the targets began disappearing below the waves. It was possible that they were in the process of submerging when first sighted so just one attack was possible. Vaclav was provided with the best view possible as the Liberator followed through with its diving attack but regrettably he was unable to report any positive action. The attack had been over in an instant, harsh recompense for the hundreds of hours spent all alone in his turret searching for such elusive targets.

Five days later, Flying Officer Irvin was to take off for his last sortie with the squadron. It must be presumed he was tour expired following that last sweep over the bay, but once again Vaclav would need to fly with another pilot. It was also a day that reminded both pilots and aircrews of the dangers of wartime flying. Liberator BZ754, an aircraft in which Vaclav had frequently operated within, crashed shortly after taking off. From the nine men on board, only one survived albeit with serious injuries.

Sadness turned to joy as Vaclav teamed up with another pilot, his good friend from two years ago when he was bombing Germany in 1942, Flying Officer Zezulka. In August 1944, the squadron transferred from one end of the country to the other, being sent to Scotland for reconnaissance roles over the Baltic and the North Sea. In addition they were also briefed for convoy protection duties,

WARRANT

The Right Honourable the SECRETARY OF STATE FOR AIR

To 𝔙𝔞𝔠𝔩𝔞𝔳 𝔖𝔭𝔦𝔱𝔷

By virtue of the Authority to me, by the King's Most Excellent Majesty in this behalf given. I do hereby Constitute and Appoint you to be a Warrant Officer in His Majesty's Royal Air Force Volunteer Reserve from the Second *day of* December 19 45, *and to continue in the said Office during the pleasure of the Right Honourable the Secretary of State for Air. You are therefore carefully and diligently to discharge your Duty as such by doing and performing all manner of things thereunto belonging, as required by the Established Regulations of the Service, and you are to observe and follow such Orders and Directions as you shall receive from your Commanding, or any other, your superior Officer, according to the Rules and Discipline of War.*

GIVEN *under my Hand and Seal of the Air Council this* First *day of* January 1946

Stansgal

The warrant issued by the Secretary of State for the Air in January 1946 appointing Vaclav Spitz to the rank of Warrant Officer in the RAFVR.

escorting vessels sailing northwards to the Soviet Union. The reunion with his old friend Zezulka was short-lived as on 25 September, Vaclav was himself posted to St Athan. This was a training establishment for aircrew trades as well as a holding unit for Czechoslovak Air Force personnel. Vaclav was deemed to have completed his full second tour of duty and was rested from operations for the prescribed six month posting. Very few rear gunners achieved such a feat during the Second World War.

On 3 April 1945, Vaclav once again returned to serve as a rear gunner in 311 Squadron, in effect commencing his third operational tour of duty. He was provided with the opportunity to fly on three operational sweeps in the closing weeks of the war. Those final sweeps over the North Sea were with Flying Officer Polivka. Vaclav's flying logbook was later endorsed by the Commanding Officer of 311 Squadron on 31 May 1945, evidencing that Flight Sergeant Vaclav Spitz has completed ninety-five operations against the enemy and had flown a grand total of 1,010 hours and 25 minutes. His dedication, although recognised by the previous recommendation of the Distinguished Flying Medal, was never re-submitted. He was however to become a warranted officer – a form of recognition which should probably have taken place long before December 1945 when his promotion to Warrant Officer was approved.

311 Squadron was officially disbanded on 15 February 1946, however the majority of personnel had previously been transferred into the newly formed Czechoslovak Air Force in August 1945. On 14 August, Vaclav was provided with the opportunity to return to Czechoslovakia but what he saw displeased him. The immediate post war Czechoslovakia was a shadow of its past and the communist threat was sufficient for many men like Spitz to seek authority to live in England. These brave men should have spent their remaining years as national heroes back in their free homeland but it was not to be. Vaclav Spitz went into exile and was required to register his presence in the United Kingdom as a registered alien.

In February 1948, the Communists staged a political coup in Czechoslovakia and took control of the government and the other instruments of state. As far as the new regime was concerned, anyone who had fought with the western allies was at best a suspect and at worst a traitor. Suspicions ran high in the unstable political hot bed of Czechoslovakia and within days of the coup, leading figures across the country were arrested and tried for fabricated crimes. An example of this was the head of the Czechoslovak Inspectorate for the RAF, Karel Janousek who was tried by the communist regime and sentenced to fifteen years in jail. Many airmen were immediately dismissed from the newly formed air force and the majority of those men were victimized for their service in the Royal Air Force. Their record of gallantry in fighting for their country remained virtually unknown for the ensuing years. It became commonplace for those men who retained uniforms or flying logbooks, to hide them securely or burn them to remove possible evidence that could be used against them.

Photograph of Vaclav Spitz, *c.* 1946.

Air Gunner's Association reunion at RAF Cosford, 14 October 1995. Vaclav is seen standing third from the left sporting an impressive moustache. (*Vaclav Spitz*)

The Czechoslovak awards were added to the British Campaign medals – 1939-45 Star, Air Crew Europe Star (Bar Atlantic) the Defence Medal and War Medal, creating a most impressive set of medals to a dedicated rear gunner.

As a registered alien in the United Kingdom, Vaclav Spitz was successful in re-joining the RAF. In November 1948 he was granted a five-year service period as a General Duties Aircraftsman. On 23 November 1948 he took the oath and declaration but just six months later, at his own request he was discharged. Vaclav remained in the United Kingdom and became an active member of the Air Gunners' Association for many years.

Despite the unfortunate lack of official recognition for the DFM, Vaclav's impressive operational statistics were outstanding. He had completed 732 hours and 32 minutes within his Perspex turret. His home country eventually recognized his extraordinary commitment and awarded him with the Czechoslovak War Cross 1939 with two bars, the Czechoslovak Gallantry Medal with one additional bar, the Czechoslovak Medal of Merit and the Czechoslovak Commemoration Medal. The author would suggest that ample evidence existed to recognise the immense dedication and extensive hours spent by Vaclav Spitz. He served two full tours of duty, within two Commands and the RAF failed to recognise a gallant Czechoslovak volunteer who was willing to give everything to protect his home country and the United Kingdom.

27

Sergeant Frank Bell DFM

Rear Gunner, 58 Squadron

Frank Bell was a well-educated young man who had been brought up in Nether Edge, Sheffield. He had grown up in a small family with his only sister Olive, with whom he had a very close relationship. Upon leaving school, Frank started out on his career as a junior traveller with local builders and contractors Dyson and Co.

At the outbreak of war, Frank was twenty years of age, and he swiftly volunteered for aircrew duties in the RAF. The transition into service took place and Frank was selected for training as an air gunner / wireless operator, the standard dual role requirement for an air gunner at that time. Frank attended the initial Gunnery Course at Newton Down, Dorset in July 1940 and during the following four weeks he gained experience in the large Whitley bomber. Frank appeared to excel in gunnery, gaining a final examination grade of 79 per cent and classed as an above average air gunner.

The natural progression at that early period in the war, for an under-training air gunner would have been to serve on an Operational Training Unit. Towards the end of August, Frank arrived at RAF Abingdon, near Oxford where he received his training in wireless operation. Abingdon was the home of No. 10 Operational Training Unit where he gained further experience flying in the Whitley. Promoted to the full rank of Sergeant, Frank departed Abingdon having received an operational posting to serve in 58 Squadron, Linton-on-Ouse Yorkshire. This squadron was equipped with Whitleys, an aircraft that Frank knew exceptionally well. But having entered service with the RAF in 1937, the Whitley was only capable of 250 mph at 16,000 feet with a range of 1,500 miles, and was regarded as an out-dated aircraft, capable of carrying a relatively modest maximum bomb load of 7,000 lbs. But more importantly for Frank it was armed with only one light machine gun in its nose turret, and four Browning .303s in the rear powered turret.

Frank Bell's first operation with 58 Squadron was to bomb the Skoda works at Pilsen in Czechoslovakia on the night of 20 October 1940. No doubt, with the nervous anticipation of his first full bombing mission over occupied Europe, Frank checked and re-checked his equipment. Frank's turret and guns needed to function without fault as working in the dark on a mission was normal and

Left: Frank Bell sitting far right wearing his air gunner half brevet on his uniform. (*Simon Muggleton*)

Below: The Whitley bomber illustrating the unusual flying attitude of this aircraft – the rear gunner's turret being elevated in normal flight was a most unusual and unique characteristic of this particular airframe. (*Simon Muggleton*)

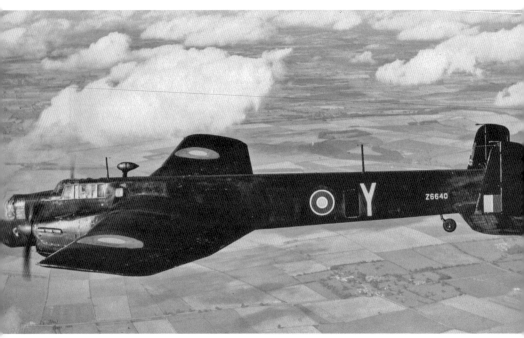

The crew getting ready to fly in their Whitley. Various clothing is being worn including an early white flying suit and a short-sleeved, short-legged flying suit which was developed pre-war by the GQ Parachute Company. Incorporated in the design was provision for the clip-on seat or chest-type parachute packs. Manufactured in drab olive-coloured robust cotton, and referred to as the 'GQ Parasuit', it was produced in limited quantities and superseded by the similar Irvin harness suit in 1940. The crew's observer, far right, is pulling on the all in one Sidcot suit. (*Simon Muggleton*)

Frank needed to know exactly where every control was positioned. The reality of sitting in isolation at the furthest position possible from the pilot would have come home after his initial intercom check with his pilot. On looking out, he must have felt like he was suspended in space, as the Whitley slowly gained the required height in the sky. On this occasion, the stark reality of his vulnerability suddenly came to light as the turret became unserviceable resulting in Frank advising his skipper. The decision was taken to return to Linton-on-Ouse. To take a defenceless Whitley into enemy skies was inviting disaster. Whitley bombers had been at the forefront of Bomber Command's early night offensive against Germany and their losses had been significant.

Three days later Frank again climbed into his rear turret and went through the same procedure of checking his equipment in anticipation of a planned operation to bomb Stettin. There was no faulty equipment this time but the mission proved a non-starter due to bad weather. It was to be a further three weeks before Frank eventually completed his first operation. On 14 November, he endured a full seven and a half hours within the cramped rear turret, the longest period of time he had spent so far confined and restricted behind the Perspex, but this time having

Frank Bell wearing the sheep skin Irvin Flying Jacket and B Type helmet with the large earpieces that held the receivers. The Mk.III goggles complete this classic combination of flying equipment from around 1940. (*Simon Muggleton*)

been part of a successful raid upon Lorient. It was to be the first of twenty eight successful operations that he participated in with 58 Squadron. Several were very eventful and Frank recorded them accordingly within his flying logbook.

The decision by the RAF to attempt a raid upon Turin in late November 1940 caused some concern to Frank as it was only his second operation and their Whitley N1462 would need to negotiate the height of the French Alps. That apprehension was proved founded when his aircraft experienced engine trouble whilst trying to cross the mountains, forcing them to return westwards. In order to make use of their bombs they dropped them over the docks at Calais before crossing the English Channel and arriving safely at Linton.

On the night of 12 December, the Luftwaffe attacked Sheffield during their Blitz upon major city targets. Four hundred and six aircraft from *Luftlotte Kampfgruppen* (Bomber Groups) dropped over 355 tons of high explosive bombs on their chosen target. The raid was code named as Operation *Schmelztiefel* (Crucible), the first real Luftwaffe raid upon the home of British steel making. The first bombs fell at 1840 hours and the raid was completed some eight hours later. The fires in Sheffield were extensive and only brought under control at around 0615 hours the following morning. Three further nights of bombing were endured by the residents of Sheffield, with civilian casualty numbers high. Amongst them, tragically, was Frank's older sister Olive. She had been seriously injured whilst living at 12 Westbrook Bank, Sheffield, which had been completely demolished in the raid. Her mother-in-law had died in the property and Olive was rescued but with serious injuries. Olive was taken to the Women's Hospital in Leavygreave Road but died from her injuries during the following day.

The devastation after the enemy bombing that destroyed 12 Westbrook Bank Sheffield and took the life of Frank Bell's sister and her mother-in-law.

A telegram informing Frank of his sister's death arrived at his aerodrome. Between December 1940 and February 1941, Frank added only six raid entries into his logbook. On 11 February, he was briefed for a raid upon Bremen – this was to be a most significant and memorable operation for him. Climbing into the rear gunner's cockpit, Frank was unaware that he was about to experience the might of the German Luftwaffe. The Whitley K4213 took off at 1830 hours and once more Frank was scanning the dark sky and panning his turret looking for the deadly night fighters that would be hunting in the darkness. The moon was bright that night, which allowed for more visibility than normal but also meant the Whitley would stand out against the moon light. The agile night fighters used the moonlight to their advantage and once spotted, they stealthily approached towards the rear of their prey. The Whitley crossed the sea heading towards its target when Frank suddenly sighted an attacking fighter, the swastika clearly visible. Opening fire at 150 yards with a long burst, he could immediately see bullet strikes on the attacking enemy aircraft which then fell away no longer capable of flying. Rarely had a rear gunner fired his guns and succeeded in shooting down an attacking fighter on the first offensive action. The combined fear and elation was short lived as a second enemy aircraft attacked just as they crossed the Dutch coast. On this occasion it flew over the Whitley and as it passed astern, Frank positioned his guns to where he anticipated the fighter would appear. He opened fire, once again raking that section of the sky and successfully shot the enemy aircraft down.

However, just twenty minutes later truly remarkable set of events happened when Frank's captain, Sgt Fullerton, barked down the intercom reporting that a third fighter was approaching from the port beam. The pilot manoeuvred the Whitley skilfully in order for Frank to capitalise on the position and swing his rear turret around. The German fighter opened fire first with tracer bullets, but Frank instantly opened up, firing his four Browning .303 guns resulting in the attacking Me109 last seen diving steeply with smoke and flame engulfing it. As the Whitley approached Bremen, a fourth attack developed. Three Messerschmitts came up in formation on the bomber's tail. Frank was faced with a formidable target so he picked out the middle fighter and gave a terrific burst of fire. Smoke and flames were seen to envelope the fighter and it fell into the cloud which glowed red. The remaining fighters never reappeared.

Very rarely did rear gunners experience such intense combat and achieve such remarkable results. Frank had displayed the finest qualities required of an isolated rear gunner, defending his aircraft and clearly evidencing the fact that without a skilled rear gunner, there was little hope of survival over occupied Europe. Thankfully the return to England was initially uneventful until the reality sank in that fog had blanketed the ground beneath them. The twenty-one Whitley aircraft returning to Linton that night were requested to divert to several nominated airfields. Frank's aircraft was running low on fuel and calculations by the Flight Engineer Sergeant Morgan revealed that a safe landing back at any of the nominated airfields was most unlikely. The captain Sergeant Fullerton took the decision to order his crew to bale out of the aircraft. The navigator, Pilot Officer McCarrapiett calculated their position to be over Fulbeck, Lincolnshire, and this was where the crew were to 'take to the silk'. It was not the ideal way for Frank to complete what had been a truly remarkable experience, but thankfully the crew, which included Frank's fellow air gunner Sergeant Keatley, all left the aircraft safely. As so many airmen did, they imparted their trust and individual lives to a silken parachute, all landing without suffering any injuries apart from Frank who twisted his ankle on what proved to have been an awkward landing. The crew were however entitled to apply for membership of the Caterpillar Club having saved their lives in an emergency by using the Irvin Parachute. A total of six other Whitley crews from the twenty-one that had departed that night all faced that same predicament – seven perfectly serviceable Whitley bombers were abandoned and subsequently lost whilst the remaining fifteen crews managed to land at a plethora of assorted aerodromes. Clearly 11 February 1941 was a day that was most unlikely to ever be surpassed during Frank's service in the RAF.

The station intelligence officer at Frank's home base required him to submit combat reports covering the engagements that had taken place on the raid to Bremen. It was a standard procedure to do so, and one that served to highlight the incredible achievements of his gunnery ability. Frank claimed two enemy aircraft destroyed and a probable third with a fourth damaged. There were not many air gunners who shot down three enemy aircraft and damaged another in several separate attacks during one mission. Unsurprisingly, Frank was recommended for the Distinguished Flying Medal – the recommendation was well written up by his commanding officer Wing Commander Clark, and it was published in the *London Gazette* on the 22 August 1941.

> This sergeant has done some really fine work since being in the squadron. His exceptional enthusiasm and unfailing devotion to duty have been an example to all with whom he has come in contact. On 11 February, on a trip to Bremen his aircraft was attacked by a number of enemy aircraft. He succeeded in shooting down two of these and probably damaged a third. He has unfailingly shown great courage in face of the enemy and I unhesitatingly recommend that his fine operational record be recognised by the award of the Distinguished Flying Medal.

In the circumstances, the recommendation for the DFM would normally have been for an immediate award – one that was rewarded for a single act or events that became immediately recognised by the Commanding Officer and not an 'end of tour' summary award as was promulgated. However it was one of only 903 Distinguished Flying Medals that were awarded between 1940 and 1941.

The excitement was short lived on the station. Frank was scheduled to take part in a raid on 28 February 1941. The briefing disclosed that an attempt would be made to try and disable the newly commissioned *Tirpitz* battleship, resident in the harbour at Wilhelmshaven. Such a prize target was always going to be well defended, particularly by German anti-aircraft flak batteries. The *Tirpitz* had been attacked on some sixteen previous occasions by the RAF and this attack was briefed as a result of its imminent commission into the German Navy. Frank's aircraft, Whitley L4988 was one of 116 that took part in the raid. Once again he recorded a further fighter attack but it proved impossible for him to engage the enemy fighter effectively, driving it off to seek other prey.

During March 1941, in addition to two long and arduous trips to the German capital further raids upon the German warships and U-boats took place. With the limitations of height and speed imposed by the Whitley, any trip to Berlin was a most hazardous event. For Frank, it required him to be confined in his Perspex coffin for around nine hours, and in the bitter cold. Frank was constantly scanning the dark environment that completely encapsulated him. It all required an immense amount of courage. Over the target, the intensity of the searchlight beams would have completely destroyed his night vision, creating a feeling of even greater vulnerability. In March he recorded a total of 33 hours and 15 minutes cooped up inside his turret flying on operations, and during the following month, similar raids consumed another thirty hours and thirty minutes.

It was around this time that Frank adopted a dog, called Raff, not an

A poignant illustration of a mid-upper air gunner attending to his guns, with his companion at his side even whilst upon the fuselage. (*RCAF museum*)

uncommon practice for those airmen who had grown up with dogs during their young lives. No doubt many men sought any opportunity to maintain that same unique bond that exists between animals and man. Establishing that senior ranks on the station were in favour of animals was always an advantage, providing an easier route to adopt a dog into the life of busy squadrons. It is now known that this companionship extended into the air as well, and several accounts exist where dogs flew with a particular member of a crew or as a crew mascot.

Scottish Terriers were a favourite breed of dog selected by many men and the colour black at that time was thought to be lucky and was thus very prevalent. This good-natured small companion dog was accommodated in many operational bases, with many of them brought onto the airfield prior to operational activities. Crews had many superstitions prior to take off, many looking to their faithful companions to see them off and greet them upon their return. There are countless stories of dogs waiting patiently on the airfield for their crew who never returned. The loyalty to their masters brought admiration from fellow crewmembers or station staff who instinctively continued to care for the dog. Frank continued with his first tour of duty and was required to attack a further nine targets in May and June 1941. The intense excitement and extreme danger experienced over Bremen was thankfully never repeated but no raid undertaken by Bomber Command could ever be regarded as uneventful. For Frank, he endured an additional fifty-nine hours in his gunnery turret and never fired his guns against any further marauding enemy fighters. When the opportunity presented itself, rear gunners were known to attack targets of opportunity – normally a searchlight cone that could be used as a target funnelling the Browning machine gun rounds towards the ground. Towards the end of June, Frank was made aware that he was to be regarded as tour expired and his crew was to be rested from operations. Another ambiguous term used but meaning exactly the same was to be 'screened' from operations or becoming a 'screened crew'.

Taking his dog Raff with him, Frank returned to Sheffield. During some well-earned leave, Frank was informed that he had been posted to 76 Squadron at Middleton St George. At last, he would join a crew in one of Bomber Command's premier aircraft as 76 Squadron was equipped with the larger four-engined Halifax. This was the second of the four-engined heavies to enter service with Bomber Command, but it was known to be far more efficient than the large Stirling that had preceded it. The Halifax could carry a bomb load of 13,000 lbs and travel at a speed of 282 mph at 13,500 ceiling height, a truly significant improvement to the Whitley which Frank had endured for so many hours. The posting to 76 Squadron also created another unexpected selection. Frank was sent on a pilot's course, a most rare situation for an air gunner to ever experience. He also left the ranks and received promotion to Pilot Officer. This was a sequence of life changing events for Frank as he suddenly found himself promoted and qualified to act as a second pilot to a captain in the crew of a bomber. On 23 April 1942, Frank acted as the second pilot to Sergeant Clack in a duty flight in Halifax R 9486, MP-Q to Tain on the east coast of Scotland. Research within the squadron records indicates that ten Halifax bombers from 76 Squadron were dispatched to RAF Tain in order to mount further attacks on the *Tirpitz* which was now located in the Trondheim Fjord in Norway. The attacks made against the *Tirpitz* took place with other Halifax aircraft from 10 Squadron and Lancasters from 35 Squadron but the weather conditions and heavy defences deployed resulted in no hits achieved upon the warship.

It was around this time that the Bomber Command Operational Research Section gathered together some statistics in relation to casualties incurred during April 1942. The document AIR 14-4525 in the National Archives chillingly concludes that the rear gunners operating in the large bomber aircraft were without doubt the most vulnerable. Forty-seven per cent of fatal and serious injuries were from that crew position. Clearly those statistics were secured from returning aircraft and excluded the significant numbers that failed to return. By the middle of May 1942, the crews from RAF Tain returned to Middleton St George in order to carry on operations into the industrial Ruhr.

On 25 and 27 May 1942 Frank records in his logbook that he undertook duties as the second pilot to Squadron Leader Iveson and Pilot Officer Dobson respectively. On 30 May he flew on the Thousand Bomber raid to the German city of Cologne. In fact 1,047 aircraft were drawn from Coastal Command, Training Command and Bomber Command. It was regarded by the RAF as a successful operation even though forty-one aircraft were lost. Frank recorded in his logbook 'Dante's Inferno' reflecting upon the firestorm that was created by the attack. On this raid, Halifax L9574 took off almost alongside Frank's aircraft and rather unusually both aircraft returned and landed at exactly the same time. Frank saw L9574 carrying the severe damage of having been hit by heavy flak – the reality of sheer luck struck him. Both crews had seen several bombers shot down on both the outward and return journeys, but they had seen no prowling fighters. The second Thousand Bomber raid to Essen on 1 June 1942 saw Frank engaged in what was a most unsuccessful raid. Thirty-one aircraft failed to return and the bombing from the participating 956 aircraft was scattered across a large area. This was his penultimate raid as just twenty-six days later he flew over Germany for the last time with a trip to Berlin in Halifax R9485.

Frank Bell was an extraordinary rear gunner and another dramatic turn of events imposed yet another responsibility upon him. On 10 July 1942 Frank was the Wireless Operator in Halifax E 7672, piloted by Squadron Leader Iveson on an eight and a half hour flight to Gibraltar. Fifteen aircraft from the strength of 76 Squadron were detached from operations over Germany, to commence operations in the Middle East. Rommel had successfully taken Tobruk in June and the North African campaign was in serious jeopardy. The perilous nature of the situation was recognised and the deployment of aircraft from 76 Squadron formed part of the Allied response. Frank resisted the temptation to smuggle Raff along with him, and he decided to leave his trusted dog under the care of others.

Following a short overnight stay in Gibraltar, the crew departed on 12 July on a twelve-hour transit to Kasfareet in Egypt and then finally to Agir in Palestine. Here they were joined by 454 Squadron, which was at that time non-operational and acting as a servicing unit. It was later to reform as a light bomber squadron in September 1942. 76 Squadron operated from two advanced bases in Egypt, Shallufa and Landing Ground 224, situated on the Alexandria to Cairo road. The conditions were far removed from some of the comforts provided at the airfield in middle England, and the frequent sandstorms and huge contrast between the extreme heat of the day and cold during the night had to be endured. From these basic landing grounds, a series of attacks were mounted on the harbour at Tobruk. In early August 1942, 76 Squadron moved to Fayid where they were joined by 10 Squadron – combining to continue the bombing upon Tobruk Harbour. During this period, Frank had also acquired another dog which he named RAAF, clearly accentuating the term he had previously used, no doubt in honour of the new squadron in which he was operating with No. 462 Squadron, a Royal Australian Air Force Squadron operating under command of the RAF. This squadron had an unusual genesis, resulting from the two British based Halifax Squadrons, 10 and 76 who had dispatched detachments to Aqir, in Palestine, and formed

Frank Bell, centre, the only man to be wearing a cap, is holding a young dog that he called RAAF. There is a rather unusual combination of clothing worn by this group of personnel from 462 Squadron, but not unexpected from that theatre of operations. (*Simon Muggleton*)

No. 249 Wing of No. 205 Group. On 6 September 1942, the two detachments were merged to form 462 Squadron RAAF. The squadron was mainly engaged in attacks on Tobruk and Crete, and in preparation for the pending Battle of El Alamein.

Frank took part in fifteen separate night operations in this area from July to September 1942, each round trip lasting approximately seven hours. The dangers of ditching in the North Sea had been replaced with the dangers of crashing into the hostile and barren sands – both of which had claimed many lives of bomber crews. The desert and heat would have represented such terrible images of being lost and dying from thirst. On 5 September Frank encountered a heavy concentration of flak around his aircraft which was immediately followed by an engagement by fighters whilst over their target. On this occasion he was not in a position to deploy his skills in the rear turret, instead, feeling rather hopeless sitting in the wireless operator's position. Without doubt, he probably would have liked to have swapped positions with the rear gunner. On 15 September and once again over Tobruk, Frank was in the wireless operator's position once more with Squadron Leader Iveson Piloting Halifax E7672.

The squadron's operational records indicate that the raid was made at heights between 7,000 and 13,000 feet and the bomb loads were dropped upon the harbour's jetties, as no ships were visible in what were poor weather conditions. The diary entry also records that the enemy's anti-aircraft defences were twice as strong as had been previously noted and one aircraft sustained flak damage

An example of the Middle East-configured Halifax. The paint scheme and removed mid-upper turret are indicative of the modifications for that theatre of operations.

whilst directly over the target. The aircraft noted as damaged by flak over the target was Frank's – it had been seriously peppered by the anti-aircraft shell and limped back to base where it crash-landed. This was Frank's fiftieth operational mission since the start of the war – it was also to be his last.

Promoted to the rank of Flying Officer (No. 111934), Frank was rested from operations and selected for duties as an instructor. His wealth of experience was invaluable and the RAF wanted him to disseminate it upon students who were being trained as aircrew. Once more he was required to hand over his beloved dog into the care and control of another. On 25 November 1942, he was a passenger on a BOAC Caledonian aircraft flight from Cairo, along the coast of East Africa to Durban in South Africa. From here he flew to Port Elizabeth where he attended No. 42 Air School for Officers. As well as training pilots, this was an air gunnery training centre set up under the Joint Air Training Scheme (JATS).

Frank was obviously rated as an excellent air-gunner, and by February 1943 he was instructing other aircrew, flying around all parts of South Africa. In March 1944 he undertook training as a navigator, flying in Oxford and Avro Anson aircraft, mainly in the Cape Town area. On 1 January 1945 he was at Westlake Transit Camp in South Africa, awaiting transport for his return to the UK. Once more he had completed a tour of duty and after nearly three years away he was looking forward to returning home and seeing his family. Frank left the RAF with an exemplary record and having accomplished what few could achieve, surviving fifty operations and shooting down several enemy fighters, a rare event during the Second World War.

The post-war period saw Frank working with his father in his drapery business in Sheffield but compared to his eventful life flying in the RAF he found it difficult to settle. In 1951 he was successful in gaining re-employment with the RAF, obviously being respected for his outstanding service and experience, he was re-appointed to the rank of Flying Officer. He was immediately sent to No. 5 Air Navigation School at RAF Lindholme (5 miles east of Doncaster), for refresher training as a wireless operator/signaller. He further developed his skills in map reading and navigation, and occasionally acting as the second (safety) pilot. Frank subsequently achieved his full pilot status and was awarded his wings during this period.

In August 1951 Frank Bell found himself as a passenger in a York aircraft on a flight from RAF Lyneham to RAF Shaibah in Iraq, where he was posted as a navigator in a Valetta aircraft. Frank was again posted, this time to RAF Mauripur in Pakistan where the base was shared with the newly formed Pakistan Air Force and was known as No. 48 Staging Post. In late 1953, Frank returned to the UK for further training duties and received promotion to a Flight Lieutenant. Frank's skills and experience were further developed by flying in Lancaster and Shackleton aircraft engaged in Atlantic exercises during the Cold War conflict.

He later served for four years at the Royal Aircraft Establishment at Farnborough where he undertook duties with the Radio Flight-Experimental Flying Department. In May 1960, Frank was posted onto No. 42 Course of the Maritime Operational Training Unit at Kinloss, again flying Shackleton aircraft. After completing the course he was posted to 205 Squadron at Changi, Singapore. The squadron was maintaining maritime reconnaissance duties in the Far East, as well as maintaining search and rescue operations. Frank served as the Signals Leader. His second retirement from the RAF took place on 18 November 1963, having flown over 3,000 hours in thirty-eight different types of aircraft.

Frank Bell's service was extraordinary in many ways – awarded the DFM for displaying the utmost skill in the rear gunner's turret and then unusually, he served as a wireless operator, pilot and navigator. He died on 3 May 1977.

28

Flight Lieutenant John Darby DFC

Rear Gunner, 40 Squadron

The Island of Malta centrally situated in the Mediterranean had huge military significance for both the Allied and axis forces during the Second World War. As a result it was attacked and defended at an immense cost of human lives. Malta is reportedly the most intensely bombed location within the entire destructive process that took place in the European conflict of the Second World War. One of many rear gunners destined to defend Malta was John Thomas Darby who like so many others had volunteered to fight in the early stages of the war, with a desire to serve in the Royal Air Force and fly as aircrew. His journey in service would take him to North Africa and then Malta – flying in Wellington bombers sitting in the tail turret. The start of his journey commenced with being moulded into military service with initial training to qualify as an air gunner at No. 7 Bombing and Gunnery School followed by service at RAF Newton Down during August and September 1940. Upon completion of his training he had proved his capabilities by passing out of the gunnery school system with the comments, 'Qualified – Class A passed with credit, a sound air gunner' endorsed in his flying Logbook.

John was just as competent in wireless training, which he undertook at the Operational Training Unit at Harwell. In 1940 the RAF aircrew training structure was working with speed and maximum capacity to provide for the needs of the consistent stream of students. For John it would have been seen as an advantage as he was swiftly introduced to flying a range of assorted training operations in Wellington bombers, which included air gunnery exercises and drogue target flying, from his rear gunner's turret. His first expedition over occupied France took place on 20 November 1940. John's pilot, Squadron Leader Arnold, flew Wellington 4294 to Paris where they released a plethora of printed leaflets into the sky, destined to fall upon the streets below. These sorties were identified by the RAF as 'Nickel Raids' and thought at the time to be of some importance in delivering political propaganda. The five-hour night operation allowed John to experience the sights and smells of an operational environment and the views of the flak and searchlights from his privileged turret perspective. The following day, Squadron Leader Arnold provided John with another first when their Wellington

An early enlistment photograph of John Darby in uniform.

crashed back onto the runway during an attempted take-off. Luckily nobody was seriously injured and the accident did nothing to hinder an operational posting which saw John and his pilot dispatched to No. 40 Squadron, a Wellington unit operating out of RAF Wyton, on 26 November 1940.

Squadron Leader Roy Arnold took command of 'A' flight and flew his first sortie with 40 Squadron against Ostend on 21 December 1940, followed by a sortie to Bremen on New Year's Day. With John as part of his crew, they had great difficulty in locating the main target, something that was all too frequent at that time, and dropped their bomb load on what was presumed to have been a searchlight and flak concentration. Just over a fortnight later, the crew were lucky to survive an incident which saw their aircraft collide with a telegraph pole in a training flight. John wrote in his flying logbook, 'crashed hit telegraph pole and high tension wires. Plane burnt out'. The dates within the logbook are conflicting and research at the National Archives indicates that Squadron Leader Arnold crashed and swung off the runway at Wyton, Huntingdonshire on 12 December 1940 resulting in the aircraft being completely wrecked. It is presumed that injuries were sustained by John as he did not take any further flying until mid-March when he joined the reserve training flight at RAF Stradishall.

Squadron Leader Arnold had in the meantime, been posted to command 9 Squadron at RAF Honington. On 9 June, whilst operating with that squadron, he flew a reconnaissance sortie off the French and Belgian coast during which his Wellington was intercepted by Luftwaffe fighters near Calais. The Wellington was badly shot up and seriously damaged. Ordering his crew to abandon the aircraft, Arnold gallantly struggled to hold it stable in the air. His crew escaped by

The striking silhouettes of three Wellingtons flying in the evening sky, the light illuminating through the Perspex turret of the leading aircraft.

parachute but he was not able to save himself. His crew of five survived and spent the remaining years of the war as prisoners. No greater sacrifice could have been given to his crew and his country. Arnold's body was later recovered from the crash scene and he was buried in the Blankenberge cemetery, Belgium. A similar set of circumstances took place when in 1942, Leslie Manser of 50 Squadron also saved his crew at the cost of his own life and was later recognised with a posthumous Victoria Cross.

Upon arrival at RAF Stradishall, John was immediately slotted in as the rear gunner within Pilot Officer Johnson's crew. No sooner had he arrived, he was advised that they were shortly departing on a monumental 2,000-mile non-stop flight to Benghazi. This was deemed to be a dangerous trip and one of the primary safety requirements needed was to assess the exact fuel consumption that their engines would consume, information that was obtained on 21 March following a test flight of nearly four hours' duration in their Wellington T2985. John prepared for the flight with various vaccinations that were required and kit provisions. On 31 March the crew fully prepared they departed and with the aircraft holding its maximum fuel capacity, they had to undertake the flight in stages to reach their final destination – Stradishall to Benghazi, Benghazi to Tobruk, Tobruk to Cairo and finally Cairo to Ismailia where they arrived on 4 April. Upon arrival John's crew were posted onto the strength of 38 Squadron.

On 6 April 1941, the Germans invaded Greece and Yugoslavia, completely overrunning both countries within a month of commencing their aggression. The Allied strength in the Middle East was severely stretched and John was required to operate in the front gunner's position of Wellington R3291 for a flight to Eleusis, Greece on 11 April. On 14 April the British Army had been forced to withdraw to the Olympia-Servia line. The RAF's evacuation of Paramythia, just south of the Albanian frontier, and almost midway between Yanina and the island of Corfu began. On 15 April the Luftwaffe made large and successful attacks on the airfields at Larissa, Kalambaka/Vassiliki, Paramythia and Niamata with many Allied aircraft destroyed on the ground, precious losses that the RAF would not be able to sustain. The following day the situation worsened for the Allies, both on the ground and in the air, which necessitated a general withdrawal. On 17 April the last Wellingtons at Eleusis were ordered back to Egypt and John flew with his crew back to Ismailia, no doubt a traumatic experience for all. The Greek evacuation was called operation Demon and involved some 50,700 troops that were evacuated from an establishment of some 62,500 troops deployed to Greece. Of the 12,000 who were not taken off, approximately 3,000 were believed killed with a further 9,000 becoming prisoners, another serious blow to the Allied forces. Cyrenaica, Greece and Crete had been lost, however Malta valiantly continued to resist all the assaults inflicted by the enemy. The stage was set for the next round in the struggle for control of the Mediterranean and the Middle East. John and his crew would subsequently attack targets within Greece, Libya, and Crete on a regular basis. They had well and truly entered the cauldron of the Middle Eastern conflict and their next operational flight would bring them further trouble.

On 19 April the target was scheduled to be Benghazi which had fallen into German hands on 4 April. Within a matter of weeks axis forces had recaptured over 600 miles of Allied territory and surged across Libya. On 14 April 1941, Rommel had reached the Egyptian border. Lieutenant General Erwin Rommel commander of the Africa Corps was proving to be one of Adolf Hitler's most competent leaders. In addition, the Luftwaffe which had moved to Sicily in order to protect the axis shipping lanes and to defeat the British forces in Malta, were continuing to maintain their constant harassment and bombardment on that beleaguered Island. On the raid to Benghazi, John's Wellington aircraft R3291 was attacked by an enemy Me109, an attack that caused sufficient damage to the Wellington to induce it to crash in the desert near Mersa Matruh, west of Alexandria. Luckily the crew were rescued but once again John's captain appears to have been injured and was unable to continue operational flying. Pilot Officer Johnson's name never featured in John's flying Logbook again. Pilot Officer Davis took over command of the crew, and undertook a number of cross country sorties to settle in with them. John was requested to man the front gunner's turret for those sorties, but soon returned to his rear turret upon the order of Pilot Officer Davis who had decided that John was best placed to protect the rear of the aircraft and his crew. This was a common practice and captains frequently made such decisions based upon night vision tests, or the gunner's examination results which were always recorded in their flying logbooks. The rear gunners

A typical Middle East Wellington crew briefing prior to an operation. This crew are wearing a differing array of flying uniform and footwear.

position was always given a high priority with pilots keen to ensure their best gunners 'looked after the rear'. The first two raids for John, bombing Derna in Libya on 3 May and 5 May, were both abandoned due to poor weather despite several hours spent in the air trying to locate the targets.

John soon began to understand the extraordinary procedures that were required to operate safely in the desert environment. 38 Squadron were based at Shallufa, Egypt but independently operated from what were known as Landing Grounds which were coded as LG 09 and LG 60 and so on. These were sparsely equipped venues, simply used as platforms to conduct bombing operations from. The main base at Shallufa was shared with 37 Squadron, another Wellington unit deployed on the same generic targets within the Middle East campaign, as John's. Ground crews had a tough time competing against the weather and the ever-present sand that would blow into every crevice, both mechanical and human. For John and indeed for other gunners, the personal challenge of keeping his guns clean and his Perspex polished, ranked high on his list of duties. His next operation was to attack Meloai in Greece. Taking off at 2334 hours on 16 May, Wellington T2507 completed the raid in just over seven hours. They experienced no opposition whatsoever and the bomb load was accurately delivered. As was normal for operational duties the pilot landed the aircraft back at the landing ground, in this case LG09, and sometime later on the same day, returned the

Wellington and crew back to base at Shallufa where in comparison to the landing grounds, even the basic wooden huts at Shallufa were regarded as pure luxury.

Towards the end of the month, an operation was planned to take place with the target identified as Crete which had been the subject of a German airborne invasion early on the morning of 20 May 1941. However, John's Wellington T2507 had been in receipt of some hefty maintenance work undertaken by the ever-efficient ground crews and the oil and fuel consumption needed to be fully established before it could undertake the long mission. John made use of the respite from flying by studying aircraft recognition, as he needed to be confident in his recognition of both German and Italian airframe types. The Italian aircraft were quite different in their profiles to most types and it was of utmost importance to the crew's safety that he could identify them. He undertook this responsibility with great diligence.

These were desperate times for the Allied forces in the Middle East. The situation on Crete was, to a large extent, influenced by the invasion of Greece by the combined Italian and German forces. The allies had to retreat from Greece via Crete thence to North Africa. This was a difficult logistical problem and units became separated and lost as the shipping convoys were unable to facilitate the sheer quantity of movement of the men and materials. Some Allied personnel went to Crete whilst some went direct to Alexandria. Many of the units on Crete adopted the role of infantry because they no longer had their respective equipment. There was limited air support available to Crete, and what was available consisted of Gloster Gladiator, biplane fighters. The expected invasion by the axis forces upon Crete took place with the Germans utilising massive forces delivered by Ju52 transports. John Darby and his crew were again thrown into immediate bombing sorties upon the newly occupied areas held by the German forces.

On the night of 25 May, enemy troop concentrations on Crete were scheduled to be attacked, but once again the weather was the main enemy. The nine hour and thirty minute operation was recorded in John's flying logbook as DNCO – 'did not complete operation'. Just two nights later a lengthy trip to the aerodrome on the Isle of Scarpanto took place, a location where the Italian Air Force Regia Aeronautica CR.42 aircraft were based. The Italians successfully used this aircraft as a fighter and escort fighter across the Mediterranean theatre. The raid on the aerodrome was completed but in doing so, Wellington T2507 was singled out to receive heavy and fairly accurate flak. It was a terrifying experience for John sitting alone in his turret and he recorded this fact against his thirteenth operation in his flying logbook as 'quite a shaky do'.

Wellington T2507 had become the crew's regular and reliable aircraft and John liked flying in his rear turret as he had ownership over the cleanliness of both the turret and Perspex. The guns would be removed after operations or at least covered to prevent sand infiltration and he would have ensured that they were stripped and cleaned ready for the next sortie.

The trails of flak fired up into the sky attempting to shoot down the British bombers illustrate the intensity of anti-aircraft fire. The rear gunners saw these trails and witnessed first-hand their destructive power.

Operations took place to bomb Moritza aerodrome on 3 June and then to Benghazi on 9 June. Both raids were successful, but the aircraft had been targeted with fairly accurate flak over both areas. A further Benghazi run was ordered four days later and on this operation the pilot advised John that he was going to provide him the opportunity to strafe the aerodrome at Benina. The squadron were not adverse to this combination of events, and for John it would have been an exciting prospect which he undertook with some level of cool-headed accuracy. As the pilot took down the Wellington to a relatively low level, John's guns created a field of fire that visibly ran along the ground acting as a guide until they struck the parked aircraft. Even if no fires or explosions resulted, John knew that his accurate firepower had destroyed several of the targets he had selected. Unfortunately for John, the hydraulics to his turret became faulty following the raid which resulted in the crew abandoning their next allocated raid, a fortunate set of circumstances as the long awaited and anticipated leave arrived for John and his crew. They were flown to Cairo for five days well-earned rest. They then returned to their squadron to undertake further runs to Benghazi in Wellington T2507. Whilst the target was the same, on this particular raid they were specifically tasked with attacking shipping that was reportedly at anchor within the harbour. Unbeknown to the pilot, this particular operation was to become one of importance to him personally.

Just before 2200 hours, Pilot Officer Davis lifted the aircraft off the landing ground and commenced the journey with no real knowledge of any weather conditions over the target. Upon arrival, weather conditions were good so Davis decided to undertake a diving attack from 5,000 feet to just 1,000 feet. Flying in the darkness and with the knowledge that the anti-aircraft defences were known to be both capable and accurate, this was not an action that John would have relished. They survived but it had been a heck of a ride for John hanging on in the rear, the 'G' forces imposed upon him during such diving and recovery would have been unpleasant to say the least. This raid was a trigger for the Commanding Officer to submit a recommendation for a Distinguished Flying Cross to be awarded to the pilot. The recommendation submitted in the *London Gazette* on 15 August 1941, read:

> DAVIS Clive Selwyn Flying Officer RAFVR 38 Squadron. One night in June 1941 this officer carried out a successful attack on a target at Bengazi, afterwards flying on to Benina where in spite of heavy anti-aircraft fire, he machine gunned aircraft on the ground from a low altitude. This officer has carried out thirty-four operational flights and has at all times displayed exceptional keenness, skill and determination.

The reference to the machine-gunning of the aircraft relates to the actions by John in the rear gunner's turret. John's flying logbook entry made on 28 June 1941 quotes 'Captain gets DFC' and the squadron operational record book entry indicated that the pilot thought he had struck a ship lying at the end of the central mole in Benghazi harbour.

July 1941 commenced with another regular run to Benghazi on the first day of the month. These entries deserved more than the bland statement of fact shown in John's logbook as each one represented around nine hours for John in his rear turret, and the continuing repetition of raids to this target indicate just how important a military objective it was to the Allied forces. Another medal was to be awarded to a member of John's crew. On the seventh of that month, the crew were briefed to attack the Syrian targets of Alleppo and Beirut. Once again the squadron records provide more detail than John's logbook entry: 'Direct hit on petroleum tank causing terrific explosion and red fire with volumes of black smoke'. The crew's Australian navigator Sergeant Ross had once again done an amazing job and his service to 38 Squadron was recognised by the award of the Distinguished Flying Medal.

> Sergeant Ross has carried out forty-four operations in the Middle East. On every occasion he has made a success of his raids owing to his accurate navigation and bomb aiming. He prepares for his operations with meticulous care and sets a fine example to all the Observers in the squadron.

John recorded in his logbook, 'Navigator gets DFM'.

On the night of 23 July, John assisted another pilot, Sergeant Brine, by crewing with him and conducting a searchlight co-operation sortie over Alexandria. These were flights at pre-determined heights to allow the searchlight operators to calibrate and adjust the mechanisms, part of the defence structures over Alexandria. It would have been a welcome break from the Benghazi run, but as he might have expected, the last operation for him in July was a return to that very same repetitive target, Benghazi.

On 15 August, John volunteered to act as the rear gunner on a special operation to attack a reported submarine sighted off Bardia. He joined another pilot, Sergeant Couper in Wellington T1018 which flew to LG09 for a detailed briefing alongside another crew captained by Sergeant Earl. The two Wellingtons flew five bombing runs over the given position, dropping their bomb loads in a pattern to cover as best possible the entire target area. After the bombings, a large patch of oil was seen in the sea giving the crews an indication that the submarine had been hit. Although John was able to report the slick, it proved insufficient evidence to claim the submarine's destruction. Flying low over the sea whilst engaging in action would have been a welcome change for John but he modestly wrote in his logbook, 'operational bombing at Bardia'.

August continued to provide operational variations for John, much welcomed relief from the dreaded Benghazi run as well as being notified that he and his crew were to depart their base and support the beleaguered Island of Malta. A detachment strength of nine Wellingtons from Shallufa were ordered out. On 18 August, their trusted Wellington T2507 flew the 7 hours and 35 minute sortie to Malta, which was still being heavily engaged by axis aerial forces. It was indeed a most uncomfortable posting in many respects as severe and enforced rationing for just about everything possible was in place. Between 1940 and 1942, there had been thirty-five major supply operations to Malta however axis forces had inflicted significant damage on eight of these, one of which was the famous Operation Pedestal. There were long periods when no convoy runs were even contemplated and only a trickle of supplies reached Malta by submarine. John had arrived on Malta at the worst possible time – the axis forces had complete air and naval supremacy in the central Mediterranean area of conflict. John would have been advised of the constant dangers of unexploded ordinance and the ever-present time delay bombs that silently sat waiting to explode and add their own havoc to the carnage that had taken place on the island.

The Wellington was the heaviest bomber based in Malta, operating from an airfield at Luqa which was also home to several other units. The Wellington bombers were deployed on night operations, bombing the North African ports in axis hands, as well as Italian mainland targets. In the six months up to the end of December 1941, the Wellingtons at Malta flew well over one thousand sorties between them. John was also thrown into the campaign against the harbour in Tripoli. His flying logbook recorded a sequence of six raids to that target, taking place from 22 August to 4 September. The operational records indicate that

L.M.A.6   19.1.43.   F/20.   ← P.

Luqa aerodrome in Malta, seen from the air in this vertical illustration which was photographed on 19 January 1943.

John's aircraft carried a bomb load of 5,000 lbs on 4 September, a record load for a Malta based Wellington, bearing in mind the recognised bomb load was 4,500 lbs. Nine Wellingtons had flown to Tripoli and three had carried the extra-large bomb load. The raid was evidenced as successful with bombs hitting two medium sized merchant vessels and fires started as a result of the strikes. The anti-aircraft fire was intense and accurate with several aircraft damaged – nine searchlights were operational. John had experienced several raids to this target and each time, aircraft had been engaged and damaged by the efficient defences. The searchlight capability varied but the operators were very skilful and held some of the Wellingtons in their beams very well. John was frequently provided the opportunity to respond with fire towards such ground defences always seeking to fire at any gun and searchlight emplacements.

Whist returning from the last escapade to Tripoli, a motor transport convoy was sighted on the Tripoli to Homs road so the pilot advised John and he swung his turret to the best optimum position engaging the transport with the full firepower of his four Browning machine guns. The operations to Tripoli were fairly short in duration, returning to Malta within about four hours. Despite operating in the Middle East, the night operations were very cold and just as uncomfortable as any other rear gunner in service with the RAF. John's pilot had received promotion to Flight Lieutenant, but John still retained the rank of Sergeant.

Early in September he attacked another harbour installation, this time Palermo, Sicily. Then it was bombing Messina, the railway station and main railway lines. For John in the rear it was a relief that no searchlights were in action, they always had the potential to catch his aircraft and completely destroy his night vision.

Intelligence information arrived at Malta concerning an Italian convoy of ships identified as the *Bainsizza*, *Caffaro*, *Giula*, *Nirva*, *Nicolo*, *Odero*, and *Tembien*, they were believed to be departing Naples on 10 September. Rommel was convinced quite rightly that the British had broken the German codes because of the frequency of attacks on his supply lines. Berlin rejected Rommel's views, but the importance of this theatre of operations dictated that Ultra Intelligence was indeed used extensively to disrupt supplies to the Africa Corps. This particular convoy was headed for the port of Tripoli, escorted by the destroyers *Oriani* and *Fulmine* and the torpedo boats *Procione*, *Pegaso*, *Orsa*, and *Circe*. The convoy was an important target and plans to attack it were put into place. The Italian steamer *Caffaro* was attacked north west of Tripoli and sunk by 830 Squadron Swordfish aircraft of from Malta. The Italian steamer *Tembien* was damaged by a similar attack. Another Italian steamer *Nicolo Odero* joined the convoy three days after sailing and she was also damaged in the Swordfish attacks. This important target was again located some 25 miles north-west of Tripoli, and attacked by Wellingtons that had flown from Malta. Flight Lieutenant Davis was flying Wellington Z8790, and John was sitting in his rear turret well aware that this was a terribly dangerous operation. They had left Malta at two in the morning not knowing exactly where the convoy was, but once sighted the bombers rallied between 0340 hours and 0455 hours, bombing the convoy, which resulted in four ships being hit and set on fire. The escort destroyers threw up as much light flak as possible and to give an indication of how low some of the Wellington bombers were flying, the destroyers' guns were also firing close to the surface of the water in an effort to catch the bombers as they dived away after their bombing runs. John was able to supress the destroyers light flak gunfire by returning fire from his position as the Wellington passed over the targets. The crew were able to claim a confirmed direct hit upon one of the merchant vessels and so returned to

Middle East converted Wellingtons from 221 Squadron, which were operational from Luqa airfield.

Malta elated at the successful operation with the debriefing, an opportunity for the crews to relate their accounts which would have been very different had any axis forces fighters been in a position to intercept the Wellingtons.

Just three days later, five Wellingtons took off from Malta *en route* to Tripoli harbour. A plan had been devised to allow two Wellingtons to drop sea mines within the proximity of the harbour itself. Various sizes of sea mines were available, each capable of being dropped by parachute and robust enough to withstand the impact into the water without detonating. The Wellington normally carried two mines, which could be dropped independently. They were capable of being laid or dropped with delay fuse mechanisms. These were a creative way to permit shipping to use areas of water with some certainty of being safe, but after a few days the mine armed itself and the magnetic field of the next ship passing over the device initiated its detonation. Some mines also deployed acoustic methods of detonation, noise or vibration of propellers or a combination of both methods also existed. As with all armaments the sea mine developed and grew in capability through the war years.

Within the RAF, operations that involved dropping sea mines were identified as Gardening Sorties, planting mines. On this particular operation three additional

Wellingtons created a diversion by bombing, whilst the two aircraft detailed with the mines slipped into the area and planted their load. The searchlights and flak gave them no trouble but a technical fault on one of the Wellingtons prevented their mines from being dropped. All of the aircraft returned safely and undamaged, but only two mines had been laid.

On 22 September, John was amongst five bomber crews that were targeting the barracks and motor transport depot in Tripoli. They all safely left the airfield at Luqu, at around 2100 hours that evening. Wellington EZ8776 was being captained by an Australian, Sergeant Secomb, his crew consisted of Walter Brown, a 19-year-old wireless operator / air gunner, and rear gunner William Poole, both British born alongside fellow Canadians air gunner James Sheridan and Robert Toshack, navigator and finally 26-year-old Peter Bold from England who acted as second pilot. The official squadron records identify that a heavy anti-aircraft barrage was present in the sky over the harbour area. Nine searchlights were operational in support of the flak units but they were recorded as having been ineffective. That said, Wellington EZ8776 with the above mentioned crew, failed to return to Malta. The other participating crews in this raid were unable to shed light on the fate that had befallen this aircraft and her crew. Post-war investigations however established that they had been shot down near Tripoli, and all of the crew had perished in the incident. The Australian pilot Rowland Secomb lies buried in the Cemetery at Tripoli, Libya, but his remaining five crewmembers were never recovered. They are commemorated on the Malta Memorial which records 2,297 Allied airmen who lost their lives in that theatre of operations and were denied a grave.

Back on Malta, John completed his red ink logbook entry, 'Operational bombing at Tripoli four hours and thirty-five minutes'. His pilot, Flight Lieutenant Davis, announced that he was going to be temporarily absent and that a Flying Officer Hall was replacing him. Hall had recently arrived having delivered a replacement Wellington onto the island. Hall was an experienced pilot having served previously with 149 Squadron and been involved in a gallant rescue of his front gunner after crashing when returning from a raid to Cologne in March 1941. His aircraft had been damaged by flak and struggling to reach their home airfield, it clipped a treetop and fell in flames. The front gunner was trapped but Hall managed to clear and release the turret door enabling the gunner to survive from what would have been a horrific death – being burnt alive. Flying Officer Hall took his new crew on raids to Palermo harbour on two occasions, and another to Tripoli at the close of September. In October they flew to intercept an axis convoy some 240 miles east of Malta but the target was not located.

Flight Lieutenant Davis returned from his sojourn having been promoted to squadron leader, and he promptly took command of his old crew for a maximum effort raid to Naples in Italy. Sixteen Wellingtons from 38 Squadron were scheduled to bomb the important targets of the Valiana Torpedo Factory and the Royal Arsenal in Naples. John and his crew were one of just three aircraft to carry the large 4,000-lb bomb on this operation. The target area was bombed during an extended two-hour period and John recorded the event by dropping one of the first 4,000-lb bombs for the squadron on his 40th operation. The new 4,000-lb bomb had been tested and approved. A requirement of its design was that it should be able to be carried within the Wellington bomber's bomb bay. Up until May 1941 several 4,000-lb bombs had been used by Bomber Command and by August 1941, 226 bombs had been recorded as dropped with no proven failures. These Mark I bombs were formally introduced into full service in January 1942 and forthwith they were always known as 'cookies'. Upon return to base, Squadron Leader Davis, acting as the B Flight commander advised the crews that they would refuel, re-arm and return to the air for another operation that evening. Operations were planned to attack the aerodromes in Sardinia and Sicily. Luckily for John it was a short operation of only three hours and ten minutes but he would have been exhausted by this time, both physically and mentally. However his spirits would have been lifted when the news came through of orders to depart Malta, passed to the crew by Davis. At midnight on 24 October John climbed into the rear turret of Wellington Z8376 and left the beleaguered Island of Malta. Upon arrival in Egypt, Squadron Leader Davis signed John's flying logbook, endorsing that he had completed forty-three operations which had entailed a total of 316 hours and 50 minutes spent behind his Browning guns. Squadron Leader Davis respected and valued his crew and John had been his reliable rear gunner for many operations but the partnership was to end – Davis was regarded as tour expired and due a non-operational posting. He was able to fly with them for one final operation and it was quite appropriate for that to be a 'Benghazi Run', which took place on the night of 5 November 1941.

With forty-four operations completed, John knew that his 'tour expired' status would soon follow but prior to this he was captained by another pilot, this time a fellow sergeant named Dibb, who took him on a raid on 19 November to bomb Derna aerodrome. The following day, two sorties were flown to search for Wellington T2991, captained by Sergeant Lewis RAAF, and Wellington Z8711, captained by Sergeant Swingler RCAF. Both of these aircraft were missing from the operation to Derna and they could very well have come down in the desert. It transpired that Wellington T2991 had forced landed at El Imayid on 20 November and in doing so the aircraft had exploded with all six crew on board killed. John had lost another group of friends, as all those killed had been fellow sergeants alongside him in 38 Squadron. The other aircraft, Wellington Z8711 had run out of fuel but had managed to land some 200 miles south of Sidi Barrani. Fortunately for them, a searching Wellington of 37 Squadron located them and all crew were later recovered safe and well. Back at LG 09, an incident took place which claimed the lives of three ground crew. Wellington Z8720 also on the strength of 37 Squadron, was undergoing final preparations for deployment when it inexplicably exploded. Six ground crew staff were attending to the aircraft at the time of the explosion, and three received fatal injuries.

John's final operations in the desert were to undertake the bombing of troops at El Gazala, the bombing of motor transport at South Gazala, Maleme, Crete, and finally Derna aerodrome on 13 December. Returning Wellington T2507 from LG 09 to the main airfield the following day, John suffered his first complete hydraulic failure within his turret. He had conducted a great many operations in this particular Wellington, all without mechanical failure and this was the only time that his rear turret had ever let him down. John became officially tour expired or screened, from operations having accumulated the impressive total of forty-nine operational raids.

In February 1942 John was ferried to Cairo and thence to Nigeria, eventually arriving in the United Kingdom to serve as an instructor at No. 11 Operational Training Unit, RAF Bassingbourne. This posting was regarded as a rest from operations but it most certainly was not a rest from flying – in his six months duty in the training unit, John added an additional 253 hours into his logbook.

Sergeant John Darby commenced his second operational tour of duty having been posted to East Wretham, No. 1678 Conversion Unit in order to prepare him to join a crew operating in one of Bomber Command's Mk.II Lancasters. Finding himself crewed up with Pilot Officer O'Farrell, John was unexpectedly allocated the position of mid-upper gunner. Almost all Lancasters were equipped with three Frazer-Nash hydraulically operated turrets, each fitted with .303 machine guns. The FN-5 nose turret had two guns, the FN-50 mid-upper turret had two, and the FN20 tail turret had four. The nose turret was rarely used and manned by the bomb aimer if required. For John the allocation of mid-upper gunner was a change from the solitary rear turret, and most probably received on his part with some objection. The reality of only having two Browning machine guns, and not four, would have been difficult to accept. An advantage however was that in this position, John had the opportunity to see where he was going rather than looking backwards in his rear turret and with a full 360 degree view around him, John's view now took in the entire length of the Lancaster.

On 25 July, 1943 John flew his first operational sortie in the Lancaster on a mine laying 'gardening' operation close to the Frisian Islands. This was John's 50th operation and it was the final requirement placed upon the crew, before they were posted onto 115 Squadron, RAF Little Snoring. John departed the conversion unit with Pilot Officer O'Farrell and remained as his mid-upper air gunner. John once again had an opportunity to operate in an aircraft that had by choice become the crew's regular airframe, Lancaster DS675. It was an entirely different experience for John, exchanging the rear turret and now sitting on a tiny hammock type arrangement in the mid-upper turret. The Perspex was more mushroom or domed in shape with larger panels and instead of concentrating on a rearward view for aggressing night fighters John was charged with covering both flanks and to the forward positions as well. It was just as isolating, apart from the fact it was possible to see the navigator should he pop his head into the astrodome that was positioned at the rear of the cockpit section. John clocked up

A post-raid photograph illustrating the density of destruction and significant fires still burning in Munchen-Gladbach. It was bombed by over 600 aircraft. The accurate results were achieved by controlled pathfinder marking.

15 hours and 55 minutes in his new post with raids to Nuremberg and Milan on 10 and 12 August.

The following raid was to be Turin on 16 August with fourteen Lancasters from 115 Squadron participating. One Lancaster flown by Flight Lieutenant Anderson was shot down over the target area, another flown by Flight Sergeant Bradford was forced to abandon the raid because the rear turret had become faulty and John's Lancaster was attacked by a night fighter. John noted that the attacking fighter was driven off by the combined machine gun fire of both himself and that of his rear gunner, Warrant Officer Lionel Goldsmith from New Zealand. The Lancaster was forced to land at Wyton at 0455 hours, in order to assess the damage but five hours later they were able to depart Wyton and return to Little Snoring. These particular events, combined with the delayed arrival back at base, became the reason why John and his crew did not participate in the raid to Hitler's rocket base at Peenemunde on 17 August.

The next raids flown by John were to Berlin and Nuremberg – he and his crew returned safely but each raid had claimed another crew from 115 Squadron. Statistically 115 Squadron suffered exceptionally high losses when serving in Bomber Command, over 100 Lancasters, representing some 700-plus aircrew lives were lost. On 30 August the target was Munchen-Gladbach and John proudly recorded that their Lancaster carried one of the huge 8,000-lb blockbusting cookie bombs. It was successful and allowed John to record fifty-seven operations completed encompassing over 400 operational hours flying.

Pilot Officer O'Farrell's crew undertook training upon what was identified as G. H. radio equipment, in early September. This was later known and identified as 'Gee'. The Bomber Command notes produced in late 1943 and early 1944 on required G. H. training reported that it was 'essential' for preliminary flights to 'familiarise' navigators with the movement of the G. H. pulses, and the crew with the general principles of G. H. tracking. During this training John fell unexpectedly ill and was removed from any flying duties by the medical officer. He recorded his last entry of G. H. training on 5 September and John's position in the crew was replaced, pending his return to operational fitness. Pilot Officer O'Farrell and his crew completed the training and the squadron's next operation which they were to participate in was to be Hanover on 22 September 1943. Sergeant Harold Bean had replaced John in the gunner's position, otherwise the crew remained exactly as it had been previously. Their Lancaster DS675 took off from Little Snoring at 1918 hours, just ahead of the remaining six other Lancasters from the squadron, but it never returned. Lancaster DS675 and six of the crew were added to the horrific fatality statistics accumulated by the squadron. His crew had been attacked by night fighters over the target area. The casualties from John's crew now rest together in the Hanover War Cemetery, Germany:

Flying Officer Patrick O'Farrell, Royal Australian Air Force, Age 21.
Flight Sergeant Cornelius Ward, Royal Australian Air Force, Age 24.
Sergeant Donald Cowling, Royal Air Force Volunteer Reserve, Age 28.
Pilot Officer Reginald Fuggle DFM, Royal New Zealand Air Force, Age 26.
Sergeant Harold Bean, Royal Air Force Volunteer Reserve, Age 22.
Warrant Officer Lionel Goldsmith, Royal New Zealand Air Force, Age 27.

The two crewmembers who survived, Pilot Officer Pipe RNZAF and Sergeant Heath RAF, the navigator and bomb aimer, became prisoners of war. It could be speculated that they had been in a relatively advantageous position to escape from the forward escape hatch, which was very close to their work stations. For John, he entered October in better health and on the station he became a 'spare bod', an air gunner without a crew, but a most experienced one having completed a total of fifty-seven operational sorties. This was considered to be a

The Australian Government issued upon application a silver-coloured mother's or widow's badge. The badge was marked 'For Australia', symbolising and recognising the loss of a son or husband during the war. The RAAF suffered 11,061 casualties during the Second World War, 5,117 of those men lost their lives whilst serving in RAF Squadrons and 5,944 occurred serving in RAAF Squadrons. Canada and New Zealand also issued a similar badge, but no such token of respect was issued by the British Government.

significant and impressive number of missions to complete and very few if any men that surrounded him would have achieved such a high total. The Air Ministry directives in 1943 had set the following requirement in order to be assessed for tour completion: First tour thirty operations, second tour twenty operations and a tour within pathfinders required forty-five operations.

Flight Sergeant John Darby received promotion to Warrant Officer. This was in recognition of the time he had served which meant he was invited to apply for his commission. It is worthy to note that according to the Air Ministry directives, John was overdue in being stood down from operations. He was once again allocated duties as the spare gunner, acting as mid-upper air gunner with two needy 115 Squadron crews at the close of the month. On a raid to Leipzig he must have thought he had pushed his luck too far when his Lancaster DS765 became severely iced up causing significant handling problems for the pilot. Ice had the potential to create life-threatening conditions and to make it worse the Lancaster was bounced around in violent electrical storms. This would have been a frightening experience for John as he sat in his Perspex bubble, witnessing violent bolts of electrical discharge that were taking place around him. These electrical storms represented serious danger to aircraft as instruments and in particular navigational equipment, could malfunction.

At the close of the month John was finally screened from operations, with a grand total of fifty-nine operations and 430 hours operational flying. He was recommended for the award of the Immediate Distinguished Flying Cross. The author suspects that few DFCs had ever been more hard won than this one, despite the rather bland wording to the original recommendation which states:

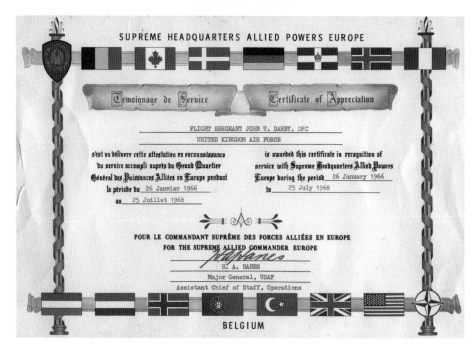

SUPREME HEADQUARTERS ALLIED POWERS EUROPE

Témoignage de Service — Certificate of Appreciation

FLIGHT SERGEANT JOHN T. DARBY, DFC
UNITED KINGDOM AIR FORCE

s'est vu délivrer cette attestation en reconnaissance du service accompli auprès du Grand Quartier Général des Puissances Alliées en Europe pendant la période du 26 Janvier 1966 au 25 Juillet 1968

is awarded this certificate in recognition of service with Supreme Headquarters Allied Powers Europe during the period 26 January 1966 to 25 July 1968

POUR LE COMMANDANT SUPRÊME DES FORCES ALLIÉES EN EUROPE
FOR THE SUPREME ALLIED COMMANDER EUROPE

H. A. HANES
Major General, USAF
Assistant Chief of Staff, Operations

BELGIUM

The personal certificate awarded to John Darby for his service with The Supreme Headquarters Allied Powers.

As a wireless operator / air gunner Warrant Officer Darby has completed a large number of sorties, many of them in the Middle East. He has displayed exceptional skill and proved himself to be a most valuable member of aircraft crew. In spite of several trying experiences his keenness remains unabated and his example has been most inspiring.

John Darby's name was published in the *London Gazette* for the award of his DFC in November 1943 and he received his medal in 1944 at a special investiture at RAF Witchford by His Majesty the King. It was not a common practice to receive an award at an operational base in front of the entire station strength. On this occasion, the royal visit was filmed by the RAF film production unit and included King George VI and Queen Elizabeth examining a Lancaster before presenting medals to the selected and most privileged recipients. This would have been a crowning moment in John's service and one that would have remained with him for the rest of his life. Warrant Officer Darby continued with instructional and staff duties from November 1943 to January 1947 when he was discharged from the service.

This was not to be the end of John's career in the RAF as four years later he was afforded the rare opportunity to re-enlist. His exemplary service had led to his selection for duty with the Supreme Headquarters Allied Powers. On 4 April 1949, twelve nations from Western Europe and North America signed the

John Darby photographed in the Hanover War Cemetery, Germany. John has placed his hands upon the headstones to his original crewmembers, men that he never forgot his whole life.

North Atlantic Treaty in Washington DC. A key feature of this treaty was Article 5, in which the signatory members agreed that 'an armed attack against one or more of them in Europe or North America shall be considered an attack against them all.' In July 1951, SHAPE's new headquarters complex in Rocquencourt opened for business. SHAPE closed its facility at Rocquencourt near Paris on 30 March 1967, and the next day held a ceremony to mark the opening of the new headquarters at Casteau, Belgium. Flight Sergeant Darby served at SHAPE 26 January 1966–25 July 1968.

John Darby was commissioned and promoted to the rank of Warrant Officer on 1 July 1969. Retirement from the Royal Air Force eventually arrived in January 1972 with John having served 20 years and 175 days. He never forgot his crewmembers who had died on that fateful night of 22 September 1943 having had a particular friendship with Patrick O'Farrell, Reginald Fuggle and his fellow Air Gunner Lionel Goldsmith. On Tuesday 10 July 1984, John Darby visited the Hanover War Cemetery where he was finally able to see the graves of his fellow crewmembers and pay his respects. Just seven months later John himself passed away on 2 February 1985. It can be speculated that his long held desire to visit his old crew had fulfilled a significant need in his life. Against the odds, fate had spared his own life and his service as a rear and mid-upper gunner in Bomber Command was exceptional in respect of the hours spent in his turret.

29

Sergeant Brian Rogers

Rear Gunner, 75 Squadron

The thought provoking image of Sergeant Brian Rogers' rear turret, is one of the most iconic Second World War photographs associated with rear gunners. The image graphically illustrates the specific dangers that rear gunners were consistently exposed to during their operational flights. Sergeant Rogers was a 22-year-old volunteer within the RAF who found himself posted into 75 Squadron becoming a member of a New Zealand led crew, captained by Pilot Officer Buck RNZAF.

75 Squadron within Bomber Command held a strong contingent of RNZAF staff. It had originated from the New Zealand Flight of the Royal Air Force and later became 75 NZ Squadron. London born Brian Rogers grew accustomed to the broad New Zealand accents that surrounded him and he quickly gained their respect and fully understood his responsibilities in protecting them when in the air on operations.

The monumentally large Stirling bombers that equipped 75 Squadron were 87 feet and 3 inches long (26.59 metres) with a wingspan of 99 feet and 1 inch (30.2 metres). Designed by Arthur Gouge and built by Short Bros, it incorporated similar strengths associated with the large flying boats for which the firm was associated. The rear turret was the Frazer Nash designed unit which in common with several other bomber aircraft had its ammunition feed situated within the fuselage. The hydraulic power supplied to the turret came from the aircrafts starboard inner engines. Unusually, beneath the area of the rear turret, sat two large twin tail wheels to support the aircrafts weight when on the ground. These were retracted into the fuselage in exactly the same way as the main undercarriage wheels once in the air. Worryingly for Brian the twin tail wheels were prone to collapse as was the main complex undercarriage and any rear gunner suffering such a fate would find their turret unceremoniously deposited onto the concrete runways. Despite the aircraft's size, the crews were not treated to a large spacious interior. There were two ways to enter the aircraft – a hatch at the front under the nose, but this was some 20 feet off the ground and required a ladder climb, or the rear port side door situated close to the tail unit. Brian Rogers and his crew naturally used the rear crew door where a small step ladder was provided. Brian

The devastated rear gunner's turret of Stirling aircraft BF517 completely destroyed by lethal night fighter cannon and machine gun rounds that had been accurately delivered by a classically executed night fighter attack. It is extraordinary that the night fighter removed the perceived threat of gunfire from the rear turret but failed in the endeavor to destroy the entire aircraft.

would turn towards the tail and negotiate another short ladder leading into a short tunnel which carried on over the tail fin spar section and into his rear turret. The remaining crew left Brian and climbed off the entrance step onto a narrow walkway fixed along the floor of the fuselage. The crew then negotiated a climb up upon what was the roof of the aircrafts bomb bay, where some 40 feet further along, the mid-upper gunner's short ladder appeared. This was to enable access into that turret but the fuselage was seriously restricted by the mechanism and size of the turret itself. The remaining crew then reached a small doorway prior to the massive wings' main spar that required clambering over before reaching the narrow walkway that accessed the wireless operator's position and the flight engineer's station. Eventually on reaching the cockpit area, sufficient space was available for the crew to stand up and accommodate the pilot and navigator. The bomb aimer progressed a little further to his station right at the nose of the aircraft. The pilot of any Stirling was challenged with the unique ground-handling characteristics created by its design and cockpit height above the runway. The Stirling was fitted with the largest tyres, manufactured by Dunlop and fitted on a British aircraft at the time.

Any emergency that involved the rear gunner would require significant and most difficult terrain to be negotiated by his fellow crewmembers in order to reach him. In combat situations with the aircraft slewing and bumping, it was far from easy for anyone to accomplish this. The flying clothing was very bulky and such efforts were invariably always in darkness and at height that required oxygen. Portable oxygen bottles for the crew were provided in the form of small cylinders which could be hooked or strapped to their clothing. However these

A Stirling bomber at RAF Newmarket. The massive and complicated undercarriage assembly can be appreciated when compared to the size of the ground crew personnel. Ground crew personnel were always exposed to lethal injury from bomber aircraft running propellers, however the height of the StIrling's undercarriage alleviated such injuries by virtue of the standing height of the wings.

only carried a maximum of ten minutes supply. First aid kits were located on the fuselage sides behind the pilot seat (two on the starboard and one on the port side). The rear gunners were very much aware of their vulnerability and exclusion from basic first aid or immediate assistance.

On the night of 26 April 1943, 19-year-old Pilot Officer Buck was flying Stirling BF517 to attack Duisburg. Brian was as usual in the rear turret and maintaining a watch across the sky that surrounded him. As the aircraft was approaching the target area, an enemy night fighter made a skillful and surprise attack from the rear. The pilot was initially unaware that the rudder and tail of the bomber had been badly damaged, and his rear gunner mortally wounded in what had been a classically executed and swiftly timed assault. A few seconds later however, a stream of tracer bullets hit the upper fuselage and the upper gun turret. In his immediate response the pilot found the rudder controls to be useless and he immediately jettisoned his load of incendiaries from the bomb bay. Without rudder control it was difficult to turn or control the aircraft, but with help from his second pilot, they managed to turn the aircraft on course for base albeit they were several hundred miles away from that sanctuary. Despite an obviously successful initial attack, the night fighter left his prey and luckily never relocated them. The pilot struggled to maintain height, and the crew jettisoned everything possible to lighten the weight. This would have included almost anything that was removable and capable of being dropped into the night sky from the emergency escape hatches. One of the engines then failed as a result of the oil pipes having been severed by the night fighters cannon fire. By skillful handling of his crippled aircraft, the pilot nursed the Stirling back to base and made a safe emergency landing at RAF Newmarket. The pilot was to be awarded the DFC for this action, and his navigator pilot Officer Symons RCAF, also won a similar award for ensuring the safe return of the aircraft despite sustaining his wounds.

The Bomber Command Operational Research Section had ballistics teams that, in cases like this, analysed the damage inflicted on aircraft that managed to return home and detailed damage reports were prepared. The reports that remain are preserved at the National Archives. The RAF gained significant intelligence from such technical analysis. In this case it was obvious that the Luftwaffe night fighter had skillfully deployed an intense field of fire direct into and around the rear gunner's turret. The intensity of 20-mm cannon shells and the smaller 7.9-mm machine gun rounds had torn the rear turret to shreds. Brian died within his turret but it was only the skill of his pilot in returning to their base that enabled his parents to grieve his loss. After the return of his body, Sergeant Brian Rogers was buried at The City of London Cemetery in Aldersbrook Road, East London where he lies in the collective grave, 108018 which is located in the central section of this extensive cemetery.

Stirling BF517 had been built and delivered to 75 Squadron within the Ministry

Squadron Leader Broadbest and Wing Commander Wells both inspect the devastated rear gunner's turret of the Stirling BF 517. The small open hatch which can be seen would have been the rear gunner's emergency escape position which appears to have been shot away by the barrage of enemy cannon and machine gun fire.

of Aircraft Production order, March-May of 1943. Following the tragic events on the night of 26 April 1943, Stirling BF517 underwent extensive repairs to the rear section. The aircraft was eventually returned to service and later served at RAF Stradishall, No. 1657 Heavy Conversion Unit. This particular conversion unit had strong connections to 75 NZ Squadron and many of the crews had passed through Stradishall prior to their operational postings. It is thought that Stirling BF517 continued to serve at 1657 HCU until the unit officially disbanded on 15 December 1944. The Air Transport Auxiliary flight crews later ferried out the twenty-four Stirling aircraft from that unit on 22 December, and aircraft BF517 was finally taken off charge by the RAF on 19 July 1945.

Another aircraft that had an eventful experience was Wellington X9764. On the night of 12 August 1941, the aircraft was rostered alongside eight other aircraft to be flown on a raid to Hanover. 75 Squadron had many colonials within its strength of aircrew personnel and had selected an Australian Pilot to captain X9764. His name was Pilot Officer Hugh Alfred Roberts, a native of Brisbane who had volunteered to join the Royal Australian Air Force in May 1940. He and his crew had completed some of the early long penetration operations of the war for Bomber Command. The rear gunner's turret was manned by Sergeant Joseph Paul Faguy, a Canadian from Quebec who had also volunteered to serve in 1940. He was an air gunner who had previously served in a different crew, captained by Sergeant Fox. The operation to Hanover was one in which Roberts crew had successfully attacked their primary target, but the weather conditions had been unfavourable with a heavy haze across the general target area. The bomb load was thought to have been accurately delivered upon the dock installations and the defenses had not been particularly troublesome to their aircraft. The return sortie also progressed well having left the target area they were heading towards the English Channel and were soon to leave occupied territory, when the situation dramatically changed over the Zuider Zee. Wing Commander H. L. Thompson subsequently recorded the events as related by the Australian Pilot.

> Without warning I saw a stream of tracer going past the fuselage between the starboard motor and the cockpit. The whole plane seemed to shudder under the impact of the striking bullets and cannon shells. Tried to turn sharply to port, but found that I could get no response from aileron control, so immediately dived. However the gunner [rear gunner] was able to get a good burst into our attacker, and as we dived, the Me110 [night fighter] went overhead and was last seen diving steeply away to starboard. I pulled out of the dive at about 10,000 feet and with the strong odour of petrol in my nostrils, tried to collect my scattered wits. The first thing I noticed was that the airspeed indicator was not registering, and the second pilot who was standing in the astro-dome, reported that petrol was leaking from one of the pipes inside the kite. The wireless operator said that several bullets had entered his cabin, and made our wireless receiver unserviceable; the Rear Gunner also reported petrol flying

past his turret in the slipstream from the starboard motor. Then looking out of the side windows I could see that the undercarriage was hanging down and the bomb doors were opened. A bullet had pierced the main hydraulic pipe, and so I knew that if we did reach England we would have to crash-land without flaps. Our dinghy had been released during the attack and was lying punctured on the starboard wing. About fifteen minutes later, as we were crossing the Dutch coast, I again checked the petrol, and it seemed that we would have sufficient to take us across the North Sea, so I finally decided to carry on for home. Luck was with us and we did get safely across the water and tried to gain more height in case my petrol should suddenly run out. It did, though the engines fired spasmodically for the next few seconds, and I immediately ordered the crew to abandon the aircraft.

Joseph sitting in the tail turret had been instrumental in the Wellington's survival. He had been alert enough to respond to the night fighters attack with an initial burst of concentrated fire from his Browning guns, and at the same time instruct his pilot to take emergency manoeuvres to escape the deadly cannon fire. The intercom connection between the rear gunner and the pilot was one of the most important means of communication that existed in any of the large bombers within bomber command. It had been a precision attack with cannon shells entering the aircraft and inflicting serious damage. The instinctive response by Joseph with his guns had been accurate and the Me110 fighter was seen diving leaving a streaming a trail of smoke. Joseph could justifiably consider the Me110 to be seriously damaged but insufficient to be able to claim it as destroyed.

The instructions to bale out by the pilot were clearly heard by the crew and Joseph immediately grabbed his parachute and affixed it to the harness hooks. He unclipped his turret safety belt that sat around his lap and fully traversed his turret which fortunately still had full power to its controls. Choosing to turn and expose his rear turret doors onto the port side, Joseph unclipped his intercom and pushed against the doors. The doors swung open into the slipstream and Joseph tumbled out backwards. He had elevated both guns upwards and this had provided a little more room for this awkward manoeuvre. Joseph had pulled his D ring on his chest parachute, and the canopy inflated but it was however a short descent to earth, he had tumbled from his turret at an estimated altitude of only 1,000 feet and was falling quickly towards some mature pine trees which he inevitably crashed into. The unpleasant landing left him with a badly broken ankle. The crew and aircraft had ended up within Norfolk's extensive Thetford Forestry Lands. All of the crew were safely located during the hours of darkness. Joseph required medical treatment for his broken ankle and was later sent to recover at the RAF hospital at Littleport.

The pilot had been left with no time for his own parachute escape, he later recalled:

Wellington X9764 having force landed on the Forestry Commission Land. The rear gunner's turret of Sergeant Joseph Faguy can be clearly seen in the traversed position following his emergency departure.

Everything was strangely quiet after the boys had gone, and I muttered a quiet prayer for something soft to land the kite on. All I could do at the moment was to keep the plane going down in something like a glide, but without an air-speed indicator I could not tell how sharply I was approaching the ground. At 500 feet I switched on the landing light, and below me I saw what I took to be a roadway, which seemed to me to be running more or less in the same direction as I was landing. I kept along the track, and in less time than it takes to tell I felt the starboard wing brushing over the tops of the wood which flanked each side of the roadway. In the next instant the plane swung sharply to the right and with a rather drawn-out crash, it came to a stop.

Joseph had sustained a badly broken ankle which required surgery. Once fully recovered and assessed fit for duty, he was posted to No. 1659 Heavy Conversion Unit, at RAF Topcliff where he undertook an air gunnery instructors position.

Wellington X9764 was dismantled and recovered from the forest. The airframe was assessed as repairable and taken to the Vickers works where it was rebuilt and returned to Bomber Command for operational duty. The Wellington was later attached to the strength of the Polish 304 Squadron, but tragically the aircraft and her entire crew of six Polish volunteers perished on the raid to Cologne in April 1942.

Joseph received a mention in dispatches award in 1944, most probably for his service as an instructor and gained an officers commission. He survived the war and returned to Canada where he lived a long and happy life; Joseph died in Ottawa, in November 2011.

30

Flight Lieutenant John Hall DFC
Rear Gunner, 106 Squadron

John Hall was a young man of 21 years who originated from County Durham. He arrived at RAF Syerston as a newly trained and fully qualified air gunner having earned the right to sew his air gunner's brevet onto his tunic on 29 September 1941. Standing just 5 feet, 5 inches tall, John was of an ideal stature to squeeze into the rear turret of a Bomber Command aircraft, and that's exactly where he was recommended to serve. His flying logbook held good proficiency and accreditation of his ability, previously achieved at the No. 4 Air Gunnery School.

Wing Commander Guy Gibson is a name that immediately conjures images of the Dam Buster raids that took place in May 1943. Gibson was to be awarded the highest award of gallantry for his part in the raid, The Victoria Cross, however prior to those famous raids he had was in command of 106 Squadron at RAF Syerston. Guy Gibson was exceptionally well liked by his men. He was just two years older than John Hall but he had already been awarded the DFC, adding a DSO whilst serving and commanding 106 Squadron. John would have received briefings and undertaken other encounters with Gibson but he was not to fly within his actual crew.

John was allocated to fly as the rear gunner in the crew captained by a Rhodesian pilot, Sergeant Noel Burton. His crew was made up entirely of Sergeants, not an uncommon situation within 106 Squadron, or indeed any other squadron at that time. Their first operation was to have been to Hamburg on 30 January 1943. John had prepared well for his first full venture into the operational arena over Germany. He had made good friends with his mid-upper gunner Sergeant Banks and John felt confident, despite the trepidation of his first raid well into the heartland of Germany. He need not have worried; Lancaster R5573, their allocated aircraft, became unserviceable soon after take-off and the crew were forced to return to Syerston. John was unable to record an operation in his logbook because 'scrubbed ops' as they were known, did not count. One of the squadron's Lancasters, W4826 never returned to Syerston from Hamburg that night. Guy Gibson personally wrote letters to the families of that missing crew, a task that he had to perform far too frequently whilst in command of 106 Squadron. Gibson would soon be invited by the highest command in the RAF to lead 617 Squadron for the special raids upon the dams, forcing an unplanned departure from 106 Squadron.

John Hall's tour of duty was still to officially commence, but two raids to Lorient enabled him to commence his count of operations towards the seemingly unattainable thirty that were required. In keeping with the vast majority of squadrons the majority of raids he was to undertake were dropping bomb loads on target markers laid by the RAF Pathfinder Force. A prime example being on the evening of 26 February when Wing Commander Gibson took off at 1835 hours from Syerston in Lancaster ED649, and led his squadron to bomb Cologne. Guarding the rear of Gibson's aircraft was Flying Officer Wickins, a rear gunner especially chosen by Gibson, despite the fact that he was well above the normal height for such duty. John Hall sat on the runway looking at several Lancasters lined up behind him on the approach sections of the runway, and at 1840 hours Sergeant Burton's Rhodesian accent crackled on the intercom. Their Lancaster W4156 commenced the operation to Cologne – the operational record, Form 540, quotes:

Lancaster ED649. Weather good, slight ground haze, but river and ground detail seen. Red and Green T. I. target indicator bombs seen. These were in sights, bombing in a straight, fast run from 16000 feet at 2121 hours. Bombs seen to burst near aiming point. Concentration was achieved and it seemed that the target had been accurately bombed. Heavy flak encountered in barrage form. This was pilots [Guy Gibson] 70th bombing raid. Bomb load: 1 x 4,000 lb; 12 SBC small bomb containers (30 lbs).

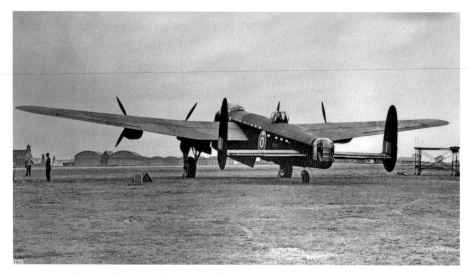

Lancaster W4126, this aircraft originated from the same production sequence as W4156 and as such was identical to the aircraft that John Hall and his crew operated within on several operations.

Lancaster W4156. Bombing conditions were good although there was some haze over Cologne. Red and green T.I. bombs were seen and these were bombed from 18,000 feet at 2122 hours. Own results not observed as aircraft was coned by searchlights on bombing run. Attack appeared to be successful and concentrated. Bomb load: 1 x 4,000 lb; 12 SBC (30 lbs).

The 4,000 high-capacity bombs dropped on Cologne were little more than huge cylinders full of explosives. They were designed to create a surface blast effect in order to cause damage to buildings, primarily blasting the roof off buildings and destroying wall structures. John and his crew were consistently to drop this particular type of bomb during their tour of duty. The 4,000-lb cookie was an important weapon in Bomber Command's arsenal. Plans had been made during the inter war years for a bomb weighing up to 4,000 lbs, but without an aircraft capable of lifting such a load to Germany, the concept was not fully progressed. That was until the Luftwaffe began dropping its huge parachute G mines on England in 1940. In the autumn of that year, a firm commitment was given by the Air Ministry to proceed with the production of the 4,000-lb bomb and it was ready for use at the end of March 1941.

The only readily available high explosive to utilise in these large bombs was Amatol, which had been developed during the First World War, but it was progressively replaced by newer explosives such as Cyclonite. A mixture of Torpex, Amatex, and Minol – Minol was a mixture of 40 per cent TNT, 40 per cent ammonium nitrate, and 20 per cent powdered aluminium which was added to increase the blast effect. Various developments led to differing proportions of these basic components. These mixtures proved to be a relatively insensitive type of explosive but it allowed armourers some level of safety during manhandling, transit and storage. The fuse, or initiator, designed to set off the cookie, was made from a far more sensitive explosive and deserved far greater respect. This was only ever fitted at the time of loading the bombs into the aircraft's bomb bay.

The additional load of small bomb containers (SBC) that accompanied the cookie, held incendiary bombs which would be deployed by tumbling from the containers. Incendiary bombs were designed to ignite after impact and to be capable of generating a great deal of heat in the immediate area where it had fallen. The 4-lb bombs contained thermite pellets within a magnesium alloy body. After the pellets had reached a high enough temperature, the magnesium case also ignited and continued to burn for seven to ten minutes thereafter. At the start of the war in 1939, the RAF possessed a stock of 5 million 4-lb incendiary bombs, and factories were geared up to produce as many as 60,000 per week. The RAF's consumption of these small bombs was monumental during the war. The bomb loads carried by 106 Squadron was the normal and most commonly deployed Lancaster blast and incendiary combination which were coded and identified as 'usual'. The RAF had coded references for the various configurations of bomb loads deployed during the war. That system enabled the armourers loads to be communicated in a simple and easily understood procedure. Guy Gibson was soon to be made aware of another most secret bomb code – the name 'Upkeep' was used to identify the bouncing bomb that he would use to attack the dams in Germany.

John Hall's next operation with 106 Squadron was to be Berlin. The reality of attacking the capital of Germany at the very start of his tour was slightly perturbing. Stories amongst the squadron gunners with whom he circulated, were not complimentary towards such excursions to Berlin. Having been coned in searchlights over Cologne, John had experienced a most unpleasant raid already, and the account of one crew, captained by a Sergeant Reed having his rear gunner torn to shreds in his turret by a night fighter, did nothing to help his inner thoughts. The raid to Berlin saw John secured in his rear turret for eight hours. He found the experience completely exhausting but the most frightening experience so far was the exposure to very heavy flak. The German anti-aircraft gunners were themselves experienced in placing barrages of exploding flak shells at the correct heights. John was jostled about as the blasts caused the aircraft to be buffeted in the air and the danger of white hot shrapnel tearing into his turret was a distinct possibility. John felt like he was sitting amongst the flak explosions, his turret was little more than a viewing gallery within a massive display of explosive terror. However once again his crew dropped their cookie on the coloured pathfinder markings and returned safely. Bomber Command committed 302 aircraft to this operation to Berlin, and within that figure 156 aircraft were Lancasters and of these seven of them failed to return. Forty-two lockers and personal belongings would be stripped and cleared away as those airmen were never going to use them again. This was a well-rehearsed practice on all stations and it began the procedure of informing the next of kin.

Bomber Command's struggle to destroy the heart of Germany was exacting a high price in men and aircraft. It was acknowledged that there were three battles being fought targeting the Ruhr, Hamburg and Berlin. Sergeant John Hall sitting in his rear turret was to take part in all. With the usual black humour the Ruhr valley became known ironically as 'The Happy Valley' by bomber crews and March 1943, saw a concerted effort to destroy the mighty industrial resources that occupied that valley. It covered a vast territorial area and Germany protected this vital area with batteries of anti-aircraft guns and searchlights on all the predictable routes to and from the valley. The night fighter activity was also increased and their capability was never in doubt. In early 1943, Bomber Command's strength of four-engined squadrons had risen to thirty-four. Sixteen Lancasters, eleven Halifax's and seven Stirling. Despite this the grand total of aircraft remained the same as the previous year, but significantly the bomb load capacity had increased enormously, and as such Bomber Command could now conduct more effective operations.

Essen was the next target to be written in John's logbook. It was another of the well-known targets for the command. The pathfinders dropped their slow burning yellow target indicators which were clearly seen by the main stream of bombers. John saw an enormous explosion below him, which created a massive orange glow and dense black billowing smoke. From his height of 19,000 feet it illuminated the sky, and never before had he seen such a concentrated raid. He was able to pick out the muzzle flashes of the flak guns that sent up their explosive shells towards the bombers. The flak emplacements were frequently grouped into rings of six to twelve with blast wall defences surrounding the individual fortresses. One of the twelve aircraft from 106 Squadron engaged in the raid to Essen was flown by Flight Lieutenant Bill Picken, another Rhodesian. Bill's Lancaster W4918 was either damaged by flak or fell prey to a night fighter. It was simply noted on the squadron records as 'failed to return'. *The Bomber Command War Diaries* by Middlebrook and Everitt advise that 442 bombers participated in the raid to Essen and Bill's Lancaster was one of fourteen that failed to return and additionally it notes that this raid was the 100,000 th of the war thus far. Crucially one of the primary targets, the Krupp Works, had been badly damaged across an area that extended over 160 acres.

Four nights later, John climbed back into another Lancaster, W4842 intending to fly the eight-plus hours to bomb Munich. After approximately two hours into the operation he reported to his captain that he had lost all operational controls within his turret. The value of the rear gunner was always foremost in any pilot's mind; it was rarely acceptable to endanger any crew by continuing a raid with such a serious defect. Sergeant Burton advised they would return to Syerston, but in leaving the bomber stream it left them completely isolated and vulnerable. John remained in his turret even more aware of his personal responsibility to watch for enemy fighters. The crew landed safely and faced robust questioning as to why they failed to complete the operation. This situation presented itself again to John on 8 April but this time within Lancaster W4256, whilst *en route* to Duisburg, but the crew had in the meantime bombed Nuremburg, Munich, Stuttgart, with two visits to Essen and then Kiel.

Lancaster R5677 safely took John to Duisburg on 9 April, but three days later when tasked with a 'gardening' operation to plant mines in the Bayonne Area, the aircraft presented the flight engineer with problems as the bomb doors would not open. The two accompanying Lancasters dropped their mines successfully and all three aircraft returned safely.   Mechanical faults were always a possibility; the Lancasters were worked exceptionally hard and they were complex structures to maintain. The month was completed with raids to Stuttgart, Pilsen, La Spezia on more than one occasion, and then Stettin. John calculated that with just a handful of additional operations the crew would have reached the level required to be screened and rested from operational duty – the targets visited had been some of the most difficult and costly to complete.

John sat approximately 65 feet away from the cockpit section of the Lancaster. He was never any more than a hand's width away from the open sky that surrounded him. It was a unique existence perched on the edge of infinity.

Operations to the Skoda factories at Pilsen, Dusseldorf, Essen and once again
Dusseldorf allowed him to move closer to achieving the seemingly unattainable
status of 'tour expired'. It was Essen that almost saw the demise of John and his
crew – on 27 May 1943 they reached the target and complied with the instructions
to conduct a timed bombing run from the pathfinder green markers. On that
bombing run their Lancaster R5677 was successfully held in a lone searchlight,
and others immediately joined in, holding the aircraft in a cone of intense light.
The heavy flak guns then targeted them with some success, and the Rhodesian
pilot ordered the bomb load to be dropped short of the completed timed run. The
Lancaster was seriously compromised over Essen and John did what he could by
attempting to disrupt the searchlights. It was the most dangerous of situations
that his pilot had managed to extract them from.

John had survived a complete tour of duty, enduring nearly 200 hours in
the air, yet he had not fully engaged a night fighter. It was not uncommon for
the pilot to be selected for a medal to acknowledge the completion of a tour of
duty. It must be recognised that crews attaining such an achievement amongst
the sickening loss rates and general casualty statistics were by no means regular
events. Sergeant Noel Burton was recommended for the Distinguished Flying
Medal on 26 May 1943. The publication of the award, which appeared in the
London Gazette, reflects upon the entire crew:

> Sergeant Burton is a Rhodesian Pilot who has consistently displayed courage
> and resolution. Over a period of four months, he has flown on most of the
> routine and more important raids. Berlin, Nuremberg, Stuttgart, and Naval
> bases in Germany, Italy and occupied France are some of his targets. He
> took part in all three of the successful raids on Essen in March and April,
> 1943, and recently attacked Duisburg, Spezia (twice) and the Skoda Works
> (twice). By his exemplary courage, Sergeant Burton has captained with
> success a fine crew, which has achieved excellent results.

Sergeant John Hall was posted to perform instructional duties at No. 1660
Conversion Unit but the six months slipped past very quickly and on 27
December 1943 he was posted operational into 44 Squadron. Rather ironically
it was a squadron with an affinity to Rhodesia and was officially identified as 44
(Rhodesia) Squadron.

John immediately commenced operations to the primary targets within
Germany, many of which he had previously visited. It was almost as if he had
never ceased operations – the orders were almost identical except the pathfinder
markings were a little more elaborate. In February 1944 he was personally
selected as the rear gunner to the newly arrived Commanding Officer, Wing
Commander F. W. Thompson. It was not uncommon for ranking officers to select
their own crew and John was probably the most experienced rear gunner on the
squadron. John's logbook saw consistent primary capital targets entered upon its

Flying low over the North Sea, this 44 Squadron Lancaster displays the exhaust trails over the impressive wing span indicating this aircraft to have seen some significant service. The rear gunner has swung the turret to one side illustrating the regular scanning of the rear quarters.

pages – Berlin, Brunswick, Leipzig Stuttgart, Schweinfurt, Augsburg – and then came Nuremberg on the 30 March 1944. This date was to haunt high command. On Thursday 30 March 1944, the various station commanders, flying navigation leaders, bombing leaders, signals and gunnery leaders, the intelligence officer and the meteorological officers were all involved in delivering operational briefings at a great many Bomber Command bases. Each briefing followed the standard security procedures and outside the closed doors and shuttered windows, armed RAF Police stood guard. The crews were isolated from the rest of the station, and the station itself was isolated from the outside world. What would be said was regarded as secret and access to public telephones was from that point onwards prohibited. John found himself once again facing daunting prospects, another major maximum effort raid to Germany.

The code name of the target that night was 'Grayling', it had been securely sent to all group commanders and in turn to stations and squadron commanders. Ten squadrons in No. 1 Group, eight squadrons from No. 3 Group, seven squadrons from No. 4 Group, twelve squadrons from No. 5 Group, nine squadrons from No. 6 group and twelve squadrons from No. 8 Pathfinder Force Group were to participate – altogether 820 heavy bombers were scheduled to take part. In addition fifteen Mosquitoes would adopt an intruder role to seek out enemy night fighters whilst *en route* to the target area. Nuremberg was some 90 miles to the north of Munich. It was a military centre for general and electrical engineering, the famous M.A.N. works were producing armaments of all kinds, and the Siemens plant has stepped up production of its electric motors and searchlights. Nuremberg was a prime industrial target in the heartland of Germany.

The navigation leader issued the complex instructions to the men charged with the responsibility of getting the Lancasters over the target at precisely the correct times. It was a most detailed briefing with turning points, speeds, heights and bearings all of which needed to be fully understood and complied with.

The Bombing Leader advised on the bomb loads, weights and fuel loads. The Pathfinder Force were tasked with marking strategy and colour identifications. These were initially red markers with incendiaries, then green markers turning yellow, and then these would be further fed by red markers, with target illuminators enforcing the colours as required. The meteorological officer briefed that a fairly stiff crosswind could be expected on target. The more technical weather aspects were provided in detail but in summary, the outward flight was to expect broken cloud except over Southern Germany where it was expected to be layered. Local industrial smog was to be expected with valley fog accumulating towards dawn.

The Intelligence Officer provided a detailed and precise outlining of operation Grayling which has been taken from the report compiled by Wing Commander F. Lord, DFC, and Flight Lieutenant P. Fox who had participated in the operation to Nuremburg.

The very direct nature of the route to the target tonight has been the subject of weighty discussion between Bomber Command and Group Commanders. In particular Air Vice-Marshal Bennett, head of 8 PFF Group strongly advocated a far more indirect approach. His views, however, were opposed by other Air Officers commanding, including the Hon. Ralph Cochrane, head of 5 Group. They supported the Commander-in-Chief's plan on these grounds: The distance involved precludes wasting time and fuel on too many doglegs; the present route suggests a number of perhaps more vulnerable targets to the German defences, thus persuading them to disperse and thin-out fighter concentrations; the sheer simplicity of this route will surprise the Germans and keep them off-balance sufficiently long for you to complete the operation without too much trouble. I think you deserve this explanation and it may help to dispel any misgivings you have about the direct route as laid down.

As a further encouragement, I can tell you that just ahead of you when you cross the coast, Mosquitoes will open the night's proceedings with low-level attacks on the known night-fighter fields in Holland at Leiuwarden- Twente-Deelen and Venlo in a bid to keep them on the ground until you're well past.

At the same time off Texel and the Heligoland Bight, a force of fifty Halifaxes will start dropping mines as a diversionary move to keep German ground controllers confused. Additional to this, and a while before the main force reaches the target, Mosquitoes will make a feint attack on Cologne between 2355 and 7 minutes after midnight. A further force of twenty Mosquitoes will also drop fighter flares, markers and 'window' on Kassel between 26 and 28 minutes after midnight in an attempt to spoof the German controllers into believing the main attack is to be the Ruhr, and thus lead them to send the bulk of the fighters there.

So far as ground defences are concerned, we've tried to route you over the coast both going and coming back where flak and searchlights are believed to be thin and the use of 'window' here will help to blur the picture from the ground. Again, the route takes you across the southerly end of the heavy Ruhr defensive area. Obviously much depends on the accuracy of your course-keeping and your ability to maintain a well bunched-together pattern and no straying away from the main stream.

Night-fighters can as usual be expected, but with cloud-cover and the Mosquito attacks to keep them grounded, the danger from these, we believe, will be minimized. Keep a sharp lookout for them, however, and wireless operators, make sure your fishpond is working at all times.[1.]

'Fishpond' was a radar device which potentially identified enemy aircraft. This type of briefing was echoed across the plethora of aerodromes and the great many Nissan huts where close on 6,000 men across Bomber Command sat in smoky companionship. John Hall was just one solitary rear gunner from this massive group of aircrew personnel. After the briefing, he like the vast majority, sat and ate their traditional egg and bacon pre ops meal. Then some time later joined his crew in the crew room to put on their flying kit and check parachutes. The special bond between crewmembers was most evident on occasions like this. Frequently the good luck charms or other similar artefacts were taken from their lockers and safely tucked into their flying gear. Several men developed procedures that they followed with precision prior to every operation. Superstition had its own value and was respected accordingly amongst all of the men.

Wing Commander Thompson gathered his crew together and they climbed aboard one of the crew buses that took them to their Lancaster parked at the dispersal. The aircraft were always dispersed across the aerodrome, but they would gather together after they ran up their engines and taxied towards the runway. At 2209 hours on the evening of the 30 March, Wing Commander Thompson applied full power to Lancaster ND515 and it officially commenced the raid to Nuremburg. For John, sitting in the tail it was no more than another raid to Germany, it was however to become a tragedy for Bomber Command. Despite his awesome accumulation of completed operations, John was to experience sights from his turret that he had never seen before. There was very little, if any, cloud cover, and the moon was as bright as he had ever seen it on any operation. Visibility from his turret was as good as it could possibly be, as was the case with

The sergeant seen in the centre of the photograph is wearing Irvin sheep skin trousers. When the jacket is also worn, it creates a significant layer of thick sheep's wool to provide optimum warmth.

John, he had ensured his Perspex was as clean as possible having had the ground crew polish it prior to this operation.

From the force of 782 heavy bombers that had taken off from the many airfields for Nuremberg, 725 crossed the Belgian coast *en route* to the target. The remaining fifty-seven aircraft had aborted for various and in some cases, predictable reasons that were always likely to arise on any major operation, engine failure, oxygen supply problems, and unserviceable rear gunner's turrets. As the bomber force flew due east, progressing onwards from one of the allocated turning points, they began to drift north of the correct track and to fall behind schedule. The leading pathfinders were detailed to transmit the winds that they experienced to their Group HQ, who would in turn broadcast these to all the bombers on the half hour. The wireless operators however received very few such messages. The information process completely broke down and just after midnight, the first bomber was shot down by flak over Liege. At the same time, over 200 Luftwaffe night fighters were on their way as directed by their controllers who were predicting the bombers progress. The diversionary measures taken by Bomber Command had completely failed in their efforts to fool the Luftwaffe defences.

The official summary of the raid reflects:

In their Wurzberg sets, the Germans detected intense air activity as far away as the Norfolk area before Bomber Command crossed the English coast and they began to put the night fighters in a state of readiness. German ground controllers, under General Schmidt, were not fooled by the British diversionary attacks, and by the time that Bomber Command's main force crossed the coast they had their night fighters circling their beacons and ready for interception. Contrary to met expectations, there was no cloud cover at all so that, in bright moonlight, Bomber Command flew into an ambush as soon as the 725 Lancasters and Halifaxes crossed the enemy coast and were involved in a running fight over the next 750 miles with a force of 246 night fighter aircraft. Higher velocity than forecast winds (80 to 90 mph) also upset navigation, and heavy cloud disturbed the accuracy of the bombers that managed to reach the target. Loss of life and aircraft were heavy.

31 March 1944, became known as Bomber Command's Black Friday. One hundred and eight aircraft failed to return. Ninety-four had been shot down by a combination of night fighters and flak over enemy territory. John Hall sitting in Lancaster ND515 witnessed the destruction of many aircraft, always eager to see any possibility of parachutes being deployed but never having long to take his eyes off the most dangerous of skies he had ever flown in. Black Friday had claimed around 750 Allied aircrew personnel who never came home with John.

Squadron Intelligence Officers compiled the debrief information and each individual aircrafts accountability on Form 540, operations record books. These now form an important part of post war research into operations conducted by men like John Hall. The 540 account written and recorded by 44 Squadron for his part in operation Grayling is factual, as was his red ink entry into his flying logbook. It was a sortie of 8 hours and 21 minutes, and in true reality for John it was no more, or less, than another trip recorded towards completing his second tour of duty. It was however, the day in which the highest gallantry medal possible was awarded to a participant of Bomber Command who flew to Nuremburg. The King was graciously pleased to confer the Victoria Cross in recognition of most conspicuous bravery to Pilot Officer Cyril Joe Barton 168669, RAFVR, 578 Squadron, (deceased).

On the night of 30 March, 1944, Pilot Officer Barton was captain and pilot of a Halifax aircraft detailed to attack Nuremberg. When some 70 miles short of the target, the aircraft was attacked by a Junkers 88. The burst of fire from the enemy made the intercommunication system useless. One engine was damaged when a Messerschmitt 210 joined in the fight. The bombers machine guns were out of action and the gunners were unable to return the fire.

Fighters continued to attack the aircraft as it approached the target area and in the confusion caused by the failure of the communications system at the height of the battle, a signal was misinterpreted and the navigator, air bomber and wireless operator left the aircraft by parachute.

Pilot Officer Barton faced a situation of dire peril. His aircraft was damaged, his navigational team had gone and he could not communicate with the remainder of the crew. If he continued his mission, he would be at the mercy of hostile fighters when silhouetted against the fires in the target area, and if he survived he would have to make a four-and-a-half-hour journey home on three engines across heavily-defended territory. Determined to press home his attack at all costs, he flew on and on reaching the target, released the bombs himself.

As Pilot Officer Barton turned for home the propeller of the damaged engine, which was vibrating badly, flew off. It was also discovered that two of the petrol tanks had suffered damage and were leaking. Pilot Officer Barton held to his course and, without navigational aids and in spite of strong head winds, successfully avoided the most dangerous defence areas on his route. Eventually he crossed the English coast only 90 miles north of his base.

By this time the petrol supply was nearly exhausted. Before a suitable landing place could be found, the port engine stopped. The aircraft was now too low to be abandoned successfully. Pilot Officer Barton therefore ordered the three remaining members of his crew to take up their crash stations. Then, with only one engine working, he made a gallant attempt to land clear of the houses over which he was flying. The aircraft finally crashed and Pilot Officer Barton lost his life, but his three comrades survived.

Pilot Officer Barton had previously taken part in four attacks on Berlin and fourteen other operational missions. On one of these, two members of his crew were wounded during a determined effort to locate the target despite the appalling weather conditions. In gallantly completing his last mission in the face of almost impossible odds, this officer displayed unsurpassed courage and devotion to duty.

Just five days after the horrors of Nuremburg, Flight Sergeant Hall once more attended a briefing, and after the final checking of his equipment, entered his rear gunner's turret. The raid was to Toulouse which proved to be uneventful for him, it was followed by further operations to Tours, Salbris, Ameins, Brunswick, Maisy, La Perelle Etampes, Auny and Beauvoir. When night operations like these were announced, the battle order or roster list of aircraft and crews nominated was posted at about 1000 hours. The target was a closely guarded secret but the fuel load would be known to everyone as a result of the close working relationships the aircrews had with the ground crews. 1,700 gallons would be the Ruhr valley or somewhere around that area of Germany, 1,900 gallons somewhere middle

44 Squadron Lancaster seen displaying a bomb tally painted to the front of the fuselage. Several aircraft recorded their operational raids with bombs or other symbols, painted on by their ground crews. This particular airframe has some personal artwork additionally applied by a crew or ground crewmember.

Distinguished Flying Cross, 1939-45 Star, Air Crew Europe Star, Bar France & Germany, Defence Medal, War Medal and the Queen's Cadet Service Medal with two Bars.

distance, and when it was over 2,000 gallons you knew the target was a deep penetration into enemy territory. The Lancaster consumed an average 180 gallons an hour, and the aim for any Flight Engineer was to get one mile to the gallon. The maximum capacity of fuel that could be carried was 2,154 gallons.

John had sat alone with the heavy responsibility of guarding his crew for forty-six sorties into enemy held territories. He has seen endless crews lost in some of the most tragic of circumstances. He harboured the hope that many would have survived, and would be in a prisoner of war camp somewhere in Germany. No doubt he questioned his own survival many times. John's official recognition finally arrived when he was recommended for the Distinguished Flying Medal in June 1944. The recommendation made mention of his extensive operations completed during his two arduous tours of duty – shortly after the recommendation John was to receive a commission and promotion to Pilot Officer. His award was therefore upgraded to that of the Distinguished Flying Cross, as awarded to officers.

Following additional training and instructional duties the war concluded with John having risen to the rank of Flying Officer. After he left the RAF he had a desire to serve as an instructor in the Cadet Forces in Hemel Hempstead and did so for a great many years. John was awarded the Cadet Service Medal in 1962, a clasp was added in 1971, and a second clasp in 1979. Flying Officer John Hall, DFC, served in the RAF with distinction and extended bravery and is a worthy contributor to the story of rear gunner during the Second World War.

31

Sergeants John McKenzie and Jack Cantor

Rear Gunner and Mid-upper Gunner, 550 Squadron

Lancaster DV305 had been delivered as a new aircraft direct to 100 Squadron, at RAF Waltham, near Grimsby where Sergeant McKenzie and Sergeant Cantor were both air gunners to the pilot, Flying Officer Morrison, and they soon regarded DV305 as their own Lancaster. Sergeants McKenzie and Cantor had been through training together having met at No. 18 Operational Training Unit, and then at the Conversion Unit 1667, it had become a natural assumption for them to be in the same crew.

Towards the end of November 1943, Bomber Command initiated a new squadron, 550 Squadron, which was to be formed and based at Waltham and several crews from 100 Squadron were transferred onto its initial strength. Lancaster DV305 was one of the unit's aircraft that transferred into the newly formed squadron. Operationally both 100 and 550 Squadrons were being sent to the same targets and working from the same airfield. This was the situation on 26 November when both squadrons were charged with bombing Berlin.

At 2130 hours, flying at 22,000 feet and in clear visibility, Lancaster DV305 was coned by searchlights. Whilst dazzled by bright searchlights, McKenzie sighted an unidentified fighter 200 yards dead astern. A violent corkscrew was called even though the Lancaster was already attempting to evade the searchlights. McKenzie managed to fire eighty rounds of ammunition at the fighter. Just four minutes previously, another 100 Squadron Lancaster, JB596, had a combined attack from an Fw190 and a Me210. Their troubles were serious as both air gunners' turrets had been made inoperable as a result of severed hydraulic pipe lines. The Luftwaffe fighters had intercepted and mingle within the bombers creating the ultimate danger for all of the rear gunners.

Life on station at RAF Waltham changed very little for the newly formed squadron personnel. That was until 550 Squadron received a posting order to RAF North Killingholme in early January 1944. Fortunately the new base was not a great distance away and ties remained with fellow crews from their original squadron. Both McKenzie and Cantor had been early volunteers to enlist in the Royal Air Force and both men had over four years of service experience at that time.

Jack Marshall Cantor had a rather special reason to volunteer and fight against the Third Reich. His father Abraham had been born in Russia, into a Jewish family. The persecution of the Russian Jews saw his family flee to England and settle into an impoverished life in Mile End, East London. It was there that Jack was born in 1920. He grew up knowing of his family's heritage and his father Abraham lived the rest of his life with the chosen name Alfred. No doubt this was a means to distance himself from any possible persecution during his new life in England. His skills as a cabinet maker became well recognised and his work led to some improvements in the family lifestyle. The reports of anti-Semitism brought fear back into the Cantor family – they were also the seeds of hate that grew into genocide and mass extermination of Jews in the concentration camps that flourished in the lands of occupied Europe.

Jack served as an air gunner capable of operating in the rear or mid-upper turrets of his squadron's Lancasters. His fellow air gunner John McKenzie favoured the rear gunner's turret. He was two years older than his fellow gunner and grew up living in Southall, London. On the night of 28 January 1944, their trusted Lancaster DV305 took them once more to Berlin. For Jack this was another raid to the heart of Germany, the capital where such terror had been planned and executed. For John, it was a target that represented the ultimate in defensive anti-aircraft fire, searchlights and night fighters. No operation to Berlin was ever going to be an easy run and that proved to be the case with this particular raid. As they proceeded to the target it became obvious that aerial combats were taking place around them as the general visibility was good and concentrations of searchlights were nearby and very active. It was prime night fighter conditions and inevitably, at approximately 900 yards on the port quarter a Ju88 appeared on an attacking run towards their Lancaster. The mid-upper gunner commenced firing at some 800 yards and then the rear gunner sighted another Ju88 approaching from the same quarter. Firing commenced at around 600 yards, both creating a hail of gunfire that caused both enemy fighters to break away whilst on their attack trajectory. The Browning machine guns in both turrets had worked impeccably with 700 rounds of ammunition fired between them. No enemy fire had been sustained to the Lancaster, but the night fighter that was fired upon by the rear gunner broke away at approximately 200 yards and smoke was seen to be trailing from its engines. This was sufficient to compile the combat report (AIR/50/292) and make a claim as 'probably destroyed'.

On the evening of 30 January 1944 the two gunners sat through another operational briefing. The target was once again Berlin, but in their favour was the fact that there would be just one of over 500 bombers from the command flying to the target that night. Within that figure, 440 were Lancasters, a marginally smaller number than had recently been sent to Berlin during the six previous raids of that month. The Battle of Berlin as it became known saw thirty-two raids to central Germany, sixteen of which were to Berlin conducted between November 1943 and March 1944.

Returning to the operation on the evening of 30 January, this particular raid was later to be regarded by Bomber Command as having been successful, but it was at a cost – thirty-three aircraft had failed to return. Lancaster DV305 was not amongst those statistics, but the operation had cost the lives of McKenzie and Cantor following a devastating attack on the aircraft. The pilot, Flying Officer Morrison had only just managed to reach the emergency landing field at Woodbridge. It was a dire situation that had forced Lancaster DV305 to commit to an emergency landing and the events that had taken place over Berlin that night are explained by the recommendation for an immediate award of the Distinguished Service Order to the pilot:

The King has been graciously pleased to approve the following award in recognition of gallantry displayed in flying operations against the enemy:

Flying Officer Godfrey Arnold Morrison. 150107 RAFVR 550 Squadron. This officer was the pilot of an aircraft detailed to attack Berlin one night in January 1944. When nearing the target area the aircraft was intercepted by fighters. The bomber came under heavy cannon and machine gun fire and the mid-upper and rear gunners were killed at the outset of the fight. Flying Officer Morrison succeeded in evading the attackers but his aircraft had been repeatedly hit. One engine was out of action and the intercommunication system, the compass and the air speed indicators were useless. All the controls also sustained some damage. In spite of this, Flying

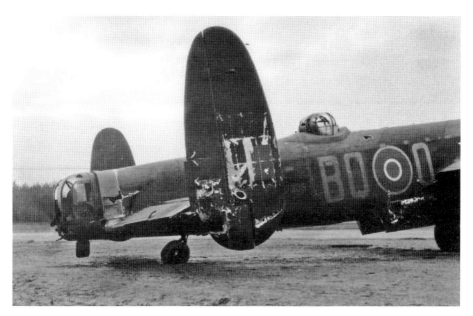

Both gunners' turrets seen with the damage caused by cannon fire penetrations and the starboard side fuselage and tail section all illustrating the direction of fire inflicted by the night fighters. (*550 Squadron Association*)

The rear gunner's turret seen from another angle and the devastation caused. The tail section clearly illustrates the cannon fire that penetrated and almost severed the tail completely. (*550 Squadron Association*)

Officer Morrison executed a successful bombing attack and afterwards flew the badly damaged aircraft back to base. This officer displayed skill and courage of a high order and his iron determination to complete his task successfully set a very fine example.

During the melee of the fighter attack and the violent manoeuvres that immediately followed, the crew's bomb aimer, Flying Officer R. Warren assumed that his fate and that of the aircraft had been sealed. Anticipating an emergency escape was required. He exited from the aircraft and parachuted to safety from the forward emergency escape hatch. Probably unknown to him thereafter was the fact that his pilot had managed to recover control of their Lancaster. Richard Warren was to spend the remaining period of the war as a prisoner in Stalag Luft III. He was included in the extensive force march from Stalag Luft III to Tarmstadt, 80 km south of Berlin, undertaken between 27 January 1945, and 4 February 1945. He was eventually liberated from the camp by the advancing Allies on 10 April.

The survival of Lancaster DV305 had obviously been a remarkable achievement. The awful situation of extracting the bodies of the two air gunners, Sergeant Cantor and Sergeant McKenzie, from their respective gunner's turrets took place with as much dignity and respect possible. Both men were later laid to rest in their London districts of the Willesden Jewish Cemetery, and the Havelock Cemetery respectively.

32

Pilot Officer Virgil Fernquist and Sergeant William Crabe CGM

Rear Gunner and Mid-upper Gunner, 550 Squadron

Lancaster NG202 was built by the Armstrong Whitworth Aircraft Company Limited under contract with the Ministry of Aircraft Production. It was one of 400 Lancasters to be built and delivered between July 1944 and February 1945. Lancaster NG202 was subsequently delivered to 170 Squadron and within her crew were two Canadian air gunners. Separated by rank, the rear gunner Virgil Fernquist was an officer, and the mid-upper gunner William Crabe, a Flight Sergeant, a factor that influenced both of their lives when on the ground, but in the air it had little, if any bearing on events. The crew's pilot was Flying Officer John Dixie, a Canadian from New Westminster, British Columbia.

On 1 February 1945, Lancaster NG202 was engaged upon a raid to bomb the railway marshalling yards at Ludwigshafen. The raid had progressed well, the bomb load had been dropped and they were negotiating the homeward track back towards their base at RAF Hemswell, Lincolnshire. Feeling relieved that the flak and searchlights had been beaten once again, sitting in the rear turret, Virgil took on the heavy responsibility of guarding the skies behind them, knowing that each minute was bringing them closer to home. Without warning, the unthinkable happened; the rear turret was sliced into by the massive propeller of another Lancaster. Catastrophic damage was caused to the rear section of the aircraft which included the tailplanes and rudder. Lancaster NG202 was thrown into what seemed uncontrollable turmoil, however the pilot managed to gather control after what must have been a terrifying sequence of events. It became clear that the rear section of the Lancaster had sustained serious damage, primarily by propellers which had torn away sections of the tail. The mid-upper gunner had been in a position to see the aftermath of collision and recognised immediately the need to rescue his fellow gunner from the remains of his turret. William Crabe assessed that the rear turret had been wrecked and in order to try and rescue Flying Officer Fernquist, he needed to cut his way into the turret from within the fuselage. With the assistance of another crewmember they cut away the required section, and then tying a rope around himself he climbed into the wrecked turret. The slipstream was tearing at everything and with no outer side to the turret it created very difficult conditions. William was not able to wear a parachute as

A Lancaster NG202. The rear turret and both rudder fins carrying significant damage. This aircraft sustained so much damage it is quite remarkable that it remained stable and capable of being flown. (*550 Squadron Association*)

it would have prevented him from being able to manoeuvre through the hole they had cut and would have made any rescue of his friend Virgil impossible to achieve. In almost impossible conditions, William was able to release the body of Virgil whilst preventing him from falling into the vast expanse of sky, virtually no turret enclosure remained. He managed to extract Virgil and recover him into the safety of the fuselage. Unfortunately his fellow gunner had suffered fatal injuries and the gallant actions in saving him had been in vain.

The pilot managed to fly the severely damaged Lancaster back to England. His efforts were duly recognised with the award of a Distinguished Flying Cross. The recommendation for which was published in the *London Gazette*, 16 March 1945.

One night in February 1945, Flying Officer Dixie was pilot of an aircraft detailed to attack Ludwigshaven. On the return flight his aircraft sustained severe damage to the entire tail assembly. The port rudder, half of the port fin and most of the rear part of the fuselage were also damaged. The aircraft dived steeply but Flying Officer Dixie regained control and by skillful airmanship flew it to base where he landed safely without incurring further damage. Flying Officer Dixie set a fine example of courage and coolness in difficult circumstances.

Four days later the *London Gazette* published the name of Flight Sergeant William Crabe as being awarded the Conspicuous Gallantry Medal for his rescue attempt in trying to save the life of his fellow Canadian Rear Gunner. Pilot Officer Virgil John Fernquist, aged 20, was buried in the cemetery at Harrogate. His Commonwealth War Graves Commission headstone proudly displays the crest of the Royal Canadian Air Force, and at the base of the headstone, a private inscription chiselled, words chosen by his family far away in Canada.

The Lancaster that had taken Virgil's life was RA502, operational with 550 Squadron, and flown by Flying Officer Lohrey from New Zealand. After the collision, RA502 fell away out of control, five crew were sighted as having abandoned the aircraft early enough to save their lives by parachute. Two crewmembers were not so lucky, and perished in the subsequent crash. The bodies of Sergeants N. Tinsley, and A. James were never found and they are commemorated on the Runnymede Memorial, both aged 20. The rear gunner Sergeant Allan Jarnell owed his life to his bomb aimer who managed to get back through the aircraft's fuselage to open the jammed rear gunners doors, allowing him to escape from his turret. They both managed to bale out of the main door at the rear of the fuselage. The doomed Lancaster plummeted to the ground and it was only in 1997 when new road works were being completed in the Nancy area of France that the wreckage was discovered. Patrick Baumann, a French Aviation Historian was responsible for a great deal of work to confirm the identity of the Lancaster. Patrick arranged the erection of a Memorial Stone at the crash site, to honour the three men from both aircraft who had lost their lives in the collision thus providing for a fitting tribute for the unfortunate rear gunner, Pilot Officer Virgil Fernquist RCAF.

33

Sergeant James Hughes DFM

Rear Gunner, 57 Squadron

James Hughes was born in Dewsbury, Yorkshire on 27 March 1920. His father originated from Drumcondra, Dublin, and worked in the Yorkshire coalmines, and in all probability that was where his son's destiny had lain. Throughout his life, James was known either as Jimmy or Paddy as he had retained an identifiable Irish accent from his father. However, his destiny took an unexpected turn and the declaration of war with Germany saw James immediately volunteer for service in the Royal Air Force Volunteer Reserve. James was allocated the service number 984589, this number fell within an extensive allocation of service numbers for United Kingdom enlistments at both Cardington and Padgate during September 1939.

From this moment onwards, James life was to change and it was to lead him to an award from the King, recognition of his services by the Queens Silver Jubilee medal and gaining freedom to the City of London. His service life started with the normal assessments and training and volunteering to fly as aircrew, choosing to become an air gunner, the expectation was for him to become operational in the shortest time period possible.

However once selected he was unexpectedly sent to Canada, and trained at No. 6 Bombing and Gunnery School, mountain View, Ontario. He was of normal stature and it would be fair to say that he was an ideal frame for the small rear gunner's Perspex pod. Qualifications in gunnery skills evidenced James to be well versed in all aspects of that trade, his night vision was deemed to be excellent and he had developed a natural ability for air gunnery. He returned to the United Kingdom on one of the regular convoys, later attending No. 16 Operational Training Unit, RAF Upper Heyford. Shortly followed by No. 1660 Conversion Unit at Swinderby where he gained experience converting onto the impressive Lancaster bomber.

James was posted to 57 Squadron on 17 February 1943, and joined in a particular Lancaster crew that was very closely linked together; their pilot was Flying Officer Jeavons and his crew: Pilot Officer Dougie Warwick, navigator, Sergeant Bob Hood-Morris, bomb aimer, Pilot Officer R. Gibbons, wireless operator, Sergeant George Cooper, mid-upper air gunner and himself Sergeant

'Paddy' Hughes bringing up the rear in the tail turret. The squadron's Operational record book (Air27/538) evidences that that on 13 and 14 March 1943, Lancaster Mk.1 W4201 was shot up by a fighter off the west coast of Denmark. Extensive damage was caused to the aircraft which subsequently crash landed just off the aerodrome (RAF Scampton). No severe injuries were sustained to any member of the crew, but the rear gunner was wounded in the fighter attack.

An extract from the squadron's operations report (AIR 540) provides further detail:

> F/O Jeavons was intercepted by an unidentified fighter when about twenty to thirty miles off the west coast of Denmark on the return journey. The aircraft was extensively damaged by cannon fire. Although handling was difficult and all Wireless aids had been made useless, the aircraft was brought back over base and crash landed just off the aerodrome. The rear gunner Sergeant Hughes was wounded, and the flight engineer and Captain injured in the crash, but none of them seriously.

This particular operation was later recounted by the crew's flight engineer, Sergeant Nick Carter and retained amongst the memorabilia associated with James during his post war years.

> That night, 13 March 1943, we were once again detailed for mine-laying. The main bomber force were going to the Ruhr again but that was cancelled because of weather conditions over their target. This was just before their take off time – we had departed some three hours earlier. It must have been a last minute cancellation for them because when we arrived back we found a number of them in line on the perimeter track, but more on this later. This time we were going to Danzig Bay carrying only four mines because of the distance involved, we flew over Denmark and over the southern end of Sweden, which of course was a neutral country, and we could see all the towns' street lighting, it looked so nice after our British blackout.
>
> We arrived without any problems at Danzig and commenced our level flight to drop the mines, when a dense curtain of flak burst around us. We had never experienced this before – it was the German Navy taking exception to our presence. It took under a minute to drop the mines but it was a very long minute. However, we were not hit and then started back on the return journey, once again over Sweden and then at 7000 feet over Denmark. We had left the Danish coast about fifteen minutes earlier and Paddy had just said that it wouldn't be too long before we were having our eggs and bacon, when it happened.
>
> A Ju88 night fighter fired at us from slightly below and behind, neither Paddy nor George spotted it until we were hit. The aircraft went into a steep dive, the cabin was full of smoke and flames and the side windows had been

blown out. Our cabin lights were flashing on and off, mainly on, and the wing tip lights were on. Bill seemed to be having a hard time pulling out of the dive and I tried to assist, she finally came out at what I thought was 700 feet [Bill said years after that he thought it was 500 feet]. We both agreed we could see the waves far too clearly. Flying level we then had to worry about the fighter. We concluded some days later that after seeing all the flames and lights he had decided we were finished.

Meanwhile, Dougie had been dealing with the flames which turned out to be signal cartridges which had been hit by a cannon shell, so we had a wonderful, but very much unappreciated, fire-work display of all colours. Dougie tried various methods to get rid of the burning cartridges and finally ended up putting on several pairs of gloves, picking up the cartridges and throwing them through the now windowless side of the cabin. I had to do something about the flashing lights and having quickly opened the fuse panel taking out what fuses I could, smashed others which I couldn't remove which were giving trouble. We worked out later that the 20-mm cannon shells, which had set fire to the cartridges and blown out the windows, must have missed Dougie and me by about 24 inches.

Now it was time to see what other damage had been done, the intercom was dead, which was not a good start but not too much of a problem. It was when I went down the rear of the fuselage with my flashlight that I found the problem: the elevator and rudder controls were square sectioned tubes passing down the port side and located in supports made form a material called Tufnol. Between two of these supports the elevator control had been completely severed with about a ten-inch gap, the supports had been blown 40 or 50 degrees out of line and had jammed the rudder control. Then I went forward into the bomb aimer's compartment, from there I could check the aileron controls. More problems – the chains had formed a loop and severely restricted the movement. No wonder Bill was complaining that the aircraft was difficult to handle. I reported back to Bill and suggested that I could try to do something with the rudder control but he said to leave it alone, he was coping and didn't want to take any chances that might make it worse. Dougie by this time had collected his Gee maps, which had blown down the back because of the wind coming through the missing windows, and was trying to find out where we were. Luckily the Gee equipment was still working. I thought perhaps we could do something to prevent the wind from giving us so much trouble. The lower part of the cabin below the windows had some fairly stiff panels so I unscrewed them and to my great surprise (and Bill's) managed to jam them into the blank spaces where they stayed for the rest of the flight.

The next problem to overcome was communication. Dougie had to give Bill changes of course, but this was solved when I suggested that I would be standing next to Bill and Doug could tap me behind either my right or left knee using one tap for each degree of turn, I would then change the needle of the directional compass as required. This worked very well and when I changed the reading, Bill would give me an OK nod. By very careful engine control Bill managed to fly the aircraft quite well. It was a case of decrease power to lose height, increase to climb, to turn port open up the starboard engines and the opposite to turn starboard. After what seemed like ages we crossed the Lincolnshire coast, I wasn't sure if they were still working but I flashed out an SOS message on the downward identification lights. Although we didn't know at the time, the signal was seen by the observer corps, who phoned the local RAF Stations to ask if they had a Lancaster missing. There were only eleven Lancasters in action that night and so Scampton were standing by when we approached. Then Bill, having decided that a landing with no flying controls would be very tricky, decided that we should bail out. It was then that I had to tell him that I couldn't because my parachute had been used by Dougie to smother some of the burning signal cartridges. Bill then wanted the other five crewmembers to bail out while he and I attempted to land. This they refused to do saying that they would stick with us but would, of course, take up crash positions between the front and rear wing spars where they passed through the fuselage.

We prepared for landing as soon as we could see the airfield. By now it was six thirty am, and fairly light. On Bill's instructions I selected flaps down and that was OK, the next thing was to get the wheels down. Nothing happened so I moved back to the wireless operator's position to where the emergency hydraulic hand pump was on his left hand side. All I found was a hole in the side of the fuselage where the pump should have been. There was one more thing to try, a last resort, a compressed air system that if used would blow all the oil out of the hydraulic system and hopefully lower the wheels. However, this meant that they could not be retracted. It worked, they came down but the starboard tire had been slashed by the cannon shells which didn't help the situation. Now it was more or less up to Bill. Aas we came closer to the airfield, losing height for touchdown, we found we were making directly for the line of aircraft left in situ when ops were scrubbed for that same night. All Bill could do was to use the engine power to gently make a 360 degree turn to make another approach, it was probably a ten-mile radius and we were not happy to find that we were still lined up with the Lancasters on the perimeter track.

It was then that Bill took drastic action. We were at about 1000 plus feet and he suddenly opened the engines up to nearly full power. The aircraft banked to port in the required direction in what was a twenty or thirty degree bank. Now we had to straighten up and so at Bill's nod I put the port engines at nearly full power, reducing the power on the other side. Nothing happened, we just slid sideways straight into the ground. I had tried to jam myself between the back of the pilot's seat and the navigator's table watching the ground come close and thinking bloody hell, this is it. The next thing I knew I was laying full length on my back in the bomb aimer's compartment feet facing forward, with the front gun turret which had come off its mounting sitting on my legs. I looked over my head towards the back of the aircraft and there was Dougie trying to open his escape hatch but turning the handle the wrong way. I yelled to him to turn it the other way, which he did and promptly left. I then found I was the only one left in the aircraft and could see that there was some smoke coming out of the starboard wing. I tried to free my trapped foot, the left one, but without success and then had a sudden brainwave, I unzipped the flying boot and out came the foot unharmed. Then it was a simple matter to exit via the pilot's escape hatch and slide down the side of the fuselage, except I hadn't unplugged my intercom from the socket and found myself suspended about a foot above the ground by my leather flying helmet. At that moment Paddy and George ran back and while Paddy held me up George removed the helmet. It really is very strange but we had come to rest in a field next to our own dispersal point and there was our own ground crew coming through the hedge to help us, plus an ambulance crew who had been waiting at the control tower with the fire engine and another truck with cutting equipment.

Although I felt fine and I am sure we were all glad to be alive, in my travels from behind the pilot's seat to the aircraft nose my face must have come into contact with the four throttle levers and also the four propeller pitch levers cutting me over the left eye and eyelid and also across the mouth. It looked much worse than it proved to be but the medics insisted on stretchering me back to the ambulance. All the crew were with me and on arrival at the medical centre I was taken into the operating room and though Bill stayed with me the others went for debriefing and then to the officers' or sergeants' mess. I was placed on a flat padded table to allow the very young doctor to see what he could do. I remember Bill gripping my right arm above the elbow and me feeling embarrassed because I had a hole in the sock on my left foot. The doctor said he would have to put some stitches in but couldn't give me an anaesthetic because of shock. I think Bill felt it worse than I did.

After that I was given a large morphine tablet and woke up 24 hours later in a hospital bed. One of my earlier thoughts was that this episode should be worth a few beers. I hadn't been awake very long when there was a huge explosion from somewhere on the airfield and later we found that a cookie, a 4,000-lb bomb, had blown up one of the aircraft, destroying, I believe, three other Lancasters. My head was bandaged up so that just my eyes and mouth were visible. I did get to look when the doctor was checking progress. After he'd left I nipped out of bed and viewed my reflection in the brass finger plate on the door. Later I heard that during breakfast of the morning of the crash Paddy had complained that his legs were a bit painful. He ended up in a local hospital where he had small pieces of his rear turret removed from the knee area, a cannon shell had passed under his seat and exploded. One foot higher and Paddy would have been killed. I still think of him and wonder why the heck he should volunteer when he came from Southern Ireland. I believe he survived the war, he was a great chap. He and George had carried me from the aircraft to and through the hedge before the medics took over.

I was then given some sick leave and ordered to report to Emmanuel College, Cambridge to have the stitches removed at the end of my leave. The college was being used as an initial training wing for aircrew cadets. With my small suitcase I stood at the bus stop by the Scampton gate when a large Rover car pulled up and the driver asked if I would like a lift. This, of course, was very welcome and he started a conversation by stating that a Lancaster had crashed into one of his fields a few days before. I said I know I was in it. 'Well I'm darned,' he said, or something like that, if you've got time before your train, I'm going to buy you a lunch. Which he did and I still think how nice it was of him.

The day before, I had walked over to the site of the crash, I could see where the wing had first hit the ground and could work out what had probably happened. On first contact the reaction had righted the plane to level attitude. It had torn across a field, then knocked down a derelict cottage and passed through a small orchard. Then it had reached the road past the airfield, which being higher than the field took the undercarriage off allowing us to pass over the road like a flying boat. We then knocked down a telegraph pole and went through the barbed wire boundary fence, which was about fifteen feet high. This wrapped itself around the two outboard engines and tore them off, the fuselage ending up in the field next to our dispersal area. I went into what was left of the aircraft and found a ground engineer writing a report and sitting in the pilot's seat. Now the funny thing was, just prior to the trip I had got an empty dope can and painted it in blue and white stripes so that any of us at the front end could use it if we were taken short. We had used it and I had wedged it behind Bill's seat, it was still there and I remarked about it as I took it away. The officer said he had been puzzled by the awful smell. Why it stayed in place while I didn't was, I suppose, a matter of weight!

The night fighter attack took place approximately 33 miles west south west of Tyboron at 0350 hours. In all probability the Luftwaffe unit involved had been IV/NJG3 operating from Fliegerhorst Grove with Ju88 aircraft. James had survived his fifth operational sortie but it had been a close call, the thoughts of surviving a minimum of another twenty operations to complete his tour would have been a most daunting prospect. To his great disappointment, his close knit crew never reformed. James became the rear gunner to Sergeant Moore's crew, a crew composed entirely of sergeants. Almost immediately James was in the thick of action with another engagement with a night fighter. His combat report

Lancaster W4201. The crewmember far left is the bomb aimer as he is carrying the Bomber Sextant. The serial number W4201 is seen on the fuselage to the right of the crew door. W4201 was written-off as a result of the damage sustained on 13 March and James Hughes was most certainly lucky to have survived. (*J. Hughes*)

located in the National Archives Air 50/190 has the following report for 22/23 June 1943:

Lancaster 'Q' ED777 No. 57 Squadron on way to Mulheim on night of 22/23 June 1943, 51.26 N, 06.54 E. at 19,000 feet and at 0152 hours.

Three-quarter moon, broken cloud below, some industrial haze and searchlights to port and starboard, flak gradually increasing over target area. Rear Gunner [Sergeant Hughes] reported single engine enemy aircraft, identified as a Me.104 [Me.109] moving up from starboard beam level about 75 yards and coming in to attack dead astern. Rear gunner immediately opened fire (firing 800 rounds) and a few seconds later mid-upper opened fire (firing 200 rounds). Both rear gunner and mid-upper observed tracer bullets to enter nose of enemy aircraft (which carried no lights and did not open fire throughout the combat). Enemy aircraft then dipped its wings and broke away diving to port and was not seen again. At this point the flak was getting pretty hot as Lancaster was running up to the target, but both mid-upper and rear gunner claim enemy aircraft as damaged. Lancaster was preparing for bombing run at time of attack but as enemy aircraft came in to attack, rear gunner told pilot to corkscrew.

This particular operation to Mulheim claimed 36 Bomber Command aircraft that failed to return safely. The Luftwaffe night fighters were highly active and James was lucky to have fought off the enemy to avoid becoming one of the loss statistics. One Stirling, EH889, had been shot down over the Ijsselmeer, Holland's largest artificial lake. Two crewmembers from that aircraft were never located and lost in the waters, whilst five of the crew were later recovered from various locations along the shorelines during the following month. Within the crew were two air gunners. Twin brothers, Robert and Richard Tod who had volunteered together, trained together and crewed together. The twins were issued with consecutive service numbers and it must be wondered why their mother was burdened with receiving one telegram notifying both of their deaths together in the same aircraft, they now lay alongside each other in the Medemblick Cemetery.

It is interesting to note, on 26 October 1939, the Member of Parliament Mr J. Griffiths asked a question during the House of Commons debate, asking the Minister of Labour whether his attention had been called to the number of recent cases in which two members of the same family had registered for service under the National Service Act and whether he would consider granting exemption to one of the members in such cases.

This question obviously has a direct relationship to the question of twins and brothers enlisting and serving together. The Minister of Labour, Mr E. Brown replied:

> I am aware that there are cases where two members of the same family may register for service at the same time. The act does not provide for exemption on this ground, but application may be made for postponement in cases where exceptional hardship would arise.

On a separate raid to Cologne conducted within a matter of weeks after the raid to Mulheim which had claimed the twin brothers, James submitted a combat report for the night of the 8/9 July 1943:

> Aircraft was Lancaster 'M '57 Squadron FD308, position 50.51 N, 06.49 E, height 19,500 feet, time 0126 hours. Conditions were half-moon, 10/10 cloud below, some searchlights below cloud. Rear gunner [Sergeant Hughes] and pilot saw tracer passing under their aircraft. The rear gunner then saw enemy aircraft which was identified as a Ju.88, at the same time the mid-upper [Golding] saw a single-engine aircraft which he identified as a Me.109. The Ju.88 was dead astern and the Me.109 was on the starboard quarter. The Me.109 then closed to 200 yards and opened fire with a short burst, the Ju.88 still astern but did not close or open fire. The pilot took immediate evasive action doing a diving turn to starboard with the rear gunner firing at the Ju.88 and the mid-upper firing at the Me.109. The Me.109 dived under the Lancaster and was not seen again. The Ju.88 was lost for a few moments

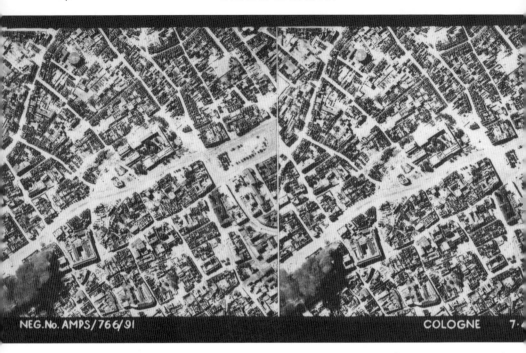

NEG.No. AMPS/766/91   COLOGNE   7∙

The photographic departments were able to print stereo images from cameras carried by some aircraft. These selected cameras provided the opportunity to view images in extraordinary detail. The images were viewed by utilizing twin magnifying lenses on a metal stand. (*J. Hughes*)

but was then picked up again by the rear gunner breaking away astern and below and was not seen again. During the action the rear gunner fired 1,000 rounds and the mid-upper about 100 rounds. No claims were made by the gunners.

The damage to the Lancaster was as follows: Starboard Rudder holed. Starboard outer engine put out of action and starboard mainplane holed. Mid-upper gunner's turret put out of action due to starboard engine being stopped.

James was promoted to the rank of Flight Sergeant and became the first member of his crew to wear the crown above the three chevrons on his arm.

On 17 August 1943, fourteen crews from 57 Squadron were briefed for a special raid which included James. The target was Peenemunde, a secret rocket research establishment. This raid was to be one of the most important carried out by Bomber Command during the Second World War. The destruction of the workshops and administrative complex dealt a severe blow to the enemy's advance in the field of rocket and pilotless aeroplane development and Germany's plans for a saturation onslaught of rocket bombs calculated to destroy Great Britain's resolve. Six hundred aircraft of Bomber Command took part in the highly secret operation during the night of 17-18 August 1943. 57 Squadron provided fourteen Lancasters for this raid of which just one failed to return – the aircraft piloted by the squadron's commanding officer, Wing Commander W. R. Haskell DFC. A total of forty-one Allied aircraft failed to return from the raid, the vast majority of whom fell prey to German night fighters over the Baltic Sea. For James, in Lancaster DV201, it was to be a sortie of just over six-and-a-half hours with the visual display of coloured pathfinder markers and the intense deployment of incendiaries no doubt providing an amazing pyrotechnic display, the like of which he would not have seen previously. Little did James realise that night on seeing the pathfinder operations that he himself would later become a member of that elite force. His Lancaster skilfully added their own bomb load of a single 4,000-lb cookie bomb and 720 individual 4 lb, and 136 individual 30-lb incendiaries onto their aiming point. Peenemunde had been an immense and demanding operation but the operational demand was high at this time and having only touched down safely back at base at 0423 on the morning of 18 August, James once more climbed back into his Lancaster that evening and flew to Berlin for another major raid.

The following month he undertook a further six raids to central Germany. He completed his 33rd operational raid on 19 October 1943 with a sortie to Hanover which enabled him to record a total of 215 operational hours flying in his rear turret, a most eventful tour of duty which had not escaped the attention of the Group Captain Commanding his squadron. On 23 November James was recommended for the non-immediate award of the Distinguished Flying Medal.

Flight Sergeant Hughes has taken part in attacks on some of the most strongly defended targets in Germany, such as Berlin, Hamburg, Cologne, Mannheim, Peenemunde, Kassel, Essen and the towns of the Ruhr. On 22 June 1943 attacking Mulheim and again on 8 July 1943 attacking Cologne, he damaged an Me109 in each case, seeing his tracer strike the enemy aircraft which immediately broke off the attack. Flight Sergeant Hughes has shown great determination in attacking the enemy, and is a most skilful air gunner. On various occasions he has volunteered to fly on operations with other crews when these crews were short of a gunner.

Wearing the ribbon of the DFM on his tunic James served his well-earned rest from operations as an instructor. Promotion and commissioned he later posting to RAF Warboys, a station near Cambridge, and home to the Pathfinder Force Navigation Training Unit. He was duly posted operational onto A Flight, 35 Pathfinder Squadron on 19 July 1944, operating from RAF Graveley, a typical Bomber Command airfield with the standard layout of a triangle of runways which allowed take-off and landing from six different directions. It was one of very few stations to be fitted with FIDO (Fog Investigation and Dispersal

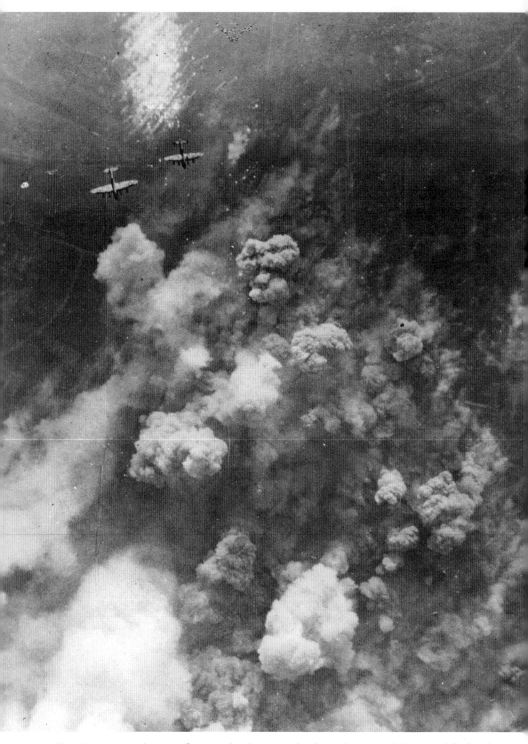

Two Lancasters about to fly over the dense smoke from the target below, pathfinder sky markings appear in the photograph just behind the aircraft. (*Air Ministry, November 1944*)

Operation), the device previously mentioned at RAF Woodbridge which allowed aircraft to land in thick fog or snow. A network of pipes were laid along the edge of one runway and, when foggy conditions prevailed, fuel was pumped through the pipes and ignited. The heat generated caused the fog to rise up to 200 feet, and the flames would highlight the outline of the runway. In addition to the emergency airfields this system was fundamental to the survival of many bomber crews who managed to successfully land in conditions that would normally have induced abandoning the aircraft in the air.

Flying Officer James Hughes joined a crew that consisted only of officers, two squadron leaders and six flying officers. It was an experienced crew who between 23 July 1944, and the 6 November 1944, flew thirty operations carrying out the various duties required of a crew with the Pathfinder Force. These included the delivery of primary markers to nominated targets, backing up marking to enforce the correct bombing by the primary bombers from Bomber Command, deputy master bomber duties, shadowing the master who was in charge of the entire operation and finally the awesome responsibility of master bomber. This

James Hughes in company with two Luftwaffe Fighter Aces at Biggin Hill aerodrome in 1968. General Adolf Galland seen second from the left and to the right of Galland the famous ace, Gunther Rall. James is standing third from the right. Lancaster Guy Gibson stands behind the group. This airframe was built in 1945 and carried the serial NX611. This aircraft is now preserved at the Lincolnshire Aviation Heritage Centre and is instantly recognized as 'Just Jane'. (*J. Hughes*)

Distinguished Flying Medal, 1939-45 Star, Air Crew Europe Star, Bar France & Germany, Burma Star, Defence Medal, War Medal and the Queen's Silver Jubilee Medal.

resulted in an extended time over a target, circling monitoring and directing the bomber stream. The Luftwaffe were well aware of the pathfinder role and the responsibilities of the master bombers, making them particularly vulnerable when over the target areas.

James had completed sixty-one operational sorties when he was regarded as having completed his second tour of duty. On 5 January 1945, he was posted to the Aircrew Allocation Centre, a type of holding unit for aircrew personnel. He was later sent to Burma where he served until the completion of the war in the Far East.

The Pathfinder Association was formed in the immediate post war years and subsequently developed communication links with some Luftwaffe pilots, including high profile figures like Adolf Galland. James 'Paddy' Hughes DFM subsequently met with Galland and developed a friendship in the late 1960's.

James Hughes DFM served as the president of the Pathfinder Association between 1977-1980 and as Honorary Vice President to Air Marshal Sir Ivor Broom KCB, CBE, DSO, DFC, AFC. The Queen honoured James with the award of her Silver Jubilee Medal for services to the Pathfinder Association in 1977.

As a direct consequence of his civilian career in banking, James Hughes was nominated to the Chamberlain's Court, Guildhall and duly received the Freedom of the City of London. The unique certificate for this prestigious honour which dates back to medieval times was proudly displayed in his office, alongside it was the warrant for his wife's MBE, awarded for her long service as secretary to the Pathfinder Association.

34

Night Hunters of the Reich

The German High Command entered Second World War with such confidence that they predicted the war would be quickly won. Without doubt, no consideration whatsoever was applied to the Luftwaffe being able to conduct aerial combat at night. The RAF changed that when Bomber Command, having suffered appalling losses in daylight, turned to attacking under the cloak of darkness.

By mid-1940 the Luftwaffe was forced to hurriedly form its first night fighter wing utilising the Messerschmitt Bf110. Thus began the long road to engage the RAF at night and the focus of attention by the Luftwaffe upon the rear gunner who were charged with guarding the various RAF bombers from such attacks.

The Luftwaffe's development of specialised equipment to aid in that task continued throughout the war years. Initially Luftwaffe pilots relied on visual acquisition, simply detecting enemy aircraft with the aid of a searchlight. Those primitive measures were not hugely productive and new electronic methods of navigation and detection were developed, and the night fighter capability grew. By the end of 1942, the German night fighter force had almost 400 aircraft engaged in the night skies. Almost 1,300 British aircraft primarily from Bomber Command were destroyed in that year alone. The experienced night fighter crews would carefully choose their prey, stalk and close for the kill. With every combat they gained more skill and ability which enabled them to play the deadly game of hide and seek amongst the darkened skies with ever greater proficiency.

The main difficulty for night pilots was to catch and attack the enemy in total darkness, because searchlights on the ground concentrated on specific areas of the sky. There was no ground control capability at this time and any interception were entirely handled by the pilot or crew engaged in the air. The pilots could patrol the sky near the operational searchlights hoping to spot a bomber silhouetted against the sky. This was a flawed strategy as the RAF pilots obviously chose to avoid the searchlights if at all possible and thus escape any interception by the Luftwaffe.

The German developments in radar installation, especially the Wurzburg and the Freya created opportunities of differing strategies, which heralded darker times for the RAF and in particular the rear gunners. All of the night fighter proactive responses were supported by the Luftwaffe Anti-Aircraft flak units which themselves accounted for destroying many aircraft over Germany. At the end of 1941, almost all of the Luftwaffe night fighter units were equipped with the Messerschmitt Bf110.

Wolfgang Falck, a Knight's Cross recipient pilot, was responsible for the day and night fighter defence of the Reich in 1943. He was a gifted pilot and instigated various tactical defensive methods to combat the raids upon Berlin at that time. One audacious and disturbing strategy was for the Luftwaffe pilots to follow Bomber Command's bombers on their way back home, waiting until they reached their airfields and attacking them at the most vulnerable moment, while landing or circuiting their own airfield. The Ju88C proved to be an excellent aircraft for the Luftwaffe when used for these intrusions over England.

To illustrate the effectiveness of these demoralising Luftwaffe tactics, the following account taken from later in the war, led to the loss of life of a rear gunner flying from RAF Shepherds Grove in 196 Squadron. The Stirling bomber had long since been removed from Bomber Command's first line of operational aircraft, but there were of course exceptions, and on 21 February 1945, Stirling LX126 took off from the Suffolk airfield carrying twenty-four 500-lb bombs. The target was identified as Rees in the Ruhr valley and nine aircraft departed for the target. The raid itself proved to be a piece of cake. The return to Suffolk was uneventful, with the flight engineer confirming to the captain that the fuel load was excellent, some 400 gallons of fuel remaining, providing a large safety margin. After crossing the English coast the pilot switched on the navigation lights, it was standing orders to do so, designed to reduce the risk of collision with so many aircraft returning to the airfields over Central England. The wing tips and tail lights were advantageous to all in the sky. Having circled the airfield, Stirling LX126 was given permission to land, and on the final approach, the runway lights were on as normal. With the massive undercarriage down and flaps deployed, the approach speed was reduced to approximately 135 mph. The crew's job was done and they waited for the last few minutes to tick down.

With the aircraft at 600 feet altitude and no more than a minute or two away from touching down upon the runway, disaster struck from behind and on the port side. A cloud of sparks and a sequence of solid vibrations struck along the fuselage of the Stirling. The entire port side of the aircraft had received raking fire from a German intruder, and both cannon and machine gun fire had penetrated the length of the aircraft. The bomb aimer let out a scream identifying the German aircraft as a Ju88 as it sped past. Fortunately, the machine gun fire had not hit any forward crewmember, or disabled any vital flying controls, but it had started a fire, which quickly took hold inside the fuselage. The pilot made the decision to continue with the runway landing, ordering the escape hatches to be opened. The presence of 400 gallons of fuel still in the tanks would have crossed his mind immediately. The air bomber duly opened the hatch above the pilot's position, and the wireless operator opened the astro-dome. The descent of the last few hundred feet provided enough time for the fire to take a significant hold, the pilot, navigator, bomb aimer and wireless operator were all forced by the torrent of flames to be squeezed into the cockpit area and in fact right against the pilot's seat.

The rear gunner was no doubt having his own problems as the fire progressed in both directions down the fuselage, but it would have been fanned towards his position with great vigour by the airflow down the massive fuselage. Flames and fumes passed over the heads of the crewmembers as it tore towards the escape hatches. At last the aircraft touched the runway, with its speed reduced as quickly as possible through the application of the brakes. As the aircraft finally halted, the bomb aimer, navigator, and pilot immediately fell from the cockpit escape hatch, landing 22 feet below and managed to run from the scene of devastation. The flight engineer and wireless operator chose to run out upon the wing and jump that same 20 feet or more onto the runway below. Both of these men sustained horrific burn injuries.

There was no sign of the Canadian rear gunner, warrant Officer McGovern, and nobody had heard anything from him during the entire episode. The rear gunner had not seen or reported the attacking night fighter, but like the remaining crewmembers he was no doubt considering the operation complete and was in no way expecting to be attacked just a few hundred feet from the home station. Warrant Officer John Bruce McGovern had perished in the mid-section of the aircraft. He was 22 years old, having volunteered to serve from his home in Ontario and his death in the most tragic of circumstances occurred when he had thought he was the least vulnerable. Afforded a full military funeral he was laid to rest thousands of miles from his home in the military cemetery in Brookwood, Surrey. The Luftwaffe intruder activities required the RAF to limit night flying training in East Anglia, Lincolnshire and Yorkshire. In addition it placed further strain upon Bomber Command's rear gunners requiring them to remain vigilant until their aircraft actually completed the landing at their home airfield.

Returning to occupied Europe and Germany, the defensive series of German radar stations, running from central France to Denmark, covered this large area in segments known as boxes, operated with searchlights. The Freya radar was used to pick up targets on their way to the Reich, assisted by the Wurzburg radar, which gave indication of speed and altitude of the incoming bombers. This radar had a master searchlight allocated to it and the RAF were able to identify it by the differing beam of light when compared to the supporting manually controlled searchlights which always followed their master radar controlled beam.

The Luftwaffe night fighter pilot's chances of a successful interception depended to a certain extent on the experience and skill of the ground controllers. The pilots however still needed to hunt with their own eyes in order to actually locate the RAF bomber and execute the attack. It was during this last phase of the hunt that the rear gunners played their vital roles. The Luftwaffe tried to give night pilots their own 'night eyes' in the form of the Liechtenstein radar, which had

An early war period Luftwaffe Searchlight and Flak Unit. The searchlight illustrates the manual controls required to traverse the beam across the sky.

an ability to vector the fighter towards the proximity of the bomber. However the production and training requirements associated to this new equipment were difficult to sustain and it took a lot of time for units to become fully established and effective.

The Messerschmitt Bf110, the main night fighter of the Luftwaffe, was not being produced in sufficient numbers to satisfy demands of the Luftwaffe. This was a consequence of the increasing efficiency of the Allied bombing campaign. The replacement design for the old Bf110 aircraft was to be the Me210, which did not live up to its high expectations and this resulted in the development of the Me410. This aircraft proved to be highly popular with the crews and updated electronic capabilities made it a most effective aircraft towards the end of the war.

On 31 May 1942, Bomber Command carried out its first 1,000-aircraft raid, attacking Cologne. The 1,042 bombers flew in a concentrated stream towards the target, a strategy designed to reduce the efficiency of the Luftwaffe's night fighter controllers. It was considered successful, just forty-four bombers were shot down, and this change in strategy influenced by Bomber Harris, led to other similar raids. This led to the development of further 'electronic warfare' measures which were being conceived and constructed. Bomber Command created the Pathfinder Force, allowing the main force to bomb their target marking flares and create far greater control over the target areas. In order to do so, pathfinder bombers were equipped with the Gee, a radio navigation system. Pathfinder crews later found their electronic system had been jammed by a German counter defensive measure which was so successful that the RAF was force to abandon Gee, and develop a new improved navigation system which was called Oboe and was immune to jamming. In addition, the bombers started to be fitted with the Tinsel, which was able to interfere and jam radio transmission between fighter pilots and ground controllers.

Despite all the electronic developments, the isolated and vulnerable rear gunner was one of the most important individuals deployed within Bomber Command. His skill at interpreting enemy aircraft approaches, and his ability to quickly and accurately deploy his Browning guns, increased the margin between life and death for entire crews. Luftwaffe fighter pilots remained consistent in their endeavours to eliminate these men throughout the entire war. The Commander in Chief of Bomber Command, Sir Arthur Harris, paid a tribute to a most significant technical factor that thwarted the Luftwaffe. 'I would say this to those who placed that shining sword in our hands: Without your genius and your efforts, we would not have prevailed – the Lancaster was the greatest single factor in winning the war.'

A striking image of a squadron of Lancasters about to join the main bomber stream in a daylight raid into Germany.

LANCASTER BOMBERS NOW RAID BY DAY

R.A.F. night bombers are now being switched to day operations and are taking part in the all out Allied air attacks on German troops and transport in Normandy.
A squadron of Lancasters starts off to join the main bomber stream in daylight raid.

35

Luftwaffe Flak

The abbreviation 'flak' is recognised across the world, culled from the German word meaning 'aircraft defence gun'. It is a word still used in modern communication and within modern military conflict. During the Second World War and in particular to aircrews serving in the Allied air forces, it was a word that identified a most specific threat to their lives. When seen in the distance and in daylight, the black puffs of smoke that hung in the sky belied their deadly capability.

Initially Germany had no expectation of requiring great numbers of anti-aircraft artillery units or searchlight batteries to protect their homelands, or the industrial valley in the Ruhr. They felt they had a good structure of anti-aircraft artillery that was unlikely to need additional strengthening and their 88mm gun was an exceptionally versatile weapon. However the Royal Air Force forced a change in these thoughts and perceptions. The gradual build up in strength and ability in Bomber Command saw offensive operations take place attacking Germany's ports, aerodromes and factories. Although not always accurate at the start of the campaign, Bomber Command became much more effective as time passed. Navigational and bombing equipment developed alongside improved aircraft, enabling intrusions into Germany on a scale that had never been anticipated by the German High Command.

The Luftwaffe were responsible for Flak Units which were labour intensive. It has to be born in mind that a static gun battery was likely to require between 120 to 140 personnel, with units replicated many hundredfold across multiple districts and borders. The basic Flak Unit was made up from several types of weapon – heavy artillery, light anti-aircraft, a combination of both, and searchlights. The heavy weapons were aimed using predictor equipment, designed to estimate where the aircraft were likely to be in the sky at the time the explosive round reached the height of the aircraft. The shells contained time fuses and a high explosive which ripped the thick metal casing apart creating deadly shrapnel which was capable of inflicting fatal damage to both the thin aluminium skinned aircraft and the men within.

Above: An example of one of the Luftwaffe's heavy flak guns. This particular gun displays successful engagements by its crew on the barrel markings.

Right: The twin dangers of searchlights probing the sky and the flak guns manned by experienced Luftwaffe personnel are illustrated in this period photograph.

During the summer of 1942 the RAF carried out a number of large scale raids across the Third Reich including specific operations to the industrial area of the Ruhr Valley. By way of an example, the award of the Immediate Distinguished Flying Medal on 24 September 1942 to a Lancaster rear gunner, Sergeant Stanley James Thompson demonstrates graphically, the perils of flak at that time. He was flying in Lancaster R5724, 61 Squadron.

Sergeant Thompson was the rear gunner to Flight Sergeant Campbell on the night of 24/25 September, 1942. When the aircraft was hit by anti-aircraft fire, a bit of shrapnel entered the rear turret and hit Sergeant Thompson in the leg. Such was the velocity and strength of the flak fragment that it broke his leg in addition to tearing at his flesh. Almost immediately the aircraft was engaged by fighters and cannon and machine gun fire entered the rear turret. The aircraft was out of control at the time, and it was impossible for Sergeant Thompson to operate his guns under those conditions. Despite his injuries, he reported the position of the fighters to the pilot and thereby enabled the pilot to successfully escape from the fighters. Sergeant Thompson was seriously injured but he never grumbled or asked for assistance and when the other members of the crew came to take him out of the turret, he helped in every possible way to facilitate their task ... It is considered that Sergeant Thompson displayed outstanding gallantry and devotion to duty when being subjected to the fire from the fighter aircraft and his efforts undoubtedly contributed largely to the aircraft escaping into the clouds.[1]

The recommendation for Flight Sergeant Campbell, the Lancaster's pilot provides a rather more comprehensive overview of events and states:

Flight Sergeant Campbell was Captain of a Lancaster aircraft detailed for mine-laying in the Baltic on the night of 24-25 September 1942. After successfully completing their allotted task, course was set for home. While crossing Denmark at a height of 6,000 feet, they were engaged by anti-aircraft fire. A shell exploded in the bomb compartment. A fire of considerable proportions started in the fuselage of the aircraft and reconnaissance flares and distress signals commenced to burn. At the same time, another shell burst in the nose of the aircraft blowing in all of the Perspex nose and the majority of the Perspex of the pilot's cupola with the exception of the front windscreen. The air bomber, who was seated in the nose of the aircraft at the time, was blown back beside the pilot. The second pilot, who was standing beside the pilot at the time, was blown back onto the floor beside the Navigator. The pilot, the second pilot, the navigator, and the wireless operator all received facial burns from the explosion of this shell. The aircraft was full of smoke and the pilot was unable to see his instruments.

At this moment, the aircraft was attacked by two fighters. The aircraft was hit by cannon and machine gun fire. Cannon fire entered both rear and upper mid turrets. The aircraft stalled and lost 2,000 feet before the smoke cleared and the pilot was able to regain control. He immediately dived for some clouds just below them and escaped from the fighters and anti-aircraft fire. There was now a big fire in the fuselage and in addition to the fire, ammunition was exploding in all directions in the aircraft. The rear gunner was seriously wounded and had a broken leg. The combined efforts of the navigator, the air bomber, and the mid-upper gunner were then directed towards getting the fire under control so as to be able to reach the rear turret. They fought their way through the fire and pulled the rear gunner out of the turret and carried him to the rest chair. The fire was still of considerable proportions and the fire and the fuselage was largely burnt away. The efforts of the navigator, the air bomber, and the mid-upper gunner were then redirected to keeping the fire under control, which they did without being able to extinguish it completely. With the Perspex missing from the nose of the aircraft, there was a terrific draft blowing through. All maps, navigation and wireless logs, and documents had been blown out of the aircraft when the shell exploded in the nose.

The wireless operator, though considerably burnt about the hands and face, remained at his post throughout and contacted his base aerodrome from the Danish coast. He maintained contact with base throughout the rest of the homeward trip, obtaining bearings regularly from the pilot. The pilot handed over control of the aircraft to the second pilot after the latter had taken stock of readings of all instruments. The pilot took over control of the aircraft when over this country and, despite conditions of bad visibility, made an excellent belly-landing at an aerodrome without further injury to any members of the crew. The whole of the hydraulic and emergency gear for the operation of the undercarriage and flaps were completely destroyed. It is considered that the captain of the aircraft displayed outstanding qualities of gallantry, devotion to duty, and leadership in bring this aircraft and crew safely home under these conditions. It would have been possible for some of the crew to bail out over Denmark but some of the parachutes were burnt and the rear gunner was too badly injured to jump. All members of the crew therefore gallantly stuck to their posts. Finally, it is desired to pay tribute to the outstanding qualities of the construction of the aircraft and engines, which enabled it to fly back home after the damage that had been inflicted.

This entire crew of non-commissioned officers were to be each awarded Distinguished Flying Medals, presented personally by the King, on 24 November 1942. Sadly however on 10 November 1942, four of those brave recipients which included the pilot, Flight Sergeant Campbell, were killed returning from a mine-laying operation in the Bay of Biscay when their Lancaster W4244 crashed in poor visibility. Having survived the flak and fighters, it was the fog that ultimately claimed their lives.

As a result of the concentrated raids by the RAF in 1942, Germany created the concept of home guard flak units, in effect bolstering the Luftwaffe's flak units by providing mixed civilian entities of both elderly and young with anti-aircraft guns to deploy against the Allied bombers, eventually including females and young boys. Factory workers provided the means of manning flak units to defend their places of work. In addition to their shift requirements within the factories or other facilities producing Germany's war effort, the workers covered the gunnery duties as well. The RAF were suffering losses of bombers on a regular basis and any enhancement of flak capabilities would have obviously increased the intensity of flak fire. Accuracy may have been an issue for these impromptu units, but for the Allied aircrews, flak represented harrowing belts of shell fire to fly through. The sight of fellow crews falling to the ground, possibly with their aircraft on fire or simply disabled by damage, would have created scenes of pure horror for the Allied aircrews. The noise and buffeting of exploding shells would have been continuous whilst flying over the target areas. Unbeknown to the RAF at that time, Germany was embarking on a programme of increasing their flak units even further with increased effectiveness. This was being influenced by the Luftwaffe's Flak Development Committee charged with the responsibility of improving the performance of the flak force. This strategy, combined with the developing night fighter capabilities was to lead to even greater losses for the RAF.

Another measure to increase the ability of flak anti-aircraft defences was the enormous concrete constructions built in Berlin, Hamburg and Vienna, each one holding four heavy guns. Known as 'flak towers' and accompanied by a further tower that provided the radar and fire control equipment, both towers were additionally provided with the smaller four-barrelled 2 cm light flak guns. The huge complex structures facilitated as civil defence headquarters and air raid shelters. The standalone gun towers were manned by very capable crews and represented a serious threat to any aircraft that was to fall within their zones of operation.

Flak did not need to actually strike the Allied bombers, as its presence alone created sufficient threat to induce potential inaccuracies in the actual bombing of the target. The effect, recognised as 'creep back', was where bomb aimers dropped their loads just short of the primary target, a condition that was always likely to be influenced by heavy flak. The bomber crews were always exposed on a bombing run as they were prevented from taking evasive action in avoiding flak. Even when the bomb load had been dropped, the run continued in order to secure the photographic evidence that recorded an individual crew's accuracy. Only then could they take evasive action to escape flak, and commence their homeward route to safety.

All members of aircrew within Bomber Command were vulnerable to injuries sustained by flak, but the rear gunners were particularly exposed as they sat

The Luftwaffe's light flak units, which were very capable of creating significant damage to any Allied aircraft that came within their range.

in their Perspex bubble surrounded by exploding projectiles. Small pieces of sharp, jagged, metal shell casings, fractured and blown apart by the internal high explosives caused fatal and life threating injuries. Flight Sergeant Patrick Dwyer was in his rear turret over Kiel on 21 June 1941 when his body, already penetrated by four separate pieces of shrapnel, received a further injury when a large piece of flak sliced into him, creating a compound fracture of his right femur. The fragments were white hot and potentially lethal. For Patrick Dwyer, he survived these terrible injuries but his name was ultimately added to the casualties of war when his Lancaster W4247 was lost whilst attacking Hamburg in November 1942. His entire crew of seven were later buried in the Ohlsdorf Cemetery in Hamburg.

The flak crews, far below the bombers, gauged their results by the number of aircraft seen to be struck, and either damaged or destroyed. In many instances these were the aircraft coned in the beams of the searchlights, such aircraft had concentrated fire directed towards them. Damage inflicted on the remaining aircraft, or indeed to the men inside, was in the main, unknown to the flak crews. Bomber crews frequently returned with fatalities, in some instances incredibly horrible injuries inflicted by flak. The vulnerability of the rear gunner is particularly well illustrated in the case of Sergeant Lorenzo Bertrand. On 8 April 1943, this airman was the rear gunner in a Wellington aircraft detailed to attack Duisberg. Whilst over the target area the aircraft was hit by accurate anti-aircraft fire and the bomber started to vibrate violently. The situation became critical and the pilot gave orders to prepare to abandon the aircraft. As no response was received from the rear gunner, the navigator went to investigate and found that the flak damage had caused the rear turret to fall away from the fuselage resulting in Sergeant Bertrand falling to his death. The Wellington incredibly survived this terrifying encounter with flak and managed to reach their base safety.

Many aircraft would leave German air space but then crash in France and the Low Countries or in the English Channel, purely as a result of damage inflicted by these despised exploding shells. Other bomber crews thinking they had escaped unscathed found that flak had inflicted small, sometimes undetected, nicks in fuel or oil lines, which created slow but consistent seepage creating an immediate need to undertake an emergency landing once they managed to reach England. For the crews engaged in these bombing operations, the certainty of flak being present was guaranteed and the mental strength required to cope with it was without doubt demanding and in some cases debilitating to the individual. The noise of small flak fragments exploding and striking the thin metal skin of the bombers fuselage would have created a noise over and above to the usual din that was clearly audible to the crew, despite wearing the helmets and earphones. In 1943, the Luftwaffe introduced controlled fragmentation'flak shells. These were manufactured with grooves cut on the inside face of the casings and when the charge detonated, the case broke up into a smaller number of larger fragments. This fragmentation round was far more effective against heavy bombers than the

Wellington HE239 with the rear gunner's turret torn from the fuselage. This devastating damage was caused by flak and resulted in Sergeant Bertrand suffering a terrible death. The apparent fragility of the aircraft's construction becomes apparent in this image, it was, however, an exceptionally strong concept of engineering. (*Ron Bramley*)

regular high explosive rounds. Towards the end of the war the Germans developed the incendiary shrapnel round, a thin-walled projectile containing numerous small pellets. When the shells detonated, the pellets were blown outwards and forwards at incredible velocity. The pellets were designed to pierce the skin of the aircraft and enter the fuel tanks to ignite the fuel. These incendiary shrapnel rounds proved to be far more effective than the controlled fragmentation rounds that had attempted to create the same effect.

It is ironic that the Luftwaffe was teaching the skill to shoot down RAF aircraft in a significantly large Flak School complex constructed very close to the RAF prisoner of war camp, Stalag Luft I, Barth. A substantial number of the aviators caged at Barth and all the other prisoner of war camps were there as a result of flak damage.

Another certainty for operational bomber crews was the presence of the searchlights, an integral component of the Luftwaffe's arsenal of defences against the RAF night bombing campaigns. The development of the master-light, which was operated by radar location and supported by other subordinate searchlights spread some distance apart, created the ability to locate and hold a bomber in intense broad cones of light. These were terrifying for the crews and every effort to escape them was taken at the earliest opportunity and bombers who failed were inevitable seized upon by the flak gunners. Searchlights were also used by the Luftwaffe as a means to lure the RAF bombers onto phony or dummy sites. Berlin had some sixteen fake targets constructed around its districts, each designed to draw the bombs away from the main target areas. These decoys were elaborate sites, able to replicate the effects of bomb burst and substantial fires. Indeed the RAF did frequently bomb these decoy sites, which were supported by searchlights distributed in an authentic fashion. As the war progressed, the Luftwaffe developed the ability to mimic the coloured pathfinder flares, as well as develop and construct very effective and efficient smoke generators which were capable of making target identification very problematical for the RAF.

There was a natural process of education in relation to target identification for all crews in Bomber Command. After each raid, the photographic departments developed and printed bomb run photographs, which were images that required the crew to maintain its bomb run over the target, exposing them to additional dangers whilst awaiting the bomb payload to fall and reach the target below. They were an important means of assessing the damage caused on each operation. The photo interpreters were excellent at establishing a great deal of detailed information from the photographs. Copies were sent to the Group HQ where the Command Photographic Interpretation Section would carry out an in-depth and detailed analysis in order to extract the maximum amount of information from each photograph. Every individual photograph had an automatic imprint to record the detail of the pilot, altitude of the aircraft and date of the raid, thus making them identifiable. The station intelligence officer would use china pencils to note comments across the photographs. These were then pinned up for viewing in the information or briefing rooms. There was a great deal of pride in the crews, and to see their efforts marked 'bombed dummy site' would have been a most undesirable state of affairs. Examination of these results, in particular by the bomb aimers became invaluable in educating and subsequently improving on the subtleties of dummy site recognition. Although the object of a decoy target complements the concept of camouflage, the two differ significantly. Camouflage endeavours to hide the actual target from visual reconnaissance, or recognition, whilst a decoy target was intended to be used at night to divert bombing attacks upon itself.

36

Decorated by the King

A wartime investiture at Buckingham Palace was inevitably a rather daunting but awe inspiring event for those individuals lucky enough to be invited. Most gallantry award recipients would have hoped for an invitation to the palace, but to give every recipient their award personally would have been a physical impossibility for the Sovereign. In many instances though, the award was sent to the operational station to be presented to the recipient, with the official Buckingham Palace note duly named to the individual and enclosed with the award. The status between ranks was reflected in the quality of the cases in which the medals were sent. The Distinguished Flying Cross was encased in a fitted velvet lined box, the box lid embossed with the letters 'DFC'. The equivalent award to non-commissioned officers, the Distinguished Flying Medal, was sent in a cardboard box with no particular fittings other than tissue wrapping.

Occasionally the King presented medals during official visits to operational units, and these arrangements were particularly noteworthy, as the entire squadron strength was inevitably present at such an important event. At Buckingham Palace the situation was very different in respect of who could attend. The recipients included men and women from across all of the fighting services, civil defence workers, Merchant Navy and others whose bravery had merited official royal recognition. Each medal recipient was entitled to nominate one or two close relatives or friends who were allowed to witness the ceremony. Entry was without question only provided to individuals in possession of a numbered and stamped entry ticket. These small tickets were issued in differing coloured card to enable easy recognition for the staff managing the presentation ceremonies.

Weather permitting, several of the Buckingham Palace ceremonies took place in the quadrangle. His Majesty presented the decorations on a small raised platform, while relatives and friends looked on from a short distance away. When investitures were held inside the palace, the King received each individual separately in the grand hall. An official would read a summarised account of the deed for which the honour was being conferred before the King pinned the medal to the recipient's tunic. Recipients would have received instructions to attend in their normal service dress with air raid wardens and other civil defence

BUCKINGHAM PALACE.

I greatly regret that I am
unable to give you personally the
award which you have so well earned.
I now send it to you with
my congratulations and my best
wishes for your future happiness.

George R.I.

Squadron Leader Jack S. Belton, D.F.C.

The official Buckingham Palace enclosure note sent to those recipients not able to receive the award in person. The enclosure was duly named to the individual and accompanied the actual medal.

609
BUCKINGHAM PALACE.

Admit one to witness the

Investiture

(at 10.15 o'clock a.m.)

13 JUL

Lord Chamberlain.

The small entrance ticket as issued to the recipients of the award which provided access to the ceremony for family or guests.

The King presents a Distinguished Flying Medal to Flight Sergeant Elwyn Rees, from Glamorgan, South Wales. As a rear gunner he had completed an eventful full tour of duty and his DFM had been announced in the *London Gazette* on 21 April 1944. The table with the awards to be presented is being attended to by one of the King's aides, Sir Harry Stockley. Waiting at the head of the queue is another member of the RAF, his brevet clearly indicating him to be air crew.

heroes attending in uniform, often with tin hats scarred as a result of their heroic work. On 4 March 1943, permission was granted for this previously most private function, to be photographed for the very first time.

Several months, and in some instances years may have elapsed between the valiant deed to merit the award and the actual presentation of the medal. Decorations conferred by the King (or on his behalf) were not given lightly and before a recommendation for an award was accepted officially, it was given careful consideration by a committee set up soon after the outbreak of the war. Apart from the decision whether a decoration had been earned or not, there was the degree of heroism which needed to be determined. Detailed reports of the circumstances were examined and judged in the light of the stringent regulations that concerned each individual medal. There was also the question of grants for consideration – several decorations carried monetary awards or pension entitlements which were implemented at the discretion of the committee.

The Distinguished Flying Cross and Distinguished Flying Medal awards could be recommended in two respects – immediate and non-immediate, the latter also known as a periodic. Immediate awards were for conspicuous deeds or individual

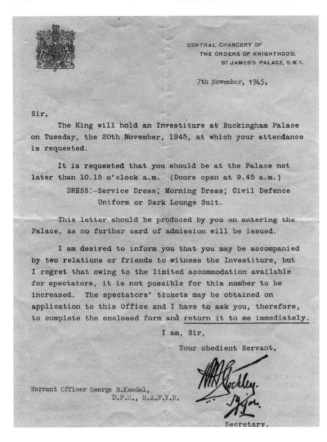

CENTRAL CHANCERY OF
THE ORDERS OF KNIGHTHOOD,
ST JAMES'S PALACE, S.W.1.

7th November, 1945.

Sir,

The King will hold an Investiture at Buckingham Palace on Tuesday, the 20th November, 1945, at which your attendance is requested.

It is requested that you should be at the Palace not later than 10.15 o'clock a.m. (Doors open at 9.45 a.m.)

DRESS:—Service Dress; Morning Dress; Civil Defence Uniform or Dark Lounge Suit.

This letter should be produced by you on entering the Palace, as no further card of admission will be issued.

I am desired to inform you that you may be accompanied by two relations or friends to witness the Investiture, but I regret that owing to the limited accommodation available for spectators, it is not possible for this number to be increased. The spectators' tickets may be obtained on application to this Office and I have to ask you, therefore, to complete the enclosed form and return it to me immediately.

I am, Sir,

Your obedient Servant,

Warrant Officer George B.Kendal,
D.F.M., R.A.F.V.R.

Secretary.

The official correspondence sent by the Central Chancery of The Orders of Knighthood, St James's Palace, London, to the recipients fortunate enough to be invited to Buckingham Palace.

acts. Periodic awards were more commonly made on completion of a first or second tour or recognition for a long term of competence. Awards were rationed and allocated on the basis of a mathematical formula – the number of hours flown by a squadron and how many awards were available. An award began with a recommendation made by the squadron commander. The recommendation then passed through several hands increasing in seniority – station commander, base commander, group commander, and in the case of Bomber Command awards, ending up in front of Bomber Harris.

In practice, the original recommendation was supported by those going up the line, but occasionally changes were made. For example a DFC was substituted for a recommended DFM because the recipient had been commissioned. In other cases an award being upgraded or down-graded was a practice that tended to be associated with immediate as opposed to periodic awards. Once the recommendation had been approved by the Air Officer Commander-in-Chief, the confirmation of the award was published in the *London Gazette*. For recipient's fortunate enough to be invited to Buckingham Palace they would eventually receive a letter from the Central Chancery of The Orders of Knighthood, St James's Palace, London.

A document distributed by 6 Group, Royal Canadian Air Force on 7 June 1943, advised on how recommendations were to be made, including comments on specific types of awards. The appendices to the document are particularly interesting and provide detailed information which deserves full quotation for the reader to understand the imposed requirements:

> Victoria Cross (VC) – Awardable to all ranks for most conspicuous bravery or some daring or pre-eminent act of valour or self-sacrifice or extreme devotion to duty in the presence of the enemy. The Air Council has advised that in their opinion, this decoration should be awarded more often for getting into danger (i.e. in the furtherance of operations) than for getting out of the kind of desperate situation which is latent in all operations. Exception to this general rule may however be made, when there is clear evidence of actions of the highest gallantry. Commanding officers should consider whether any officers or airmen under their command might be regarded as suitable for recommendation for the VC for sustained gallantry over a long period, rather than for some specific act of gallantry alone. It will still be desirable that officers or airmen so recommended, should have performed some outstanding act, but this should be the climax to a series of gallant exploits, e.g., a large number of sorties in the face of heavy opposition. The outstanding act need not of itself justify the highest award, but it would do so in a context of prolonged and heroic endeavor.

The author is aware of several instances where, even though a Victoria Cross recommendations had progressed through the system with glowing and well evidenced material, the committee was not in agreement with the recommendations and a lesser award was agreed and subsequently awarded. In some of these most exceptional cases where the individual was killed in action, the subsequent award was most likely to be the standard Mention in Despatches.

> Distinguished Service Order (DSO) – Awardable to officers (usually not below rank of Squadron Leader) who have been mentioned in despatches for distinguished services under fire, or under conditions equivalent to services in actual combat with the enemy.

> Distinguished Flying Cross (DFC) – Awardable to all Officers and Warrant Officers, for exceptional valour, courage or devotion to duty whilst flying on active operations against the enemy.

> Conspicuous Gallantry Medal (CGM Flying) – Awardable to Warrant Officers, N.C.O.s and aircraftmen as an award superior to the DFM for conspicuous gallantry whilst flying on active operations against the enemy.

Distinguished Flying Medal (DFM) – Awardable to all Non-Commissioned Officers and aircraftmen, for exceptional valour, courage or devotion to duty whilst flying in active operations against the enemy.

The appendix which set out the above criteria also laid down some administrative procedures for submitting recommendations. It advised officers submitting these to provide as much detail as possible, including sorties flown by those recommended, and degree of injuries and where they were sustained. It stated that recommendations for posthumous awards could not be submitted except when a Victoria Cross or a Mention in Despatches was involved. However the processing of recommendations for other awards went forward, even if the person involved had in the meantime been killed, but only on condition that the initial recommendation had been submitted while the person was still alive. This was a rule which was evidently relaxed on many occasions to allow what would otherwise be ineligible posthumous awards. It is occasionally evidenced in such awards with 'Since Deceased' against the official announcement procedures.

Apart from the obvious decorations, there were periodic awards of other honours. These were either for gallantry (acts of physical courage) or meritorious service (fine performance of duties that may have involved no physical risk or where risks were incurred in the absence of the enemy). Such awards were:

Companion of The Most Honourable Order of the Bath – Awardable to Group Captains and above.

Commander British Empire (CBE) – Awardable to Group Captains and above.

Officer of the Order of the British Empire (OBE) – Awardable to Wing Commanders and Squadron Leaders, and to Matrons of the Nursing Service.

Member British Empire (MBE) – Awardable to Flight Lieutenants, Flying Officers and Warrant Officers, and to Senior Nurses, Sisters and Staff Nurses of the Nursing Service.

Air Force Cross (AFC) – Awardable to all officers and Warrant Officers for exceptional valour, courage or devotion to duty whilst flying, though not in active operations against the enemy.

Air Force Medal (AFM) – Awardable to all Non-Commissioned Officers and aircraftmen for exceptional valour, courage or devotion to duty whilst flying, though not in active operations against the enemy.

British Empire Medal (BEM) – Medal of the Order of the British Empire for Meritorious Service. Awardable to airmen below Warrant rank for specially distinguished or meritorious service of a high standard. The faithful or zealous performance of ordinary duty is not sufficient in itself. There must be either special services of a high degree or merit, such as the discharge of special night duties, superior to ordinary work or highly meritorious performance of ordinary duties when these have entailed work of a dangerous or specially trying character.

Appendix IV covered awards for acts of gallantry on the ground. The VC, DSO, MC, DCM, and MM could all be granted to air force personnel for ground actions in which they were in direct conflict with the enemy 'including engagements with enemy aircraft'. This would have included such personnel like anti-aircraft gunners. It is interesting to note that the DFC and DFM were not included in the list of decorations to be granted for ground combat. The appendix also dealt with awards of a very different nature – those for acts of gallantry on the ground but not in contact with the enemy. It particularly singled out 'gallantry in effecting rescues from burning aircraft and in disposing of unexploded bombs'. The awards so covered were:

George Cross (GC) – Awardable to officers, airmen, members of the Nursing Service and civilians for acts of the greatest heroism or of the most conspicuous courage in circumstances of extreme danger. It is intended primarily for civilians and is awarded to service personnel for actions for which purely service honours are not normally granted.

George Medal (GM) – Awardable to officers, airmen, members of the Nursing Service and civilians for acts of great bravery. Like the GC, the GM is intended primarily for civilians.

Order British Empire (OBE) – Awardable to officers of the RAF and WAAF (usually limited to Wing Commanders, Wing Officers, Squadron Leaders and Squadron Officers) and to Matrons of the Nursing Service, for gallantry on the ground but not in actual conflict with the enemy.

Member British Empire (MBE) – Awardable to officers and Warrant Officers of the RAF and WAAF (usually limited to those not above Flight Lieutenant or Flight Officer rank) for gallantry on the ground but not in actual conflict with the enemy.

British Empire Medal – Awardable to NCO's, aircraftmen and airwomen for gallantry on the ground but not in actual conflict with the enemy.

Mentions in Despatches (MID) – The most common way of posthumously honouring personnel. It was to be granted in three circumstances:

(i) For gallantry on the ground in conflict with the enemy, including engagement with enemy aircraft.

(ii) For gallantry on the ground, but not in actual conflict with the enemy, and particularly for gallantry in effecting rescues from burning aircraft.

(iii) For specially distinguished or meritorious service of a high standard. The faithful or zealous performance of ordinary duty is not sufficient in itself. There must be either special services of a high degree of merit superior to ordinary work or highly meritorious performance of ordinary duties when these have entailed work of a dangerous or specially trying character.

To assist Commanding Officers in drawing up recommendations, in Appendix IX of the same document were a compilation of fifty phrases deemed useful for the task. Whilst probably helping superior officers who may have had limited literary talents, the list would also have been seen as inhibiting the drafting of exciting and heroic accounts. The similarity of many citations suggest that they were either written or edited to adhere to a formula. The phrases used:

1. By his fine fighting spirit.
2. His coolness under fire.
3. Complete disregard for personal safety.
4. By his coolness and presence of mind.
5. His fearless courage in combat.
6. This Officer's (NCO's) dogged determination, skill and devotion to duty.
7. Showed a magnificent example by.
8. Regardless of imminent danger.
9. By prompt action and with complete disregard of personal safety.
10. By skilful airmanship under most trying conditions.
11. Displayed exceptional skill and coolness in extricating his aircraft from a most perilous situation.
12. By his skill, courage and determination, he extricated his crew from a perilous situation.
13. To which action his crew undoubtedly owed their lives.
14. Thereby saving the lives of his crew and much valuable equipment.
15. His superb captaincy and airmanship.
19. Undeterred by intense flak.
20. In spite of physical suffering through intense cold, or hunger, or fatigue, or heat, or lack of oxygen, or thirst, or loss of blood, etc.

24. The successful completion of this operational flight was due to the initiative, resourcefulness and skillful airmanship of this officer (or NCO).
35. Gallantry of the highest order.
36. Fine record of achievement.
42. Proved himself to be an outstanding member of a gallant crew.
45. Handling his guns with cool determination.

Appendix XI of the document covered foreign awards. In effect it stated that awards (or their ribbons) granted by foreign powers could be accepted and worn, provided that the foreign country was not an enemy state. The order of wearing dictated that any foreign medal, once approved, must be worn submissive to their own countries awards, including gallantry, campaign and long service.

Campaign Medals and stars for service in the Second World War were accordingly governed by rules determined by the monarch on the advice of the British Government. Winston Churchill's words on the subject of medals made on 22 March 1944 are worthy of consideration.

> The object of giving medals, stars and ribbons is to give pride and pleasure to those who have deserved them. At the same time a distinction is something which everybody does not possess. If all have it, it is of less value. There must therefore, be heart-burnings and disappointments on the borderline. A medal glitters, but it also casts a shadow. The task of drawing up regulations for such awards is one which does not admit of a perfect solution. It is not possible to satisfy everybody without running the risk of satisfying nobody. All that is possible is to give the greatest satisfaction to the greatest number and to hurt the feelings of the fewest.[1]

In June 1946, a United Kingdom committee known as the Committee on the Grant of Honours Decorations and Medals produced a document setting out the conditions for the award of War Medals and Campaign Stars. This command document was known as Command Paper 6833 (AIR 2/6723 TNA) and within the document Sir Arthur Street suggested that the Battle of Britain clasp could be uniquely awarded to Battle of Britain participants and worn on the 1939-43 Star.

The matters concerning the complicated award of the various campaign stars and their entitlements were also addressed in the same document. Sir Arthur Street had tragically lost his son who served in the RAF as a pilot within Bomber Command. His son was amongst those men murdered upon Adolf Hitler's personal orders after their capture during the famous Great Escape. Sir Arthur had experienced the loss of his son whilst on operational duty, the elation of his life being saved and becoming a prisoner of war, and then the horror of his execution. He was well aware that Bomber Command had been hugely significant in the Allied victory over Germany, yet it was a bitter statement to these men that no campaign medal for Bomber Command was ever struck to commemorate their achievements. Attlee's post war Labour government appear to have given Bomber Harris's men little recognition. Harris was particularly concerned for the ground crews who served all hours in abominable conditions only to receive a Defence Medal. It is possible that Sir Arthur's personal loss, which he carried so heavily, may have had some initial bearing on this matter, but his inspiration in recommending the Battle of Britain clasp bears witness to his foresight within this difficult area of post war analysis.

The 2012 official Bomber Command Memorial that now proudly stands in Green Park, London, is a fitting testimony to all those men that bravely served, and goes some way towards addressing the perceived failings of those who failed to honour the men of Bomber Command in the immediate post war years.

Philip Jackson's impressively detailed sculptures of three Bomber Command crewmembers that formed part of the complete memorial. Philip is standing admiring his work. Each sculpture illustrates the differing equipment and flying clothing in exquisite detail. When the complete crew of seven were finally cast in bronze they created the long overdue recognition that Bomber Command most earnestly deserved. (*Philip Jackson*)

Epilogue

It is painfully apparent that all members of an aircrew walked a tight rope between life and death, and rear gunners in particular would sit in solitude in their turrets clinging to the thread of survival. Inevitably, fate, luck and awe-inspiring bravery wove together in events that often culminated in the tragic loss of life. Other men however endured and experienced the elation of surviving a tour of duty against the statistical odds of ever doing so.

Regardless of personal experience, all of these men would have witnessed friends, individual crewmembers and entire crews losing their lives, tragically a commonplace event that took place throughout the Second World War. In many instances, the loss of an airman's life was to his family represented by just three medals, primarily the 1939-1945 Star, the Aircrew Europe Star and the British War Medal, and these would have arrived in a small brown cardboard box delivered by the Post Office addressed to their next of kin. The catastrophic loss of life within Bomber Command reached the staggering figure of 55,573 personnel, but despite giving their lives in the fight for the freedom of our country, the medals dispatched to the next of kin were not named as it was thought too expensive to do so by the government at that time.

It must however be remembered that through sheer courage and personal fortitude, many men walked away from the brink of tragedy. One such crew that serves to typify the courage of all others was that of Lancaster JB228, serving with 1668 Heavy Conversion Unit, RAF Bottesford. On 10 March 1945, the crew of eight took part in a simple cross-country sortie. Sergeant Bradley was sitting in the rear gunner's turret on what should have been an interesting but fairly uneventful training flight. However, the port outer engine unexpectedly failed. The pilot and flight engineer managed to feather the propeller, enabling the Lancaster to hopefully continue on its three remaining engines and seek a safe landing. Additional to the loss of the engine the aircraft was unable to be trimmed properly and the pilot undertook an emergency landing at RAF Fiskerton. The Lancaster swung off the runway and the under carriage completely folded beneath the wings causing the aircraft to split apart. Sergeant Bradley's rear gunner's turret was literally torn away from the fuselage and a fire took hold in the main body of

The remains of Lancaster JB228 at RAF Fiskerton. Group Captain Terrance Arbuthnot, the station's Commanding Officer, is seen removing an ammunition belt from the wreckage, the ammunition having been torn away from the tracking feed that supplied Sergeant Bradley's guns in the rear turret. White foam, the result of fire fighting, creates an unusual perspective of the mechanics of the mid-upper gunner's turret. (*Robin Arbuthnot via RAF Fiskerton website*)

the aircraft. Miraculously, all the aircrew managed to escape from this accident with their lives, but two young sergeants suffered serious injuries.

The terrifying experience for Sergeant Bradley in the rear turret and those that survived the fire from within the aircraft's fuselage was not unique and these men like so many others were required to climb aboard another bomber and continue with their duties. Little did they know that just a few weeks after their escape, Winston Churchill was to announce in the House of Commons on 8 May 1945, Germany's unconditional surrender.

Bibliography

Bowyer, C., *Guns in the Sky*, Dent, 1979

Carter, N. and C., *The DFC and How It Was Won*, Savannah, 1998

Chorley, W. R., *Bomber Command Losses*, Midland Counties, 1996

Clarke, R. W., *British Aircraft Armaments*, PSL, 1994

Cooper, A. W., *In Action With The Enemy*, William Kimber, 1986

Gibson, E, & Kingsley Ward, *Courage Remembered*, HMSO, 1989

Halley, J., *Squadrons of the RAF & Commonwealth*, Air Britain, 1988

Holmes H., *Avro Lancaster the Definitive Record*, Airlife, 1997

Maton, M., *Honour Those Mentioned MID Despatches*, Token Publishing, 2010

Maton, M., *Honour the Air Forces*, Token Publishing, 2004

Mason, T., *The History of 9 Squadron Royal Air Force,* 1965

Middlebrook, M. and Everitt, C., *Bomber Command War Diaries*, Viking, 1985

Oliver Clutton-Brock., *Footprints on the Sands of Time*, Grubb Street, 2003

Tavender, I., *The DFM Register for the Second World War*, Savannah, 2000

RAF Flying Training & Support Units, Air Britain, 1997

RAAF Registers AWM 237 (63) (64)

Royal Air Force 1939-1945 Vol I, II, III, HMSO, 1953

Ramsey, W., *The Blitz Then and Now*, After the Battle, 1988

They Shall Not Grow Old, Commonwealth Air Training Plan Museum, 1996

National Archives, *Recommendations for Honours and Awards*, under the terms of the Open Government Licence.

Wallace, G. F., *The Guns of the Royal Air Force*, William Kimber, 1972